Foreign Capital Inflows to China, India
and the Caribbean

Foreign Capital Inflows to China, India and the Caribbean

Trends, Assessments and Determinants

Arindam Banik and Pradip K. Bhaumik

HG
5182
.B36
2006

First published in 2006 by
PALGRAVE MACMILLAN
Houndmills, Basingstoke, Hampshire RG21 6XS and
175 Fifth Avenue, New York, N.Y. 10010
Companies and representatives throughout the world

PALGRAVE MACMILLAN is the global academic imprint of the Palgrave Macmillan division of St. Martin's Press, LLC and of Palgrave Macmillan Ltd. Macmillan® is a registered trademark in the United States, United Kingdom and other countries. Palgrave is a registered trademark in the European Union and other countries.

ISBN-13: 978–1–4039–0040–1 hardback
ISBN-10: 1–4039–0040–X hardback

This book is printed on paper suitable for recycling and made from fully managed and sustained forest sources.

A catalogue record for this book is available from the British Library.

A catalog record for this book is available from the Library of Congress.

10 9 8 7 6 5 4 3 2 1
15 14 13 12 11 10 09 08 07 06

Printed and bound in Great Britain by
Antony Rowe Ltd, Chippenham and Eastbourne

Dedicated to
Jyotsna and Ram Gopal Banik
Reba and Late Surendra Nath Bhaumik

Contents

List of Figures

List of Tables

List of Abbreviations

ACFTA	ASEAN–China Free Trade Area
ADR	American Depositary Receipt
ASI	Annual Survey of Industries
BOT	Build-Operate-Transfer
BPD	Barrels per day
BPO	Business Process Outsourcing
BPTT	British Petroleum Trinidad and Tobago
BRIC	Brazil, Russia, India, China
BSE	Bombay Stock Exchange
CARICOM	Caribbean Community
CMIE	Centre for Monitoring Indian Economy
CSA	Country-Specific Advantage
EC-6	European Community (Belgium, the Netherlands, Luxembourg, West Germany, France and Italy)
EOU	Export-Oriented Units
ESCAP	Economic and Social Commission for Asia and the Pacific
ETDZ	Economic and Technological Development Zones
EU	European Union
FDI	Foreign Direct Investment
FERA	Foreign Exchange Regulation Act
FIE	foreign-invested enterprises
FII	Foreign Institutional Investors
FIPB	Foreign Investment Promotion Board
FSA	Firm-Specific Advantage
FTAA	Free Trade Area of the Americas
GDP	Gross Domestic Product
GDR	Global Depositary Receipt
GI pipes	Galvanized iron pipes
GNP	Gross National Product
HKSAR	Hong Kong Special Administrative Region
IC	integrated circuit
ICICI	Industrial Credit and Investment Corporation of India
IDP	Investment Development Path
IMF	International Monetary Fund
IPC	intellectual property rights
LAC	Latin America and the Caribbean Economies

LIBOR	London Inter-Bank Offer Rate
M&As	Mergers and Acquisitions
MDC	More Developed Country
MEEI	Ministry of Energy and Energy Industries
MNC	Multinational Corporations
MNE	Multinational Enterprises
NAFTA	North American Free Trade Agreement
NASSCOM	National Association of Software and Service Companies
NCAER	National Council of Applied Economic Research
NICs	Newly Industrialized Countries
NRI	non-resident Indian
NTB	non-tariff barriers
OBM	Original Brand Manufacturing
ODM	Original Design Manufacturing
OECD	Organization for Econmomic Co-operation and Development
OECS	Orgnization of Eastern Caribbean States
OEM	Original Equipment Manufacturing
OLI	advantages, location and internalization
OPEC	Organization of the Petroleum Exporting Countries
PPP	purchasing power parity
R&D	Research and Development
RBI	Reserve Bank of India
RBTT	Royal Bank of Trinidad and Tobago
SBS	switching power supplies
SEBI	Securities and Exchange Board of India
SEZ	special economic zones
SIA	Secretariat for Industrial Assistance
SOEs	state-owned enterprises
TOT	Transfer–Operate–Transfer
TP	Technology Purchase
TPM	Total Productive Maintenance
TQM	Total Quality Management
WIR	World Investment Report
WFOEs	wholly foreign-owned enterprises
WTO	World Trade Organization

Preface

Foreign investment and economic growth has been a central theme of the development literature in the past two decades. In fact it has witnessed marked changes in the global organization of industry with far-reaching effects for the evolving patterns of integration of developing countries into the world economy. The relationship between industrialization and trade-orientation, due to foreign investment across economies and regions, are thus the emerging issues. Incidentally, the precise consequences of these developments have not yet been fully analysed or understood. This has been the case for both large economies such as India and China and relatively small ones such as those of the Caribbean.

Interestingly, India and China have often been compared in terms of their performances in the development literature. These comparisons can indeed be quite enlightening, given the similar challenges faced by the two countries in the late 1940s, and the different routes they have taken in addressing these challenges. In recent time Foreign Direct Investment (FDI) and economic growth has been a common focus of comparison between India and China. Studies on the Caribbean, on the other hand, reveal an interesting contrast due to its close geographic proximity to the developed economies. Even then these studies still reveals many characteristics of developing countries due mainly to the Caribbean's inherent internal structure and a few policy failures. The immense diverse pictures with many distinct pursuits in India, China and the Caribbean thus enable us to analyse the subject from different perspectives and offer great opportunities for study. Needless to say the promised resources of social services, education, health, infrastructure and housing – among other things – may not be compatible with the respective countries' current domestic savings rate.

The selection of focus here revolves around three specific objectives: discussing the idiosyncrasies beyond rational economic choices that determine the inflows of foreign investment; examining the various facets of inflows of FDI in India, China and the Caribbean; and revealing the insights of local and foreign firms' behaviour as they compete on an emerging level playing field. It is also definitely being argued that long-term growth prospects of these developing countries will hinge on their ability to exploit population, innovation, investment and higher education.

Many scholars and organizations have assisted us in writing the book. We owe special thanks to K. L. Krishna for his inspiration. We have benefited from the comments and suggestions from Hilary Beckles, Ramesh Ramsaran, Andrew Downes, Rajat Kathuria, Michael Howard, George Bell, Ian Hickling and Sunday O Iyare. We would also like to express our appreciation to Wayne Hunte, Don Marshall, Judy Whitehead, Stephen Harewood, and Nlundu Mamingi for useful discussions on several occasions. Our students at the Department of Economics, University of the West Indies, Cave Hill Campus, Barbados, West Indies and the students at International Management Institute, New Delhi, India were critical in classes in dealing with certain issues. They deserve special appreciation. Mr Andy Watts provided us with a lot of useful information for developing a Caribbean case. Our special thanks to him.

We are grateful to the Centre for Asian Studies, University of Hong Kong for allowing the first author to use their vast resources as a visitor. We are grateful to Valerie NG Ting Yee in this context. We would like to thank the librarians and staff of Sir Arthur Lewis Institute of Social and Economic Studies, Barbados, University of West Indies Library, Barbados Campus and Williamson Magor Library, International Management Institute, New Delhi.

Finally, the first author would like to thank his wife, Mousumi, for her support, and his son, Amitayus, for providing a fresh sense of perspective during the study period. The second author feels that this work would not have been possible but for the unstinted support and cooperation of his immediate family – namely wife Dolly, daughter Suparna and son Abhishek.

Pushpa Vinod, Jiji Abraham and Debabrata Das provided invaluable assistance in the preparation of this manuscript. We are also immensely grateful to our commissioning editor Jacky Kippenberger for her faith in us and her continued support in spite of many delays in the execution of this project.

New Delhi
30 September 2005

Arindam Banik
Pradip K Bhaumik

1
Introduction

The growing importance of FDI

The last two decades have witnessed unparalleled changes in the global organization of industry with far-reaching effects on the evolving patterns of integration of developing countries into the world economy. Much of this has been caused by relatively high rates of growth of international trade and investment flows – much higher than that of world Gross Domestic Product (GDP). Accordingly, foreign direct investment and economic growth has emerged as one of the central themes of development literature in the past two decades.

FDI affects resource allocation in several ways. The presence of Multi-National Corporation (MNC) affiliates may affect capital accumulation, industrial structure and performance, trade propensity and many other structural characteristics of the host economy. Thus it is natural to assume that MNCs do influence, at least to some extent, the observed patterns of industrialization and trade-orientation in host countries. This has been the case, for example, in the larger Latin American economies, South East Asian countries and more recently in the context of India, China and the Caribbean.

Measurement of FDI

FDI figures of different countries are not directly comparable because many developing countries do not follow the International Monetary Fund (IMF) guidelines completely in compiling and reporting FDI data (IMF, 1993). According to the guidelines, FDI consists of the sum of (a) new equity purchased or acquired by parent companies in overseas firms they are considered to control (including establishment of new subsidiaries), (b) reinvestment of earnings by controlled firms and, (c) intra-company loans from parent companies to controlled firms. The common view of practical minimum of equity for having an effective right in management is 10 per cent to 25 per cent of ownership. The aim of FDI is thus to 'acquire a lasting interest in an enterprise operating in an economy other than that of the investor' (IMF, 1993).

The ultimate objective of the investor is to have an effective right in the management of the enterprise. Investments that do not imply such a permanent relationship are classified as portfolio investments. Unlike FDI, portfolio investments are not usually made with a long-term commitment. For the purpose of this book we have used the term foreign capital inflows under the broad definition of FDI. Accordingly, the terms FDI and foreign capital inflows have been used interchangeably in the context of this book.

Rationale of FDI

The principal measure of annual changes in cross border investment activities of MNCs is FDI flows. Apart from FDI, MNCs can interact with the host country via exports, portfolio investment and licensing agreements. The distinguishing feature of FDI is that it confers upon the foreign investor effective operating control.

The theory of MNCs can be traced back to the writings of (Coase, 1937) and to the literature on barriers to entry (Bain, 1956). The two micro explanations that form the core of conventional FDI theory focus on industry structure and transaction costs. Both are market failure types of arguments.

In a world of perfect markets, the MNCs would not exist and all activity would be carried out through free trade. However, the presence of market imperfections 'for goods or factors, including among the latter, technology, or some interference by government' result in the MNC acting as a replacement for free trade (Kindleberger, 1969). Foreign entrants are disadvantaged relative to local firms because of their unfamiliarity with local conditions. According to the industry structure argument, firms in oligopolistic industries overcome the disadvantage of being in a foreign country by exploiting economies of scale and hence market power.

Alternatively, FDI and MNCs may arise because of shortcomings in arm's length markets for intangible assets (Caves, 1982). These assets are knowledge, technology, managerial and marketing skills. According to this argument, firms undertake FDI because the alternatives (trade, licensing) are less efficient. Thus, by replacing market based transactions with transactions within the firm, FDI provides the means to internalize any Firm-Specific Advantage (FSA) of the MNC (Dunning, 1984; Rugman, 1982). This is necessary because of the public good character of intangible assets like knowledge. The MNC tries to overcome the public good character of its FSA by attempting to establish property rights over its FSA, thus appropriating the benefits of its knowledge that would be otherwise lost to the firm.

Dunning's (Dunning, 1979, 1984) expansion of the internalization theory to embrace an 'eclectic' approach incorporates macro-level economic variables as well. Location specific or 'Country-Specific Advantage' (CSA) of particular host countries may make FDI in them preferable to not only other potential host countries but also to domestic investment.

In the macroeconomic perspectives, Agenor (2001) argues that the domestic investment and growth of a country may be favourably influenced by a high degree of openness that can pull international resources to the domestic economy. The general characteristics of the developing economies are well known. For example, the capacity to save is constrained by a low level of income. It is thus quite likely that net foreign resource inflows can supplement domestic saving, increase levels of physical capital per worker, and help the recipient country raise its rate of economic growth and improve its living standards as long as the marginal return from investment is at least equal to the cost of capital.[1]

In addition to this direct effect on growth, FDI may also have significant indirect long-run effects. As emphasized early on by MacDougall (1960), and more recently by Berthelemy and Demurger (2000), Borensztein *et al.* (1998), and Grossman and Helpman (1991), FDI may facilitate the transfer or diffusion of managerial and technological know-how – particularly in the form of new varieties of capital inputs – and improve the skills composition of the labour force as a result of 'learning by doing' effects, investment in formal education, and on-the-job training. In addition, as suggested by Markusen and Venables (1999), although the increased degree of competition in the product and factor markets induced by FDI may tend to reduce profits of local firms, spillover effects through linkages to supplier industries may reduce input costs, raise profits, and stimulate domestic investment.

Determinants of FDI

FDI flows are generally believed to be influenced by economic indicators like market size, export intensity, institutions and so on irrespective of the source and the destination countries. In an ideal situation, the determinants of FDI inflows in a particular country may be explained by lagged gross national product (GNP), change in GNP, lagged gross domestic investment and the variation in exchange rate. They are significant for countries like India and China where there is huge scope for foreign investment. However, the most crucial exogenous variable appears to be the trade and industrial policy of the host country.

It is useful to mention here that the structural transformation of the Newly Industrialized Countries (NICs) following the trade policy reforms is the single most important exogenous factor in explaining their economic growth. The key point that needs to be emphasized here is that the shift from inward-oriented to outward-oriented trade regime among the NICs was followed by not only faster export growth but also economic growth. Likewise, the East Asian countries also achieved significant improvements in the domestic investment and savings rate.

Quite likely, GNP is a proxy for the size of the domestic economy and is a key variable in the foreign investors' decision to invest. Its importance, however, may differ from India to China not only because China has had a head start over India on their reforms but also because of the fact that FDI inflows could be resource-seeking, market-seeking or efficiency-seeking and this may differ between India and China.

As a general principle, host countries that offer what MNCs are seeking, and/or host countries whose policies are most conducive to MNC activities stand a better chance of attracting FDI. But firms also see locational determinants in their interaction with ownership-specific and internalization advantages in the broader context of their corporate strategies. These strategies aim, for example, at spreading or reducing risks pursuing oligopolistic competition, and matching competitors' actions or looking for distinct sources of competitive advantage. In the context of different strategies, the same motive and the corresponding host-country determinants can acquire different meanings. For example, the market-seeking motive can translate, in the case of one MNC, into the need to enter new markets to increase the benefits arising from multi-plant operations; while for another, it can translate into the desire to acquire market power; and for still another MNC, it can aim at diversifying markets as part of a risk reducing strategy.

The degree of openness of a country may also be considered as an important contributory factor. The more open a country, the more likely it is to attract FDI. This may influence investment flows. Likewise, the gross domestic investment rate may have a salutary effect on inflows of FDI.

In addition, the depreciation of the domestic exchange rate may determine FDI inflow to a country. It may stimulate the nation's exports and foreign investment. However, this may further lead to a trade surplus and appreciation of domestic currency, which neutralizes part of its original depreciation.

As regards small economies, the FDI decisions are mostly strategic such as motivations, locational choices and market entry mode of MNCs. This is applicable to most of the Caribbean economies. The foreign firms in the Caribbean use their firm specific advantages in order to compete with foreign firms in the USA, Canada and other neighbouring economies. Fiscal incentives are also considered as important contributory factors. The likely investment incentives seem to be low taxes or tax holidays, and duty exemptions on industry-related equipment.

This study also looks at the FDI inflows using an alternate approach based on the concepts of neighbourhood and extended neighbourhood. Using a database, this approach contrasts sharply with others which analyse FDI inflows based purely on economic variables. It is interesting to note that the neighbourhood concepts are widely applicable in different contexts – particularly for China and India and partly in the case of the Caribbean. While a substantial fraction of FDI inflows may be explained by select economic variables, the country-specific factors and the idiosyncratic component account for more of investment inflows in Europe, China and India. This may have strong relevance in explaining possible Indian investment in the Caribbean.

Rationale for this study

India and China have shifted their development strategy from inward- to outward-orientation. This may be due to the fact that the countries, that were once legendary for their wealth are now home to some the world's poorest population. Many observers feel that in these countries, the potentials are underutilised because of excessive controls, regulations and interventions. Thus, there is a significant gap between what is possible and what exists. It is interesting to note that these economies had similar levels of development in the late 1940s but took different routes to address the challenges.

FDI and economic growth appears to be the common focus of understanding these two large economies and there is indeed much to learn from China's achievement in these areas in recent time. The Caribbean, on the other hand has historically received significant trade concessions and foreign aid, and enjoyed preferential market treatment – in particular from the US, Canada and the European Union (EU) countries. The reduction in foreign aid over the last decade and withdrawal of concessions, however, means that it will need to increase FDI as an alternative source of capital and investment. The Caribbean has attempted to shift towards a private sector-led development strategy but high levels of government debt have crowded out private investment and, in some cases, public investment as well. In some countries this has led to high levels of taxation. Thus, efficient private domestic investment as well as FDI may be the key to future growth in the region. It is also necessary to understand how the Caribbean has responded to this global challenge given the tight labour market across many island nations.

Structure of the book

This book is not addressed to the expert. On the contrary, it tries to explain the economic logic to the non-economist who is interested in understanding the massive changes taking place in the world today. After this brief introduction, Chapter 2 assesses the global trends of FDI and their future prospects. Likewise it discusses the sectoral distribution of global FDI. Chapter 3 hypothesises that economic variables alone may be unable to explain specific FDI flows and there might be other factors that help reduce the perceived risk from the home country's perspective. We define the concept of 'neighbourhood' and its evolution, list the various neighbourhoods that may explain FDI flows and then elaborate and explain extended neighbourhood that may be helpful in explaining FDI inflows to China, India and the Caribbean. It is generally observed that historically FDI 'waves' have had different outcomes across India, China and the Caribbean. Chapters 4, 5 and 6 thus seek to examine the pattern, assessment and trends of FDI in each of these. Chapter 7 discusses the important concept of technology spillovers and elaborates these through some case studies of firms in India, China and the Caribbean. These are then analysed to highlight the difference in spillovers among the economies studied. Chapter 8 forms the concluding chapter and attempts some generalizations. It also investigates the sustainability of these processes unleashed by the forces of globalization.

2
FDI: Global Trends and Assessments

Introduction

The contribution of MNCs in transforming the global economy is now a widely acknowledged reality. Indeed, since the early 1980s there has been a resurgence of FDI, directed by MNCs into the economies of the developing world. The annual average FDI inflows around the globe was about US$310.9 billion during 1992–97 as compared to US$328.2 billion of outflows during the same period (Table 2.1). This trend in FDI inflows continued unabated, soaring to a record level of US$1388.7 billion in 2000. Figures 2.1 and 2.2 reveal the trends in FDI inflow and outflow for both developed and developing countries, respectively. Global FDI inflows were however, down by 41 per cent in 2001, and fell by another one-fifth in 2002 – to US$679 billion or just half the peak in 2000. It had declined further by 18 per cent (to US$560 billion) in 2003. Interestingly, FDI outflows are appearing to be good in 2004 due to 3 per cent increase in 2003 (Table 2.2). Cross-border mergers and acquisitions (M&As) – the key driver of global FDI since the late 1980s – remained weak but have started to pick up in 2004. They rose by 3 per cent in the first six months of 2004 over the same period in 2003. There are other contributory factors that may explain the present trend – such as higher corporate profitability and reinvested earnings. In addition, equity and intra-company loans are also expected to pick up.

We analyse the trends in FDI flows in this chapter. The next section examines the regional trend of FDI inflows. Then some interesting findings regarding the future prospects of four large economies with potential are revealed. The penultimate section discusses the sectoral distribution of global FDI. Finally, the last section summarizes the chapter.

7

Table 2.1 Regional distribution of FDI inflows and outflows: 1992–2003 (US$bn)

Region/country	FDI inflows							FDI outflows						
	1992–97 (Annual average)	1998	1999	2000	2001	2002	2003	1992–97 (Annual average)	1998	1999	2000	2001	2002	2003
Developed countries	180.8	472.5	828.4	1108.0	571.5	489.9	366.6	275.7	631.5	1014.3	1083.9	658.1	547.6	569.6
Western Europe	100.8	263.0	500.0	697.4	368.8	380.2	310.2	161.7	436.5	763.9	859.4	447.0	364.5	350.3
European Union	95.8	249.9	479.4	671.4	357.4	374.0	295.2	146.9	415.4	724.3	806.2	429.2	351.2	337.0
Other Western Europe	5.0	13.1	20.7	26.0	11.4	6.2	15.1	14.8	21.2	39.6	53.3	17.9	13.3	13.3
Japan	1.2	3.2	12.7	8.3	6.2	9.2	6.3	20.2	24.2	22.7	31.6	38.3	32.3	28.8
United States	60.3	174.4	283.4	314.0	159.5	62.9	29.8	77.6	131.0	209.4	142.6	124.9	115.3	151.9
Developing economies	118.6	194.1	231.9	252.5	219.7	157.6	172.0	51.4	53.4	75.5	98.9	59.9	44.0	35.6
Africa	5.9	9.1	11.6	8.7	19.6	11.8	15.0	2.2	2.0	2.6	1.3	−2.5	0.1	1.3
Latin America and the Caribbean	38.2	82.5	107.4	97.5	88.1	51.4	49.7	9.5	19.9	31.3	13.7	12.0	6.0	10.7
Asia and the Pacific	74.5	102.4	112.9	146.2	112.0	94.5	107.3	39.6	31.6	41.7	83.8	50.3	37.9	23.6
Asia	74.1	102.2	112.6	146.1	111.9	94.4	107.1	39.6	31.6	41.7	83.8	50.3	37.9	23.6
West Asia	2.9	7.1	1.0	1.5	6.1	3.6	4.1	0.5	−1.0	2.1	3.8	5.1	2.5	−0.7
Central Asia	1.6	3.0	2.5	1.9	3.5	4.5	6.1	–	0.2	0.4	–	0.1	0.8	0.8
South, East and South-East Asia	69.6	92.1	109.1	142.7	102.2	86.3	96.9	39.0	32.5	39.2	80.0	45.1	34.7	23.5
South Asia	2.5	3.5	3.1	3.1	4.0	4.5	6.1	0.1	0.1	0.1	0.5	1.4	1.2	0.9
The Pacific	0.4	0.2	0.3	0.1	0.1	0.1	0.2	0.1	−0.1	–	0.1	0.1	–	–
Central and Eastern Europe	11.5	24.3	26.5	27.5	26.4	31.2	21.0	1.2	2.3	2.5	4.0	3.5	4.9	7.0
World	310.9	690.9	1086.8	1388.0	817.6	678.8	559.6	328.2	687.2	1092.3	1186.8	721.5	586.5	612.2

Source: Based on UNCTAD, World Investment Report 2004: The Shift Towards Services (Tables B.1 and B.2).

Table 2.2 Selected indicators of FDI and international production: 1982–2003 (US$bn/%)

Item	Value at current prices ($bn)			Annual growth rate (%)						
	1982	1990	2003	1986–90	1991–95	1996–2000	2000	2001	2002	2003
FDI inflows	59	209	560	22.9	21.5	39.7	27.7	-41.1	-17.0	-17.6
FDI outflows	28	242	612	25.6	16.6	35.1	8.7	-39.2	-17.3	2.6
FDI inward stock	796	1 950	8 245	14.7	9.3	16.9	19.1	7.4	12.7	11.8
FDI outward stock	590	1 758	8 197	18.1	10.7	17.1	18.5	5.9	13.8	13.7
Cross-border M&As	–	151	297	25.9a	24.0	51.5	49.3	-48.1	-37.7	-19.7
Sales of foreign affiliates	2 717	5 660	17 580	16.0	10.2	9.7	16.7	-3.8	23.7	10.7
Gross product of foreign affiliates	636	1 474	3 706	17.4	6.8	8.2	15.1	-4.7	25.8	10.1
Total assets of foreign affiliates	2 076	5 883	30 362	18.2	13.9	20.0	28.4	-5.4	19.6	12.5
Exports of foreign affiliates	717	1 194	3 077	13.5	7.6	9.9	11.4	-3.3	4.7	16.6
Employment of foreign affiliates (1000)	19 232	24 197	54 170	5.6	3.9	10.8	13.3	-3.2	12.3	8.3
GDP (in current prices)	11 737	22 588	36 163	10.1	5.1	1.3	2.7	-0.9	3.7	12.1
Gross fixed capital formation	2 285	4 815	7 294	13.4	4.2	2.4	3.8	-3.6	-0.6	9.9
Royalties and licence fee receipts	9	30	77b	21.3	14.3	7.7	9.5	-2.5	6.7	–
Exports of goods and non-factor services	2 246	4 260	9 228	12.7	8.7	3.6	11.4	-3.3	4.7	16.6

Notes
a 1987–90 only;
b 2002.

Source: UNCTAD, World Investment Report 2004: The Shift Towards Services (Table 1.3).

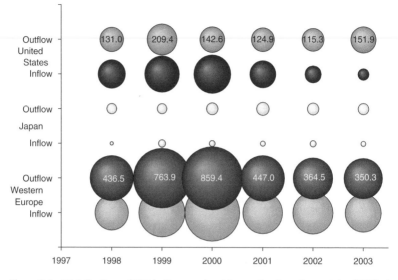

Figure 2.1 Distribution of FDI inflows and outflows: developed countries (US$bn)
Source: Based on Table 2.1.

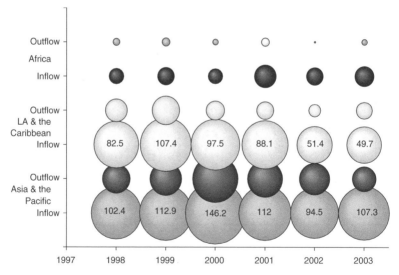

Figure 2.2 Distribution of FDI inflows and outflows: developing countries (US$bn)
Source: Based on Table 2.1.

Regional trend

Table 2.1 also shows the regional distribution of FDI inflows to both developed and developing countries during the period 1992–2003. In general it seems that developing countries are the winners in 2004 due to a 9 per cent increase in FDI in these economies. In fact, the policies on FDI continue to become more liberal in developing economies, and both countries and enterprises have been increasing their degrees of transnationality (UNCTAD, 2004). As regards the destination of FDI flows, Asia and the Pacific emerged as the most preferred and the largest host region among developing economies. It appears that most of these FDI inflows were concentrated in developing countries such as China, Brazil, Mexico, Argentina, Poland, India, Thailand and so on. The top 10 developing countries (China, Brazil, Mexico, Argentina, Poland, the Czech Republic, Chile, Venezuela, Thailand and India) accounted for about 69 per cent of total FDI flows to developing countries in 2003, down sharply from the peak of 78 per cent in 2000.

Interestingly, Latin America and the Caribbean region accounted for much of the fall in FDI flows to the developing world. This was the fourth consecutive year of decline, leading to a 53 per cent drop over the period 1999–2003. The drop in 2003 may be ascribed to a significant drop in FDI inflows to Brazil, Argentina, and Mexico. The frequency distribution according to the magnitude of FDI inflows between 1999 and 2003 has remained almost unchanged, with 9 countries receiving more than US$1 billion and 31 countries less than US$1 billion in 2003 (Table 2.3). Encouragingly, Brazil and Mexico remained the most important recipients. This variation within the region may be attributed to several factors. For example, Mexico is faced with a competitive challenge from China, notably in manufacturing. As regards small island economies, two offshore centres – namely Bermuda, and the Cayman Islands, and other relatively small countries like Ecuador, Honduras, Nicaragua, Panama and Uruguay emerge as the beneficiaries of FDI inflows. It has been a tumultuous year for Chile and Venezuela as well, but these countries recovered a large part of the declines experienced in 2002.

As regards FDI source countries in the region, the United States alone contributed one-third, followed by Spain (16 per cent), while the Netherlands, the United Kingdom, France and Canada accounted for most of the rest. Quite significantly, Spanish investment fell drastically, while it used to be a major investor from the EU.

Several factors may have contributed to the above drop. For example, the persistent slump in privatization and cross-border M&A limited FDI

Table 2.3   Distribution of FDI inflows to the Latin American and the Caribbean economies by range: 2003

Range	Economies
More than US$10 bn	Brazil and Mexico
US$5–9 bn	Bermuda
US$1–4 bn	Cayman Islands, Chile, Colombia, Ecuador, Peru and Venezuela
Less than US$1 bn	Anguilla, Antigua and Barbuda, Argentina, Aruba, Barbados, Bahamas, Belize, Bolivia, Costa Rica, Cuba, Dominica, Dominican Republic, El Salvador, Grenada, Guatemala, Guyana, Haiti, Honduras, Jamaica, Montserrat, Netherlands Antilles, Nicaragua, Panama, Paraguay, saint Kitts and Nevis, Saint Lucia, Saint Vincent and the Grenadines, Suriname, Trinidad and Tobago, Uruguay and Virgin islands (British)

Source: UNCTAD, *World Investment Report 2004: The Shift Towards Services* (Table II.7).

in the region. Indeed, the region received no privatization-related FDI in 2003, a significant slowing from the pace seen in 1998–2000, when the annual average of privatization flows exceeded US$30 billion (World Bank, 2004). In addition to that, the vulnerability of service sector FDI to financial crisis may have contributed to the slowdown in the region.

The above is only a partial explanation of the decline. In the long run, sustained growth remains elusive for Latin America and the Caribbean Economies (LAC). Growth in real GDP was below its long-term trend – the average annual GDP growth being only 0.7 per cent for the period 2001–2003 – compared with 6.6 per cent for developing Asia (IMF, 2004). Only three countries in the region are big enough to have internal markets attractive to FDI that could achieve some growth based on that factor alone: Brazil, Mexico and Argentina (IADB, 2004). The proximity of market may have also contributed to certain LAC countries such as Dominican Republic, Mexico, Honduras and Costa Rica to develop manufacturing industries in the light of the US market. Interestingly, most of the LAC countries' average per capita income levels and non-skilled worker wages are higher than those of Asian emerging economies. This may not satisfy the MNCs which have other options. This problem may be solved with the help of higher-productivity workers. It requires appropriate skills and early investment in education and human capital formation. In general the LAC countries have not invested enough in human capital to be able to compete in manufacturing industries that require more skilled labour. Some simple *maquila* industries in Mexico and Dominican Republic are losing ground in such areas as textiles to low-wage producers in Asia or Central America. To quote:

> One major concern is the level of funding available to the state to finance provision of public goods, such as education and health, but also for the administration of justice, regulation of anticompetitive practices, security etc. Several countries in the region have levels of taxation that are too low to finance a minimal level of those public goods, and their inability to do so is jeopardizing their medium-term growth possibilities. Large governments tend to dampen growth; governments that are too small can make sustained growth impossible (WEF, 2002).

Historically, FDI in the Caribbean – directed by the MNCs, has been playing an increasingly contributory role in its economic development. The entire English-speaking Caribbean comprises a mere 6 million (CARICOM, 2000) population. Its economies are monoculture specializing in activities that are especially vulnerable to the vagaries of the international economy (tourism) or ones that have lost their growth dynamics – such as sugar and bauxite (Barclay, 2000). The region is in economic crisis as evidenced by its dismal economic performance, uncertainties due to natural calamities – for example, hurricane Ivan 2004 that caused huge national loss to Grenada and Jamaica. Recent flood in Guyana in 2005 caused accumulation of national debt. With the implementation of the North American Free Trade Agreement (NAFTA), the issue of renewed flows into these countries has become even more critical.

Similarly, the region's ability to attract FDI flows in relatively labour-intensive and less technologically demanding manufacturing industries has deteriorated due to the emergence of lower cost competitors, mainly in Asia. 'The China challenge' is a strong force, even if the most affected countries respond by lowering taxes and easing bureaucratic procedures. There is a fear in certain quarters that the FTAA (Free Trade Areas of the Americas) process may further aggravate the situation. In this context, it may be mentioned here that the region has become increasingly dependent on FDI for the financing of its domestic investment. It is often argued that outsourcing by US companies may benefit the Caribbean region as it has already benefited Latin America. The attractiveness of such operations lies in low labour cost, improved telecommunication infrastructure, an identical time zone and, in some cases, a language advantage. Call centres have significant job creation impact in developing countries with particular reference to Caribbean economies with its English-speaking population.

FDI flows into Asia and the Pacific have continued to remain strong at around US$94 billion in 2002 and US$107 billion in 2003. A credible achievement is that East Asia's share of FDI to the developing world rose from 38 per cent in 2002 to 42 per cent in 2003. More importantly FDI to China continued to surge. Her share in regional FDI increased further to about 94 per cent in 2003 from 90 per cent a year earlier (Tables 2.1 and 2.4).

According to the literature, there appear to be two types of FDI – one vertical (Helpman, 1984) and the other, horizontal or market driven (Brainard, 1997; Hortsman and Markusen, 1992). Many firms carry out production activities in different countries based on cost of labour and other resource considerations. This investment decision may be termed as vertical type of FDI. Horizontal FDI, by contrast, spreads similar production activities across countries in order to gain better access to

Table 2.4   Distribution of FDI inflows to the Asian and the Pacific economies by range: 2003

Range	Economy
More than US$5bn	China, Hong Kong (China) and Singapore
US$2–4.9 bn	Azerbaijan, Brunei Darussalam, India, Kazakhstan, Republic of Korea and Malaysia
US$1–1.9bn	Pakistan, Thailand and Viet Nam
US$0–0.9bn	Afghanistan, Armenia, Bahrain, Bangladesh, Bhutan, Cambodia, Cyprus, Fiji, Georgia, Islamic Republic of Iran, Iraq, Jordan, Kiribati, Kuwait, Kyrgyzstan, Lao People's Democratic Republic, Lebanon, Macao (China), Maldives, Mongolia, Myanmar, Nepal, New Caledonia, occupied Palestinian territory, Oman, Papua New Guinea, Philippines, Qatar, Samoa, Saudi Arabia, Sri Lanka, Syrian Arab Republic, Taiwan Province of China, Tajikistan, Tonga, Turkey, Turkmenistan, Tuvalu, United Arab Emirates, Uzbekistan and Vanuatu
Less than US$0bn	Indonesia, Democratic People's Republic of Korea, Solomon Islands and Yemen

Source: UNCTAD, *World Investment Report 2004: The Shift Towards Services* (Table II.4).

markets. Often costs and market-access concerns jointly determine an FDI decision. The knowledge-capital model (Carr *et al.*, 2001) combines both cost and market-access motives in the determination of multinational production and FDI. China's large inflows of FDI may be explained by this factor due to geographical proximity (Gao, 2005) and the extended neighborhood approach, the factor which we have explained in Chapter 3.

The surge in flows to South Asia was led mostly by a significant rise in FDI to India. India's share of FDI flows to the region rose further to about 80 per cent in 2003 from 72 per cent a year earlier. The continued easing of foreign investment restrictions in the automobile, private banking, power, and telecommunications sectors contributed to the increase. In addition, FDI inflows to India in recent time may be contributed by business decisions to outsource services. During 1996–2002, India – with its low-cost, English-speaking, and IT-competent labour force attracted almost US$1 billion in FDI, some of which went into setting up of call centres (UNCTAD, 2004).

Central Asia is considered to be a region of resources. Azerbaijan, Georgia, Kyrgyzstan are the real beneficiaries as destination of FDI. The oil and gas sectors are the key opportunities for foreign investors. Recent data shows that FDI inflows to this region have recorded increase from US$4.5 billion in 2002 to US$6.1 billion in 2003. This confirms that investors may have plenty of appetite for investment in this region.

Interestingly, Asian firms of Malaysia, the Republic of Korea, Taiwan and Singapore are also investing within this region because of shifting production from higher to lower cost locations. In recent time, China and India have become important investors in the region. Indeed, India also outsources a large amount of services in contrast to the popular belief that the country is only a recipient of the business process outsourcing investment (Amiti and Wei, 2004).[1]

Europe's share in total FDI to developing economies has increased during 2001–2003 compared to 1997–98. There was a sharp increase in FDI to the Russian Federation and a steady increase in greenfield investments. A few major privatization deals were completed. For some countries in the region there was a decline in privatization boom. Flows to the first four EU accession countries such as the Czech Republic, Hungary, Poland, and the Slovak Republic dropped. This may be due to the unsustainably high flows that were helped by asset sales in the Czech Republic and the Slovak Republic in 2002 (World Bank, op. cit.). The country distribution of FDI inflows by range is shown in Table 2.5.

Table 2.5   Distribution of FDI inflows to the Central and the East European economies by range: 2003

Range	Economy
More than US$1bn	Bulgaria, Croatia, Czech Republic, Hungary, Poland, Romania, Russian Federation, Serbia and Montenegro and Ukraine
Less than US$1bn	Albania, Belarus, Bosnia and Herzegovina, Estonia, Latvia, Lithuania, Republic of Moldova, Slovakia, Slovenia and the former Yugoslav Republic of Macedonia

Source: UNCTAD, *World Investment Report 2004: The Shift Towards Services* (Table II.9).

The FDI inflows to Africa appear to have grown to US$15 billion in 2003 although the figure is still below the peak of US$19.6 billion recorded in 2001. The major oil-exporting and the other natural resource based countries such as Angola, Chad, Equatorial Guinea, Sudan, Nigeria, Algeria, the Libyan Arab Jamahiriya, Morocco, South Africa, Tunisia and Algeria are the top 11 destinations of FDI inflows in 2003 (Table 2.6). The major areas of concern that impede investment flow to Africa seem to be low labour productivity, policies for human resource development and capacity building and infrastructure development.

FDI inflows to developed countries fell partly due to less inward FDI in United States. The FDI outflows from these economies on the other hand have increased. Several factors may have caused the fall of FDI inflows to the United States such as repayment of intra-company debt as foreign affiliates in the United States reduced the debt they had accumulated with their parent firms abroad during the M&A boom of 1998–2001, and decline in equity flows. Luxembourg's position as the top recipient was due to transshipment investment (UNCTAD, 2004, p. 80). The current status of FDI inflows to the developed economies by range is depicted in Table 2.7.

Brazil, Russia, India and China – cooperation or competition?

The above findings in the previous section corroborate the startling projections made by Wilson and Purushothaman (2003). According to them, in less than 40 years, Brazil, Russia, India and China (BRIC) – the

Table 2.6 Distribution of FDI inflows to the African economies by range: 2003

Range	Economy
More than US$2bn	Morocco
US$1–1.9bn	Angola, Equatorial Guinea, Nigeria and the Sudan
US$0.5–0.9bn	Algeria, Chad, Libyan Arab Jamahiriya, South Africa and Tunisia
US$0.1–0.4bn	Cameroon, Congo, Democratic Republic of the Congo, Côte d'Ivoire, Egypt, Ghana, Mali, Mauritania, Mozambique, Uganda, United Republic of Tanzania and Zambia
Less than US$0.1bn	Benin, Botswana, Burkina Faso, Burundi, Cape Verde, Central African Republic, Comoros, Djibouti, Eritrea, Ethiopia, Gabon, Gambia, Guinea, Guinea Bissau, Kenya, Lesotho, Liberia, Madagascar, Malawi, Mauritius, Namibia, Niger, Rwanda, São Tomé and Principe, Senegal, Seychelles, Sierra Leone, Somalia, Swaziland, Togo and Zimbabwe

Source: UNCTAD, *World Investment Report 2004: The Shift Towards Services* (Table II.2).

Table 2.7 Distribution of FDI inflows to the developed economies by range: 2003

Range	Economy
More than US$50bn	Luxembourg
US$10–49bn	Belgium, France, Germany, Ireland, Italy, Netherlands, Spain, Switzerland, the United Kingdom and the United States
US$1–9bn	Australia, Austria, Canada, Denmark, Finland, Israel, Japan, New Zealand, Norway and Sweden
Less than US$1bn	Gibraltar, Greece, Iceland, Malta and Portugal

Source: UNCTAD, *World Investment Report 2004: The Shift Towards Services* (Table II.16).

BRIC economies together could be larger than the G6. In fact, by 2032 India could displace Japan as the third largest economy of the world, while by 2041 China could overtake the US as the world's largest economy.

The report finds that over the few years, economic growth in BRIC – in particular continued industrialization in China and India – could push the trend global growth rate above 4 per cent. Future world growth trend could remain above the average of last 20 years of 3.7 per cent for around a decade, though after that global demographic pressures are likely to lead to a gradual decline. Indeed, BRIC's share of world growth could rise from roughly 20 per cent in 2003 to more than 40 per cent in 2025.

The report also provides two main factors underlying India's sustained economic growth potential: the scope for it to 'catch up' with developed economies and its very favourable demographics. For India, income per capita is starting from a much lower base than in the rest of BRIC. India's dollar income per capita in 2003 was US$538, less than half of China's US$1,087. Secondly, a positive demographic backdrop weighs heavily for India. It has the only population in the BRIC that continues to grow through the projection period. What is important here is that India's working age population (the share of population aged 15–60) exhibits a 'bulge' during the projection period. In contrast, the rest of BRIC would experience an earlier and a steeper fall in working age share of population (Wilson and Purushothaman, ibid., p. 8).

Interestingly, while all the attention is on competition between India and China, the dramatic strides in cooperation have gone largely unnoticed (Figure 2.3). China now has become India's second largest bilateral trading partner, and is rapidly gaining on the US. In fact India is actually running a trade surplus with China. According to statistics issued by the Chinese customs authorities, Indo-Chinese trade amounted to US$13.61 billion in 2004. India's exports amounted to US$7.68 billion; imports were at

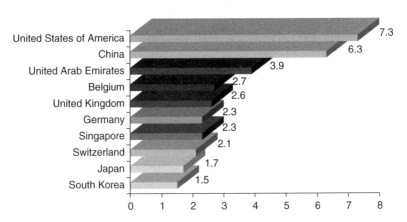

Figure 2.3 India's top ten trade partners: Apr.–Aug. 2004 (US$ bn of trade)

Source: Based on *Times of India* (9 Feb. 2005), p. 9.

US$5.93 billion. It is now widely documented that bilateral trade between the world's two most populous countries had already exceeded US$5.6 billion in just the five months of 2004–2005, a 45.2 per cent jump over the figures for April–August 2003.

Sectoral distribution of global FDI

Historically, FDI has contributed to all three economic sectors – primary, manufacturing and services. During the second half of the 1990s, global FDI flows in services have increased to overtake those in the manufacturing sector. The FDI inflows are directed not only to manufacturing and service sectors, but also towards the primary sector. The share of primary sector FDI to total FDI soared from 7 per cent to 9 per cent between 1991 and 2001–2002. Canada, the Netherlands and the United States are seen as the major source countries in 2002. The primary sector comprises two sub-sectors. One involves mining, quarrying and petroleum. About 90 per cent of inward FDI stock in the sector was in those industries both in 1990 and 2002. The other involves agriculture, hunting, forestry, and fishing. FDI has been small in this sub-sector but it rose noticeably (4 per cent to 6 per cent of total inward FDI stock) during the period 1990–2001.

The growth of FDI stock in manufacturing has been slow as compared to that in services. According to WIR 2004 (UNCTAD, 2004), developed countries accounted for more than 95 per cent of outward FDI in manufacturing in 2002. This share is lower than the 99 per cent they held in 1990. The United States still has the largest share in the cake of FDI in this sector as recipient (over US$500 billion). China's inward stock of FDI in manufacturing was more than US$300 billon in 2002.

The services sector has been seen as the major driving force in FDI inflows across select economies in recent time. These have accounted for about 60 per cent of global stock of inward FDI in 2002. The definition of the service sector is wide. It includes electricity, gas, water, transport, communication, construction, wholesale and retail trade and repairs, hotels and restaurants, transport, storage and communications, finance and insurance, real estate, renting, business services, public administration, defence, education, health, social services, information technology enabled services, business process outsourcing, social and personal service activities, and recreational, cultural, and sporting activities. Unlike the primary and manufacturing sectors, where output is tradable, services are mostly non-tradable and require close proximity between producers and consumers. That is, they are 'location-bound' and this characteristic makes FDI in services vulnerable to currency and regulatory risks. This always played a contributory role in affecting FDI inflows across regions.

The average share of services in FDI flows and in GDP is shown in Figure 2.4. It appears that the service share of both GDP and FDI inflows are in favour of developed countries. Interestingly the developing countries are also catching up. It reveals the economic logic that as income grows in an economy, its demand pattern changes from primary products to manufacturing and then to various services such as financial, tourism and so on. Quite likely, inflows of FDI are also determined by this factor. As regards East Asia and the Pacific region, the service sector data indicates that parts of the economy of the region still want to boost. Africa portrays the same trend. More interestingly, service sector appears to have made significant contribution to the region's GDP despite much structural rigidity.

Technological progress may be considered as the single most important contributor to the FDI in the service sector across regions. It has made enormous advances in transportation and communication

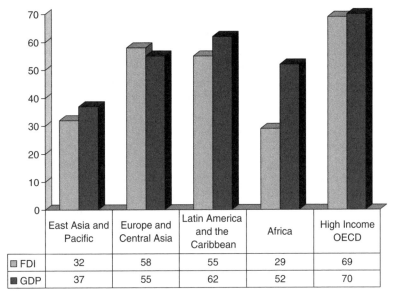

	East Asia and Pacific	Europe and Central Asia	Latin America and the Caribbean	Africa	High Income OECD
▫ FDI	32	58	55	29	69
▪ GDP	37	55	62	52	70

Figure 2.4   Average share of services in FDI flows and in GDP (%)
Source: Based on World Bank (2004), p. 82.

technologies, raised the demand for business-related services such as distribution networks, transport, storage and communications, and financial services (World Bank, op. cit.). Firms that provide these services followed their multinational clients into overseas markets by creating or acquiring subsidiaries (Esperanca, 1992; Roberts, 2001). More importantly, advances in telecommunications increased the tradability of some services, as many multinational companies began to outsource business processes to low wage countries (World Bank, 1994, 2002).

The term offshoring of services require some explanation. It may be pursued either internally through the establishment of foreign affiliates (captive offshoring) or by outsourcing a service to a third party (offshore outsourcing). Table 2.8 clarifies the concepts. Many global firms now intend to enhance their international competitiveness by outsourcing various services such as accounting, billing, software development, architectural designs, testing etc to reduce cost. Domestic outsourcing is not a new phenomenon. International outsourcing is however, recent as services become more tradable. Offshoring on the other extreme

Table 2.8 Offshoring and outsourcing – some definitions

Location of production	*Internalized or externalized production*	
	Internalized	*Externalized ('outsourcing')*
Home country	*Production kept in-house at home*	*Production outsourced to third-party service provider at home*
Foreign country (*'offshoring'*)	Production by foreign affiliate, e.g. – Infineon's centre in Dublin – DHL's IT centre in Prague – British Telecom's call centres in Bangalore and Hyderabad *'intra-firm (captive) offshoring'*	Production outsourced to third-party provider abroad, To *local company*, e.g – Bank of America's outsourcing of software development to Infosys in India To *foreign affiliate of another TNC*, e.g – A United States company outsourcing data processing services to ACS in Ghana

Source: UNCTAD, *World Investment Report 2004: The Shift Towards Services* (Table IV.1).

represents the cutting edge of the global shift in production activity, giving rise to a new international division of labour in the production of services.

Summary

FDI inflows in certain economies have significantly increased despite all the wheezing about the decreasing global trend of FDI inflows in recent time. Indicators of potential investment destinations contain hopeful signs. It appears that FDI inflows will be looking better by the end of 2005, and will perform strongly in 2006. But those estimates depend on various economic and other factors such as neighborhoods, cultures and so on. The services sector with its tradability options may be considered an important area. There is indication that it may enhance growth in both large and small economies. However, this is possible only through effective government intervention in creating highly skilled technical manpower. If pursued, this could turn out to be an unexpected advantage to English-speaking developing nations.

3
Explaining FDI Inflows – an Alternate Approach

Introduction

In Chapter 1 we have discussed the inflows of FDI in the context of the emerging global and regional scenario. The existing studies (for example Agenor, 2001; Obstfeld, 1994) have emphasized the role of select economic factors that explain investment flows. This aspect appears to be remarkably weak on some of the important questions that confront nations. There are areas where we have little or no facts but we can deduce how one action may affect another.

The temptation to examine a modified version of Isaac Newton's Law of Gravitation to predict movement of people, information, investment and commodities between cities and even continents has been strong in this context. The gravity model, as social scientists refer to the modified law of gravitation, takes into account the population size of two places and the distance between them. Since larger places attract people, ideas, and commodities more than smaller and places closer together have a greater attraction, the gravity model incorporates these two features.

The gravitational attraction between two continents, countries or regions with similar cultures and roots may explain our neighbourhood model. Such attraction, in turn, can explain certain economic flows such as investment, market access and trade.

The next section lists the various neighbourhoods that may explain FDI flows. The section following elaborates on the four neighbourhoods while the next three sections explain extended neighbourhood that analyses FDI inflows to China, India and the Caribbean respectively. The last section summarizes after contrasting the neighbourhood approach with some other similar approaches discussed in the literature.

The neighbourhoods

Historically, FDI has flowed into four distinct neighbourhoods:

1. The original neighbourhood – direct investment of USA in the manufacturing Industry of UK.
2. The intermediate neighbourhood – the formation of the European Common Market.
3. The extension of the intermediate neighbourhood – the changing pattern of FDI inflows.
4. The extended neighbourhood – the role of ethnicity when FDI became explorative and brought changes in repetitive and local experimentation with new alternatives in its wake.

The evolution of the neighbourhoods

Historically, FDI inflow in the original neighbourhood was strongly influenced by technological and economic hegemony that created competitive advantage for USA as compared with Western Europe at the end of the Second World War. The end of the war presented an opportunity for the USA. This stemmed from the fact that the economies of Western Europe had been battered during the war and so there was considerable opportunity for the expansion of US FDI. The United States has been a continental-sized country with a huge 'home market' and has commanded a substantial share of the world economy – this has made it even more difficult for other countries to compete with it.

The original neighbourhood was also influenced by historical factors such as 'preferred destination' outside North America. The United Kingdom was the single most important foreign direct investment inflow destination after the Second World War for two reasons: (i) the infrastructure and the production capacity of the UK were not damaged or disorganized, and (ii) there were sequential flows of foreign investment because of the similarity between the US and the UK firms in terms of product-markets, human resources, production technology, consumer tastes and culture in the most general sense (Davidson, 1980; Kogut, 1983).

Satisfying strategies also played an important role in terms of FDI in the original neighbourhood. Teece *et al.*, (1994) have identified two characteristics of satisfying strategies – that is, repetitive nature and local scope of experimentation. The repetitive nature suggests that private capital flow experience will be directly related to their existing organizational routines. The local scope of experimentation implies that near neigh-bourhood investment is preferred (Levinthal and March, 1993). It is the case that capital inflow in the original neighbourhood was exploitative in nature as opposed to exploratory since it added to the existing capital inflow without fundamentally changing the nature of investment patterns. Exploratory capital inflow implies changes in repetitive and local experimentation with new alternatives. As Levinthal and March (ibid.) have argued, the satisfying strategy of a firm should balance between exploitative and explorative since both are *sine qua non* for present and future viability of firms. Hence we turn our attention to the intermediate neighborhood. Interestingly, the USA was the world's biggest borrower in 1913. It had begun investing abroad, predominantly in its local neighbourhood – Canada, Mexico and the Caribbean (Twomey, 2001).

Intermediate neighbourhood

FDI inflow in the intermediate neighbourhood was strongly influenced by economic conditions, notwithstanding the opportunities for higher growth in this neighbourhood. Initially, the intermediate neighbour-hood had market conditions with which US firms were not familiar. Other factors included differences in language and business practices, lack of similarity in the GDP per capita, finite capital available for foreign expansion and high costs of establishing plant capacity in the intermediate neighbourhood relative to the original neighborhood. It was the case that US firms preferred to exploit markets with which the net start-up costs were low as opposed to new market with potential growth and opportunity to maximize profit (Dunning, 1993). However, FDI inflow into the intermediate neighbourhood improved as the economic conditions were becoming similar to the original neighbour-hood. As in the case of the original neighbourhood, it was exploitative in nature.

Another important factor that influenced FDI inflow into the intermediate neighbourhood was the formation of the common market by the *EC-6, which* provided extra incentive to establish or expand activities for the US firms. Increased FDI inflow was due to the growth of the intermediate neighbourhood economies relative to the original neighbourhood as well as the increasing homogeneous market conditions in the intermediate neighbourhood.

The preferred destination outside the original neighbourhood also played a significant role. Hagedoorn and Narula (1995) have provided empirical data to demonstrate that both the GDP growth rate and the foreign direct investment growth rate of Germany were higher than those of EC-6. What this suggests, as they argued, was that US companies preferred to invest in Germany rather than the other members of the European Community (Belgium, the Netherlands, Luxembourg, West Germany, France and Italy) (EC-6). FDI in Germany grew at over 4.3 times the rate of real GDP (1972–82), compared with 3.3 times recorded by EC-6 as a whole and US multinational firms were treating Germany as original neighbourhood.

Finally, one factor that influenced FDI inflow in the intermediate neighbourhood was the process of integration. As the intermediate neighbourhood moved towards single market, preferred destination became less important. Due to market growth potentials of this neighbourhood, US companies started to diversify their production activities to exploit the advantage of the single market (Hagedoorn and Narula, ibid.).

Extension of the intermediate neighbourhood

Historically, there have been two types of foreign capital inflow to the extended intermediate neighbourhood. These are specific and non-specific foreign capital. Specific foreign capital inflows are in the form of equity or debt specific to a particular investment project; specific in the sense that the funds would not enter the country unless that particular project was undertaken and that do not affect the general borrowing ability of the country. The non-specific or nationally controlled foreign capital are 'borrowed on the basis of the general credit worthiness of the country, fungible between alternative investment projects and constitute part of the general fund of investible resources' (Pursell, 1981).

Knowledge and practices – technical, management, and marketing – without which the project would not be undertaken, has influenced private capital inflows to this neighbourhood. Among the several forms that flow of private capital inflow can take, trend in this neighbourhood drifts towards FDI, particularly in the manufacturing sector, for the following reasons: First, FDI by its very nature entails the identification of an economic opportunity, the formulation of a productive project and its efficient implementation. Secondly, there is the argument that FDI can bestow substantial benefits on the host country where domestic management skills and entrepreneurship are embryonic and where there is no other way of organizing large-scale manufacturing. By implication, FDI is especially suitable for developing countries where technology, human skills and entrepreneurship are as scarce as lack of capital.

FDI inflow in the extended intermediate neighbourhood has been significantly influenced by financial integration or globalization of financial markets. Although there is evidence of large net capital flows from European countries to countries in the periphery for financing governments or railways in the pre-1913 period, portfolio investments were notably absent, and the flows were long-term compared with the much larger relative volume of short-term flows today (Bordo *et al.*, 1999). The process of global financial integration has been fuelled primarily by the liberalization of the markets. Bacchetta and Wincoop (1998) have shown that 'gradual nature of liberalization combined with the costs of absorbing large inflows in emerging economies leads to rich dynamics of capital flows'. The Economic and Social Commission of Asia and the Pacific (ESCAP) shows that the stock markets have assumed an increasing role in mobilizing domestic resource and providing a wider range of financial services. This has been, the survey argued, due to the deregulation, liberalization and other policies to foster the development of the stock markets. Marston (1997) also linked the progress made in integrating the financial markets of the major industrial countries – Britain, France, Germany, Japan, and the United States to deregulation and liberalization. He argued that deregulation and liberalization succeeded to an extent as interest rates in a single currency are nearly the same regardless of whether they are offered in national or Euro-currency markets. Bekaert *et al.* (1999) studied the interrelationship between capital flows returns, dividend in 20 emerging markets and concluded that after liberalization, equity flows increase by 1.4 per cent of market capitalization.

Capital inflows to the extended intermediate neighbourhood have also benefited from technological progress that improves the timeliness, accuracy, and analysis of information. Improved information and communication technology have also played major role in financial integration. Present information systems compute and store data more rapidly, and communication networks have extended their ramifications and augmented their capacity while more reliable data exchange protocols have made it possible to connect computing machines in more efficient ways.

Technological innovation and increasing cultural ties between the developing and industrial countries, has increased the range and variety of participants among emerging market countries in recent cross-border capital flows. Similarly, in many developing economies the private sector as well as the share of total capital flows that go to private borrowers is growing (Eichengreen, 1999).

Extended neighbourhood

So far our discussion of FDI inflows has focused on three types of neighbourhoods. We have learnt that FDI inflows demonstrated a preference for engaging in the United Kingdom as well as Germany, with which the US firms had the initial experience. With the formation of the EC-6, they started to diversify their production activities in order to take advantage of the single market. Likewise, at the end of the 1980s, US private capital inflows (in particular FDI) had no particular preference for either the UK or Germany and the distinction between the original neighbourhood and the intermediate neighbourhood had largely melted away.

To start with, we argue that the FDI inflows to both the original and the intermediate neighbourhoods attained their peak at the end of the 1980s. Hence FDI inflows to the extended neighbourhood became explorative and brought changes in repetitive and local experimentation with new alternatives in its wake. Similarly, linear approximation of FDI in terms of exploitation became increasingly inaccurate as the neighbourhood was extended. In this case, FDI reduced to identifying some critical variables that would make producer(s) to become competitive in the extended neighbourhood. Put differently, ability to compete started depending on the use of techniques, skills, and organizational forms compared to international levels of cost, quality, flexibility, and delivery (Lall, 2001b).

China and the extended neighbourhood

On historical grounds it can be argued that China during the first half of the twentieth century was a proto-colony; certainly a major part of the expansion of foreign investment in China after the First World War was the result of Japanese colonialist policies in Manchuria and the treaty ports.

In 1978, after nearly 30 years of largely self-imposed isolation, China finally seemed ready to rejoin the world economy. In the domestic front, the need for economic adjustment was felt due to a variety of reasons. For example, the per capita GNP had grown since 1957 at an average annual rate of 2.5–3.0 per cent, well below the average for China's neighbouring countries such as Japan and South Korea. Likewise, total factor productivity of the Chinese industry had either been stagnant or actually declined since 1957 (Kamath, 1990). By 1978, Deng Xiao-ping was emerging as post-Mao China's paramount leader. At the Third Plenum of the Chinese Communist Party's Eleventh Central Committee on December 1978, Deng successfully put economic reforms at the top of Beijing's agenda. Perhaps most importantly, he gained support for sharply reversing the Maoist policy that had explicitly rejected on nationalistic and ideological grounds relying on capital inflows from capitalist countries. A policy of 'open door' (Kaifang Zhenze) was formally adopted by the Central Committee due to the growing importance of foreign capital and advanced technologies to China's own drive for modernization.

At the second session of the fifth National People's Congress in July 1979, the 'Law of the People's Republic of China on joint ventures using Chinese and foreign investment' was adopted, granting foreign investment a legal status in China (Kamath, 1994). By 1980, four special economic zones (SEZs) had been established along the southeast coast – Shenzhen, Zhuhai, Xiamen, and Shantou. In addition to attracting foreign capital and advanced technology, these SEZs, according to an informed observer, were intended to serve at least two other very important purposes as well. First, they would serve as the testing grounds for bold, experimental economic and social reforms. Secondly their locations – Shenzhen right next to Hong Kong, Zhuhai adjacent to Macao, and the other two opposite Taiwan – suggest that they were chosen to facilitate the eventual reunification of China. In December 1982, the decision to open up China to the world economy was formally included in the 1982 state constitution adopted by the sixth National People's Congress (Cheng and Zhao, 1995).

In 1984, the concept of SEZs was extended to another 14 coastal cities and Hainan Island. In 1985, three 'development triangles' – the Yangtze River delta, the Pearl River delta in Guangdong, and the Min Nan region in Fujian – were also opened to foreign investors. In 1986, new provisions were made for the encouragement of foreign investment, of which the more important ones included: reducing fees for labour and land use; establishing a limited foreign currency market for joint ventures; extending the maximum duration of a joint-venture agreement beyond 50 years; and permitting wholly owned foreign subsidiaries. Likewise 'Cooperative joint ventures' law was passed in 1988 in order to improve the investment climate in China. In 1995, the concept of SEZs was extended to the Shanghai Pudong New Area, which is about the size of Singapore (Banik, 2003).

During the period 1979–2000, a total of US$348,300 million FDI was invested in China, about US$174,099 million (50 per cent) of which was accounted for by Hong Kong and Macao. The share of Japanese, Taiwanese and American investment in China remains more or less constant during the period. The average investment per annum was about US$16,585 million (Table 3.1).

At the initial period of opening up of the Chinese economy, only the neighbouring countries invested in the coastal regions (SEZ) due to

Table 3.1   Major sources of FDI (US$m) in China: 1979–2000

Country		79–83	84–90	91–2000	79–2000
Hongkong	Total	472.5	11 729.4	161 898.0	174 099.9
and Macao	Average p.a.	118.13	1 830.32	16 189.80	8 290.47
	% of total	52.0	60.26	49.37	50.0
Japan	Total	186.4	2 596.3	25 018.0	27 800.7
	Average p.a.	46.60	432.72	2 501.80	1 323.84
	% of total	20.0	13.34	7.62	8.00
South Korea	Total	na	na	10 326.0	10 326.0
	Average p.a.	na	na	1 032.60	491.71
	% of total	na	na	3.15	3.00
Taiwan	Total	na	na	26 160.0	26 160.0
	Average p.a.	na	na	2 616.00	1 245.71
	% of total	na	na	7.98	7.51
UK	Total	10.6	284.0	8 453.4	8 748.0
	Average p.a.	0.30	47.30	845.34	416.57
	% of total	1.2	1.5	2.6	2.5
France	Total	35.4	180.2	4 219.4	4 435.0
	Average p.a.	8.85	30.00	421.94	211.19
	% of total	3.9	0.9	1.3	1.3
Italy	Total	12.4	166.8	1 652.8	1 832.0
	Average p.a.	3.10	27.80	165.28	87.24
	% of total	1.4	0.9	0.5	0.5
USA	Total	83.1	2 204.8	27 744.1	30 032.0
	Average p.a.	20.78	367.46	2 774.41	1 430.09
	% of total	9.1	11.3	8.5	8.6
Other	Total	1 156.0	2 300.5	62 450.3	64 866.4
countries	Average p.a.	28.90	383.41	6 245.03	3 088.88
	% of total	12.5	11.8	19.1	18.6
All	Total	916.0	19 462.0	327 922.0	348 300.0
	Average p.a.	229.00	3 243.66	32 792.20	16 585.71
	% of total	100	100	100	100

Note: na: not applicable.

Source: Based on *China Economic News*, various issues.

investment friendly policies adopted by the government. However once the success cases were demonstrated across regions other countries too invested due to factors such as export-linked investment and the large market size. Indeed, the investment from the US and Europe made a significant contribution to the total investment in the country in recent times. Interestingly, non-resident Chinese population appears to be the major investor in China. It is imperative to mention here that the non-resident Chinese are mainly businessmen, with a strong representation of billionaire tycoons in Hong Kong, Macao and other South-East Asian

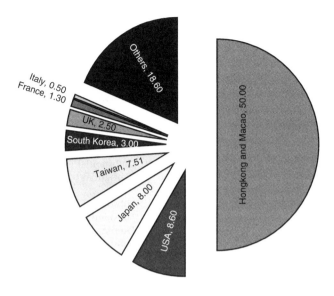

Figure 3.1   Sources of FDI in China: 1979–2000 (% of total)
Source: Based on Table 3.1.

countries (Howard and Banik, 2001a,b; Banik, ibid.). Figure 3.1 shows the major sources of FDI in China during 1979–2000 based on the data shown in Table 3.1.

The point in this context is to negotiate between the national and the global, as well as the historical and the contemporary diasporic. In order to gain more insights, one may analyse the basic characteristics of Chinese business communities such as the nature of Chinese business people, their style in order to manage organizations and then, their effectiveness and efficiency. Tables 3.2 and 3.3 present a few insights in this context.

For all practical purposes the Chinese diaspora has been the region to south of them, surrounding the South China Sea. Historically, the Americans went west, the Russians east and the Chinese south. Redding (1993) made an interesting observation in this context. To quote:

> ... the Chinese who moved have remained in some deep and significant sense still Chinese; the majority of them have not psychologically left China, or at least not left some ideal and perhaps

Table 3.2   The relative position of Chinese capital in Southeast Asia (ASEAN)

Industry	Foreign capital	Chinese capital	Private indigenous capital
Banking	Moderate	Substantial/ Dominant	Moderate/ Substantial
Property Development		Substantial	Substantial
Construction	Moderate	Moderate	Moderate
Mining	Moderate	Moderate/ Substantial	Moderate
Oil Exploration	Dominant	Substantial	Moderate
Plantation Agriculture	Minor		Substantial
Export/Import Trade	Substantial	Substantial	Minor
Manufacturing	Substantial	Substantial	Minor
Light Industries	Minor	Dominant	Minor
Machinery	Substantial	Substantial	Minor
Metals & Petrochemicals	Dominant	Minor	

Notes: Based on assessing the relative positions of (a) foreign, (b) Chinese, and (c) private indigenous capital, on a ten-point scale, such that Less than 1 = no entry; 1.0 to 2.4 = minor; 2.5 to 3.9 = moderate; 4.0 to 7.4 = substantial; and above 7.5 = dominant.

Source: Based on Yoshihara (1988), p. 51.

romanticized notion of Chinese civilization. This is the feature which unites them, and which provides them with one of their most distinct strengths – a capacity to cooperate (p. 2).

China's open door policy has catalysed the expansion of overseas Chinese investment in the mainland. Their roles are also supportive of investment being made by the original neighbourhood. In fact, the Western firms from the original neighbourhood looking at Asia seek collaboration with the overseas Chinese in business because their grips have grown increasingly strong in the region.

Table 3.4 presents the distribution of actual FDI in China according to the industrial sector during the period 1979–2000, while Figure 3.2 provides a summarized pictorial representation of the same. It reveals that FDI in the manufacturing sector in China contributes about 61 per cent of the total actual investment.

The bulk of FDI in this sector appears to be dominated by intermediate technologies. The FDI in the service sector on the other extreme contributes about 23 per cent of the total investment. On the whole, the inflows of FDI in China appear to be highly export-intensive.

Table 3.3 Occupational grouping of overseas Chinese sub-groups in Indonesia and Thailand

Occupational grouping	Indonesia	Thailand
Hokkien	Rubber, copra, coffee, pepper, tobacco, import/export, rubber & plastics, textiles, knitwear, weaving, garments, glassware, earthenware, tea processing, drugs, gold and jewelry, bicycles, trishaws, printing, hotels, entertainment, finance	Rubber, rice, import/export
Chiu Chow		Import/export, clothing, rice milling, native products, dry goods, canned food, cosmetics, hardware, jewelry, distilling, publishing, furniture, entertainment, finance, insurance, Shipping
Cantonese	Rice milling, lumber, machine shops, soap, bakeries, food canning, furniture, hardware, tailoring, photography, coffee shop, truck farming, poultry, restaurants, clothiers, piece goods, dry goods, printing, plastics, entertainment	Machine repair, construction, food and beverage, printing watches/clocks, sugar
Hakka		Leather and hides, weaving, banking, department stores, metal working, shoe manufacturing, tailoring, hairdressing, truck farming
Taiwanese	Transportation, hotels, restaurants, electronics, paper, lumber, engineering production	
Hainanese		Beverages, hotels, drugstore, furniture, hairdressing, fishing
Yunnanese		Jewellery
Kiangsu & Chekiang	Optical, clocks and watches, shoes, gifts, books	
Hupei	Dentistry	
Shantung	Piece goods	

Source: Based on Yuan li Wu and Chun-his Wu (1980), *Economic Development in Southeast Asia: The Chinese Dimension*, Stanford; Hoover Institution Press.

Table 3.4   FDI classified according to the industrial sector, China: 1979–2000 (US$100m)

Industrial sector	No. of projects	Ratio (%)	Amount	Ratio (%)
Agriculture, forestry, husbandry, fishing	10 355	2.85	123.10	1.82
Manufacturing	265 609	72.99	4 115.34	60.87
Construction business	9 059	2.59	196.91	2.91
Communication and transportation, storage, and post & telecommunications	4 027	1.11	163.86	2.42
Wholesale and retail catering	18 410	5.06	233.96	3.46
Real estate and public services	37 252	10.24	1 595.43	23.60
Health, sports and social welfare	1 030	0.28	47.73	0.71
Education, culture, arts, broadcast and film	1 336	0.37	21.23	0.31
Scientific research, technical services	2 510	0.69	21.24	0.31
Others	14 297	3.93	242.17	3.58
Total	*363 885*	*100*	*6 760.98*	*100*

Source: *Based on China Economic News*, External Services Division of Economic Daily, 21 May 2001.

The overseas Chinese community played a significant contributory role in this context.

Few insights can be mentioned in relation to technology transfer in case of China and the role of the overseas Chinese community in this context. Technology transfers in China have led to the very important transfer of 'software' – managerial and export-marketing technology. Similarly, substantial technology was transferred in the low, intermediate and even high technology areas through the establishment of manufacturing facilities, training, and 'learning by doing' aspects of technology transfer. This was the pattern of technology development for the economies of Hong Kong, Singapore, South Korea and Taiwan through the 1960s and the 1970s. China has relied on Hong Kong, and

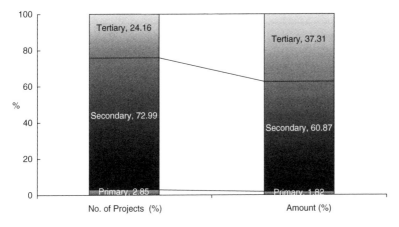

Figure 3.2 Distribution of FDI among sectors in China: 1979–2000
Source: Based on Table 3.4.

more recently on Taiwan, as its principal sources of FDI. FDI from Hong Kong has played an especially large role in Guangdong, while FDI from Taiwan has become increasingly important in Fuzian. It seems important to mention that Hong Kong and Taiwan have never been recognized as major sources of advanced technology. Similarly, these countries have been less known for adoption of new technology. Thus, the technology transfer through FDI from Hong Kong and Taiwan to China has been in the form of low or quite standardized technology (Banik and Subbayamma, 2000).

India and the extended neighbourhood

Table 3.5 presents the principal sources of FDI in India during 1979–2000 and the sub periods 1979–86, 1987–90 and 1991–2000. The average FDI per annum during the entire period in India has been reported to be US$3,463 million. The largest annual average investment is, however, reported to be US$7,956 million during the sub-period 1991–2000. Figure 3.3 shows the sources of FDI in India for the period 1979–2000 in the form of a pie-chart.

The USA appears to be the largest investor in India both during the sub-periods and the entire period (from US$119.47 million to US$20,187 million). The FDI inflows from the US constitute about 17 per cent of the total FDI in India during 1979–86. The percentage share has improved significantly to an average of 28 per cent during the period 1991–2000. The effects of reforms on trade and investment

Table 3.5 Major sources of FDI in India: 1979–2000

Country		79–86	87–90	91–2000	79–2000
USA				19 904.870	
	Total	119.47	162.74		20 187.08
	Average p.a			1 639.42	
		17.06	54.25		961.29
	% of total	21.61	28.80	20.61	27.75
UK				4 741.51	
	Total	31.15	45.56		4 818.22
	Average p.a				
		4.45	15.18	626.83	229.43
	% of total	5.63	8.06	6.62	6.63
Non-resident Indians	Total	63.97	46.97	2 854.41	2 965.35
	Average p.a	9.14	15.65	135.92	141.21
	% of total	11.57	8.31	4.00	4.08
Germany	Total	55.95	43.72	2 470.62	2 570.29
	Average p.a	7.99	14.73	274.51	122.39
	% of total	10.12	7.73	3.45	3.45
Japan	Total	76.9	27.90	3 142.57	3 247.37
	Average p.a	10.98	9.30	349.17	154.64
	% of total	13.91	4.94	4.40	4.46
Switzerland	Total	8.85	24.47	912.01	945.33
	Average p.a	1.26	7.49	101.33	45.02
	% of total	1.60	4.33	1.27	1.30
Mauritius	Total	n.a.	n.a.	8 620.06	8 620.06
	Average p.a	n.a.	n.a.	957.78	19.55
	% of total	n.a.	n.a.	12.04	11.85
Netherlands	Total	11.56	5.46	1 619.58	1 636.60
	Average p.a	1.65	1.82	179.95	77.93
	% of total	2.09	0.97	2.26	2.25
Australia	Total	0.74	4.0	1 893.28	1 898.02
	Average p.a	0.11	1.33	210.36	8.58
	% of total	0.13	0.70	2.64	2.61
Singapore	Total	0.94	6.88	1 204.87	1 212.69
	Average p.a	0.13	2.29	133.87	57.75
	% of total	0.17	1.22	1.68	1.66
Canada	Total	4.97	1.92	757.52	764.41
	Average p.a	0.71	0.64	84.17	36.40
	% of total	0.90	0.35	1.03	1.05

Continued

Table 3.5 Continued

Country		79–86	87–90	91–2000	79–2000
Other	Total	178.24	195.45	3481.30	23 854.99
countries	Average p.a.	25.46	65.15	3 142.47	1 135.95
	% of total	32.27	34.59	40.00	32.80
All	Total	552.74	565.07	71 602.60	72 720.41
	Average p.a.	78.96	188.36	7 955.85	3 462.87
	% of total	100	100	100	100

Note: n.a.: not applicable.

Source: Based on Reserve Bank of India Bulletin, various issues; India Investment Centre, India Investment Climate, various issues.

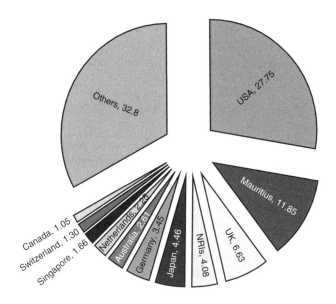

Figure 3.3 Sources of FDI in India: 1979–2000 (% of total)
Source: Based on Table 3.5.

relations with the United States have been profound. It is now not only the largest investor country in India, but also its trading partern. It appears that most of the FDI inflows to India came from the original neighborhood (USA, UK and Germany). Interestingly, Mauritius is the second largest source of FDI inflows to India in recent times. One possible explanation for the dominance of Mauritius is the double taxation treaty between the two countries, which favours routing of investment through this country. Perhaps the Indian policy makers responded positively to the role being played by overseas Indians (or persons of Indian origin in Mauritius). It can also be seen that the inflows from Japan, United Kingdom, the Netherlands, and Germany are steadily increasing during the later periods. The investment made by the Non-resident Indians (NRIs) was as much as US$2,965 million (4 per cent).

Before proceeding further, it is pertinent to mention here that the FDI figures reported for China and India (for example in Tables 3.1 and 3.5 respectively) are not directly comparable. This is because many developing countries do not follow the IMF guidelines (IMF, 1993) completely while compiling and reporting their FDI data. While it is widely recognized (Kumar, 2003) that the FDI gap between China and India may not be as large as suggested by official figures, it is only recently that the wrong signals conveyed to potential investors and the consequences thereof are being appreciated (Srivastava, 2003).

Table 3.6 presents the distribution of FDI approvals according to the industrial sector in India during the period 1991–2000. It is interesting to note that unlike China, fuel and power sector dominates (about 28 per cent of total investment) in India. The telecommunications sector too contributes about 19 per cent of the total investment during the period 1991–2000. A summarized diagrammatic representation of this distribution is shown in Figure 3.4.

India has excelled in the area of computer software and has evolved as an Information Technology hub for the world market. In recent times, 60 per cent of the total output of the IT sector is exported; another quarter of the output produced is shared between the parent multinational corporations (MNCs) and affiliates of the parent of the MNCs. On the other hand, 60 per cent of the output produced by the MNCs in all other sectors is sold in the local market providing a stronger argument that the size of the Indian domestic market will continue to play a significant role in attracting FDI (UNCTAD, 2004).

Since 1991, India has encouraged foreign investment into infrastructure but the demand for infrastructure services is still not being met. This has been blamed on skewed investments in terms of concentration in consumer durable sectors (where it is quick-yielding and withdrawal is easy) as opposed to infrastructure (investment is of long-term nature and the amount of investment needed is very high). Maitra (2003) reveals that shortage of power is estimated at about 10 per cent of the total electrical energy and approximately 20 per cent of peak capacity requirement. India's per capita electricity consumption is very low – 270 kilowatt hours/year as compared to 480 for China. India seems to have neglected the basic infrastructure such as railroad, power, road, and water management. On the whole, the emphasis on modernizing its

Table 3.6 FDI (approval) classified according to the industrial sector, India: 1991–2000 (US$m)

Industrial sector	No. of projects	Ratio (%)	Amount	Ratio (%)
Metallurgical	676	3.27	3 191.71	5.67
Fuels	860	4.16	15 994.96	27.80
Electrical equipment, etc.	4 301	20.83	5 523.12	9.77
Telecommunications	769	3.72	11 236.08	19.32
Automobile	1 377	6.67	3 978.56	7.04
Machinery, machine tools, fertilizers, dye-stuffs, etc.	4 807	23.28	4 140.24	7.32
Drugs and pharmaceuticals	467	2.26	597.72	1.06
Textiles including dyed and printed	785	3.80	709.48	1.25
Paper and pulp including paper product	183	0.89	679.16	1.20
Food processing industries	918	4.44	3 042.26	5.38
Vegetable oil, glass, ceramic, etc.	1 662	8.05	2 009.12	3.55
Financial services, banks, hospital and diagnostic centres, etc.	928	4.50	3 474.95	6.15
Hotel and tourism	509	2.46	1 006.50	1.78
Trading and miscellaneous industries	2 409	11.67	1 549.16	2.74
Total	*20 653*	*100*	*57 133.03*	*100*

Source: Based on *India's Investment Climate* (various issues), Indian Investment Centre.

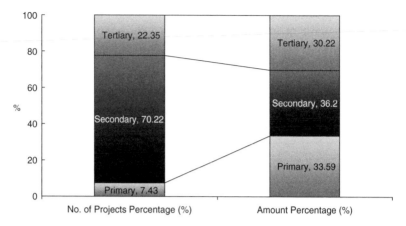

Figure 3.4   Distribution of FDI approvals among sectors in India: 1991–2000
Source: Based on Table 3.6.

basic infrastructure has been rather mild, whereas this could have been the priority in order to generate employment in both rural and urban areas.

Three types of investment projects have attracted FDI inflows in to India. The first includes projects that are invested in by the European investors. They are concentrated in the intermediate goods and machinery and equipment sectors. The EU accounted for 26–27 per cent of India's exports and 24–29 per cent of the imports during the period 1990–91 to 1998–99. The second are from North American firms, oriented towards IT and financial services sectors. Firms from USA accounted for 14–21 per cent of India's exports and 8–12 per cent of India's imports during the period 1990–91 to 1998–99. The third are from Japanese and East Asian firms concentrated in the old economy machines and equipment sector and in the new economy IT sector (Bhaumik *et al.*, 2003).

The FDI inflows are strongly influenced by India's willingness to adopt established foreign technology and management skills. It may be argued that transfer of technology and know-how is at least as likely to have an impact on India's future growth as the quantum of FDI. The issues of technological and managerial skills have been subjects of debate. Studies support the view of very little technological content in FDI investments – in particular hardware transfer. A negligible proportion of the firms spend a significant fraction of their turnover on training hence the absolute level of knowledge and know-how spillover from FDI is not significant in India. As we have seen in the case of China, firms investing in India also have very small budgets for Research and Development (R&D). It is the case that the extent of transfer of cutting edge technology to India, and the extent of spillovers by way of enhancement of skills of the labour force will remain slow for many years ahead.

The Caribbean and the extended neighbourhood

The Caribbean region is not considered to have locational advantages such as large markets, lower costs of resource or superior infrastructure. FDI decisions in the Caribbean have been strongly influenced by historical ties with member states' colonial past. Table 3.7 reveals the picture in this context.

It appears that the territories of the Caribbean continue to display inherited linkages with the original neighbourhoods, such as UK, France and the Netherlands. Interestingly, USA is the major source of imports of these island economies.

The decline in Official Development Assistance in the 1990s was offset by the increase in private flows to the region of which FDI was the most significant component compared to the debt flows (CARICOM, 2000). Table 3.8 shows the FDI inflows to the Caribbean during 1989–94 and 1995–2000. For most of the countries the figures do not exhibit a smooth upward trend. It appears that the average inflows of FDI to the Caribbean economies during the period 1995–2000 were higher than during the period 1989–1994. The only exceptions reported were for Jamaica and Antigua and Barbuda. The major recipients were Cayman Island, Netherland Antilles, Dominican Republic and Trinidad and Tobago. Interestingly, several of the major recipients (for example, Trinidad and Tobago, The Bahamas, Anguilla, Antigua and Barbuda, Cuba, Netherland Antilles, Saint Kitts and Grenadines and Guyana) have reported FDI flows in excess of that received in 1999.

It is imperative to mention here that the above movement was particularly erratic in natural-resource rich countries such as Guyana and Trinidad and Tobago. This may be due to the tendency for such projects to be fairly large and lumpy in nature, with investment lulls in between expansion phases. For example, in 1999 almost 90 per cent of the equity capital inflows reported for Trinidad and Tobago (US$488.5 million) was associated with the investment in a natural gas facility (Atlantic LNG Plant) by BP Amoco and Repsol.

Traditionally, FDI inflows in CARICOM countries have been directed to the primary and tertiary sectors namely, mining (bauxite and precious metals), energy (petroleum), agriculture, forestry and tourism services. However, over time, there has been some inflows to mainly labor intensive, medium to low-technology manufacturing such as garments and data processing activities and the resurgence of inflows into the petroleum and natural gas sector in Trinidad and Tobago.

Table 3.7 How the Caribbean is linked with the original neighbourhood

Island economy	Area (km²)	Present political status	Political classification	Link with the original neighbourhood/colonial power	Main import source	Currency
Saint Vincent & Grenadines	399	Independent from U K 1979	Independent	UK	USA	East Caribbean $
Jamaica	10 830	Independent from UK 1962	Independent	UK	USA	Jamaican $
Dominica	754	Independent from UK 1976	Independent	UK	USA	East Caribbean $
Grenada	340	Independent from UK 1974	Independent	UK	USA	East Caribbean $
Saint Lucia	610	Independent from UK 1979	Independent	UK	USA	East Caribbean $
Montserrat	100	Overseas territory of UK	Integrated	UK	USA	Eastern Caribbean $
Dominican Republic	48 730	Independent from Haiti 1844	Independent	France	USA	Dominican peso
Saint Kitts and Nevis	261	Independent from UK 1983	Independent	UK	USA	Eastern Caribben $
Turks and Caicos Islands	430	Overseas territory of UK	Integrated	UK	USA	US$
Antigua and Barbuda	442	Independent from UK 1981	Independent	UK	USA	East Caribbean $
Anguilla	91	Overseas territory of UK	Integrated	UK	USA	East Caribbean $
Guadaloupe	1 706	Overseas department of France	Integrated	France	France	Euro
Trinidad and Tobago	5 128	Independent from UK 1962	Independent	UK	USA	Trinidad and and Tobago $
Martinique	1 060	Overseas department of France	Integrated	France	France	Euro
Netherlands Antilles	960	Part of the Netherlands	Integrated	Netherlands	Venezuela	Netherlands Antillean Guilder
Barbados	430	Independent from UK 1966	Independent	UK	USA	Barbados $ pegged at 2 per US$
Bahamas	10 070	Independent from UK 1973	Independent	UK	USA	Bahamian $ fixed at par to US$
Virgin Islands	352	Territory of the USA	Integrated	USA	USA	US$
British Virgin Islands	150	Overseas territory of UK	Integrated	UK	USA	US$

Continued

Table 3.7 Continued

Island economy	Area (km²)	Present political status	Political classification	Link with the original neighbour hood/colo-nial power	Main import source	Currency
Cayman Islands	259	Overseas territory of the UK	Integrated	UK	USA	Cayman $
Aruba	193	Part of the Netherlands	Integrated	Netherlands	USA	Aruban Guilder

Sources: Based on *CIA World Factbook* (2001); CARICOM (2000).

Table 3.8 FDI inflows to the Caribbean economies: 1989–2000 (US$m)

Host economy	1989–1994 (Annual average)	1995	1996	1997	1998	1999	2000	1995–2000 (Annual average)
Anguilla	10	18	33	21	28	40	48	31.33
Antigua and Barbuda	36	31	19	23	27	27	31	26.33
Aruba	34	1	84	196	84	392	228	164.17
Bahamas	10	107	88	210	147	149	251	158.67
Barbados	11	12	13	15	16	17	14	14.5
Belize	16	21	17	12	19	56	28	25.5
Cayman Islands	179	42	1 232	3 151	4 348	6 468	4 783	3 337.33
Cuba	6	5	19	1	15	9	13	10.33
Dominica	17	54	18	21	7	18	16	23.33
Dominican Republic	161	414	97	421	700	1 338	953	653.83
Grenada	17	20	19	35	51	46	37	34.66
Haiti	4	−2	4	4	11	30	13	10
Jamaica	144	147	184	203	369	524	456	313.83
Montserrat	6	3	–	3	3	8	2	6.1
Netherlands Antilles	22	10	2 826	1 038	892	401	777	990.66
Saint Kitts and Nevis	25	20	35	20	32	42	38	31.17
Saint Lucia	39	33	18	48	83	94	75	58.5
Saint Vincent and the Grenadines	20	31	43	92	89	46	76	62.83
Trinidad and Tobago	250	299	355	1 000	732	643	662	615.17
Virgin Islands	186	470	510	500	1 348	3 656	1 483	1 327.83
Guyana	57	74	93	53	47	48	87	67
Suriname	−82	−21	19	−9	9	−18	−12	−32

Sources: Based on *United Nations (2001); World Investment Report 2001,* New York and Geneva.

The sectoral distribution of FDI inflows has, however, now begun to reflect the international trend with a concentration in the services sector, and primarily, financial services.

As we have already mentioned that the sources of FDI inflows into the community reflect the historical ties with member states' colonial past and have included the United Kingdom, USA, Canada and the Netherlands. Recently, there has been some degree of diversification in the sources from which inflows have originated and investments have been from France, Germany, Spain and India (about US$34 million in 1998). In recent time investment from South, East and South-East Asia to the Caribbean is on the rise. Incentives to export-oriented investment as well as privileged access to the United States market have played a role in attracting, for instance, garments and other labour-intensive industries from Asian to Caribbean countries. Besides, Taiwan is one of the largest investors in the Caribbean in recent times, but a large part of its investment is concentrated in tax haven economics such as the Virgin Islands.

Table 3.9 portrays the basic features of FDI inflows to the Caribbean. In the Bahamas for example, the main sectoral and industrial recipients of FDI are tourism, financial services and infrastructure. The key players are Belgium, France, Germany, Hong Kong, UK, USA and the Netherlands. Canada, UK and the USA are the major players in Barbados' tourism, agriculture, manufacturing, financial services and informatics sectors. The major players in Belize's agriculture/mariculture (shrimp farming), manufacturing (agro-processing), tourism and infrastructure (telecommunications) sectors are China, Taiwan, UK and USA. In Guyana, Canada, South Korea/Malaysia, UK, and US Virgin Islands dominate the sectors of mining (gold), forestry, Infrastructure (power and telecommunications), and trade. Tourism, mining and manufacturing in Jamaica are dominated by Canada, UK and USA respectively. In the OECS, Caribbean, USA, UK, and other European countries – particularly Italy – are the main sources of FDI in agriculture, tourism and manufacturing. The Netherlands and USA are the major players in Suriname's mining and manufacturing. In Trinidad and Tobago, energy (petroleum and petrochemicals, natural gas), electricity, transportation and communications and manufacturing are dominated by select Asian countries, Spain, UK and the USA.

To a large extent, CARICOM (Caribbean community) economies have pursued liberal foreign investment policies with limited restrictions on FDI. Some of these restrictions include: administrative foreign exchange control; land acquisition and reservation of certain sectors for local operations. The legal and institutional framework for investment promotion in the Caribbean have been well-established. While the legal framework addresses the needs of investors – particularly the offshore sectors – in the

Table 3.9   Caribbean community – sectoral and industrial recipients and sources of FDI inflows

Country	Main sectoral and industrial recipients of FDI	Main sources of FDI
Bahamas	Tourism, financial services infrastructure	Belgium, France, Germany, Hong Kong, UK, USA, Netherlands
Belize	Agriculture/shrimp farming, manufacturing (agro processing), tourism, infrastructure (telecommunications)	China, Taiwan, UK, USA
Barbados	Tourism, agriculture, manufacturing, financial services and informatics	Canada, UK, USA
Guyana	Mining (gold), forestry, infrastructure (power and telecommunications), trade	Canada, South Korea/Malaysia, UK, USA, Virgin Islands
Jamaica	Tourism, mining, and manufacturing	Canada, UK and USA
OECS	Agriculture, tourism, manufacturing	Non-OECS, USA, UK, Italy
Suriname	Mining, manufacturing	Netherlands, USA
Trinidad and Tobago	Petroleum and petrochemicals, natural gas, electricity, transportation and communications, manufacturing	USA, UK, Spain, India

Source: Based on CARICOM (2000).

form of international business legislation, the policy statements by the government translate the framework into the administrative arrangements and procedures for the approval of investments. Emphasis has been on all types of investment. The Caribbean has a very weak capital goods sector due to non-availability of high-tech and high value-added activities. In general, the Caribbean economies are classified as natural resource based or service oriented or a combination of both.

The Caribbean region has potential for high-tech industries. The FTAA – tentatively scheduled for completion in 2007 will encompass some 34 countries in the Americas, including the United States, creating a market with a population of approximately 800 million and a GDP of some $8.5 trillion (Schott, 2001). The English-speaking Caribbean economies, despite their small sizes may play an important role by providing fiscal incentives to foreign investors (with particular reference to Indian IT investors) in the areas of services and manufacturing. The decision is strategic since it will help the foreign investors to explore markets in developed economies like USA and Canada. In recent times Mexico is taking full advantage in the NAFTA region. Private investors are more interested in financing projects in the Caribbean due to little risk involved. Given the inter-island synergies between the British West Indies, economies of scale are sometimes difficult to attain (United Nations, 2001). However, the region can follow the models laid down by countries such as Canada or Ireland that have built their industries on accommodation to the United States. In this context there may be bright prospects of establishing strong India-CARICOM trade and investment relationships in the form of extension of the extended neighborhood model under the changing scenario.

India enjoys a special position in the context of the Caribbean economies due to its historical, ethnic and emotional relationships. It may be possible to develop strong economic linkages leveraging on these old relationships. The Caribbean countries need to reduce their dependence on the US (and to some extent the EU) markets for their imports and exports so as to dampen the wide fluctuations in their economic activity from year to year. The Indian economy has many complementarities *vis-à-vis* the Caribbean and these could be used synergistically to result in a win–win situation for both. On the other hand, there are many areas, covering primary, secondary and tertiary sectors of the economy where India has done exceedingly well and there is scope for developing economic linkages based on the same.

India's advantage as an extended neighbour of the CARICOM

India's share, as a source of imports and destination of Caribbean exports has been marginal. For example, exports to India from Barbados in 2001 was US$37,000 of the total exports of US$272.8 million, Imports from India was US$1.6 million of the total imports of US$1,156 million, However, there may be a vast scope to increase the existing trade pattern.

Indian diaspora are not only strong in the USA and Europe but, they also form an equally strong business community in both Africa and the Caribbean. These roots may help the Indian business community to export capital in the form of FDI of its own to the region. Under the FTAA regime more and more multinationals may shift the operation and control of key business functions away from their head office to the English-speaking Caribbean. This may happen at a rapid rate as IT skills and networks make the spread of digital information increasingly easy. Indian companies can take full advantage of the changing scenario by establishing their businesses and then explore their potential in the integrated region. This may be possible in the areas of IT and other financial services. Other possible areas of cooperation in order to create a win–win situation are, service sector development, manpower and training, Indian high technology applications – satellite remote sensing, oceanography, IT, biotechnology, Indian industrial joint ventures, offshore financial operations, oil and gas-production, refining and transportation, Indian entertainment industry (Indian Hindi films), exchange of academics, technical cooperation in economy, finance, science and technology, pharmaceutical industry. The Caribbean is the region hardest hit by HIV/AIDS in the world outside sub-Saharan Africa. India can take advantage of its cheap anti-AIDS drugs in this region. Similarly, the region may be treated as an entry point for Indian goods and services to the Latin American and North American markets.

Summary

Our analyses reveal interesting insights that explain foreign investment inflows to the countries both developed and developing. The approach in the form of neighbourhood and extended neighbourhood is deepening and widening our understanding of FDI flows.

Although there are some apparent similarities between the concept of 'psychic distance' as proposed by some Swedish economists (Johanson and Vahlne, 1977; Johanson and Wiedersheim-Paul, 1975; Vahlne and Wiedersheim-Paul, 1977) and later elaborated and extended by other authors (Child *et al.*, 2000), and the neighbourhood model proposed in this book, there are significant differences in concepts, explanations and consequences of the models. 'Psychic distance' presents a static concept, wherein investments and their sequence is attempted to be explained through the 'psychic distance' between the home country and the host country. In the neighbourhood model, the role and importance of 'psychic' or 'cultural' distance itself changes dynamically as investments move from the original to the intermediate and the extended neighbourhoods. Although developed in the context of the USA, the concept of original, intermediate and extended neighbourhoods should be equally applicable in explaining the FDI flows of other FDI sources.

Similarly, the eclectic paradigm of Dunning (2001) hypothesizes that firms make their international production decisions based on perceived Ownership (O advantages), Location (L advantages) and Internalization (I advantages) related factors. When stretched from the micro to the macro, this leads to the concept of the investment development path (IDP). As a country develops, the attractiveness of its OLI advantages change to potential investors (both inward and outward) and the country is likely to go through five relatively well-defined stages. The IDP is a useful heuristic model and attempting to find the position of a country on its IDP can lead to meaningful policy debates. In a way, the O advantages are related to the *push* factors of the home country, the L advantages to the *pull* factors of the host and the I advantages to the *how* of the involvement in so far as an international production decision is concerned. Although the basic structure of the model is very attractive, its details have been evolving over time (Dunning and Narula, 1996) and may contain too many explanatory variables – many with limited predictive value. On one side, this may be too general a theory and on the other it ignores the possibility of any special advantage for a pair of countries. Countries in the *neighbourhood* have a role in reduction of perceived risk and Dunning (1988) also argues that firms from developing countries are likely to perform activities in neighbouring countries, which are politically and economically stable.

We find there are significant common factors in explaining FDI inflows to different regions. While a substantial portion of FDI inflows may be explained by select economic variables, the country-specific factors and the idiosyncratic component account for more of investment inflows in Europe, China and India. These findings may have strong relevance in explaining possible Indian investments in the Caribbean.

As noted by Arndt (2001), one of the innovative features of the current phase of globalization is the fragmentation of production into production networks based on component specialization and intra-product trade. It offers groups of small countries opportunities to make open regionalism work by enhancing their productivity and competitiveness as well as welfare of their nationals. This concept is equally applicable to the Caribbean, although Arndt (ibid.) justifies it for the ASEAN. As production networks grow in the ASEAN region, this provides opportunity for both China and India to participate in these networks in their extended neighbourhood with their respective component specializations.

It is now open to question why some economies have attracted large FDI flows and grown fast (for example East Asia and now China) over the last forty years and others have not. The Latin American and the Caribbean economies are geographically closer to the highly developed economies. Yet, the regions could not take advantage of this physical proximity. These economies could not become part of the original, intermediate or even extensions of intermediate neighborhoods perhaps due to the fact that most of the people came from other cultures where neighbourhood was too weak.

4
Foreign Investment: China

Introduction

In Chapter 3 we discussed an alternate view that could explain the inflows of FDI in different neighbourhoods. The last two or three decades have witnessed marked changes in the global organization of industry with far-reaching effects for the evolving patterns of integration of developing countries into world economy. FDI affects resource allocation in several ways. The presence of MNC affiliates may affect capital accumulation, industrial structure and performance, trade propensity and many other structural characteristics of the host economy. Thus it is natural to assume that MNCs do influence, at least to some extent, the observed patterns of industrialization and trade orientation in host countries. This has been the case, for example, in the larger Latin American economies, and the South East Asian countries in which the presence of foreign capital is significant.

The relationship between the degree of openness and inflows of FDI in developing countries has been the subject of numerous empirical studies. Most of the studies pursued traditional causality tests using single time series or panel data. The determinants of FDI are analysed based on time series approach with the help of select macroeconomic parameters. For example, Cheng and Zhao (1995) analysed the panel data in order to determine FDI inflows in 28 Chinese regions over 1983–92. The variables were identified as geographical location, factor endowments and per capita GDP. They found that per capita GDP and the effects of SEZs[1] played a significant role in this context, in addition to an increasing importance of good quality infrastructure. Cheng and Kwan (1999) analysed the Chinese FDI data from 1986 to 1995 using the partial adjustment model. Good quality infrastructure appeared to be the dominating variable in the study. Balasubramanyam *et al.* (1999) used cross-sectional annual data averaged over the period 1965–70 for a sample of 46 developing countries and found that the size of the domestic market, the competitive climate in relation to local producers, and the interaction between FDI and human capital exerted an important influence upon growth performance.

Agenor's (2001) study is quite interesting in this context. Using the panel model, he considered the rate of growth of real GDP as a proxy for the rate of return on domestic investment, the ratio of gross investment to GDP, the degree of openness, the ratio of total debt to GDP, the real London Inter Bank Offer Rate (LIBOR) rate, the real GDP per capita and the volatility of the real exchange rate. He found that real GDP per capita has a positive effect on FDI inflows. The real LIBOR rate has no discernible effect – neither does the stock of foreign debt nor the ratio of domestic investment to output. Interestingly the rate of growth of real GDP, as well as the degree of openness, both have a highly significant impact on FDI inflows, although the degree of significance of the latter variable drops somewhat when the lagged value of FDI to GDP is added as a regressor to account for some degree of inertia in these inflows. The volatility of the real exchange rate however has a negative sign.

It is often argued that the entry of external capital may lead to greater economic activity and encourage savings, but it may also lead to the appreciation of assets (through the accompanying foreign stock and real estate market booms), which might raise consumption and reduce savings. The effect may be multiplied if the national currency is overvalued and import tariffs are lowered as this facilitates access to imported goods. The problem may be more acute if the domestic loans are consumption-driven. Obstfeld (1994) in his model viewed resource inflows either as substitutes for domestic savings or complements. As long as the marginal return from investment is at least equal to the cost of capital, net foreign resource inflows may increase physical capital per worker and upgrade technology, which in turn encourages activities in the economy.

This chapter seeks to examine various aspects of the contribution made by FDI to the Chinese economy. The next section traces the geographical distribution of FDI among different regions of China. The following section focuses on the various forms of FDI in China and also examines the performances of foreign enterprises and local firms. The subsequent four sections discuss, in turn, the impact of FDI on foreign trade, the nature of technology adoption and the role of foreign firms, the magnitude of expenditure on R&D incurred by various organizations; and the current status of Chinese economic development. The main findings of this chapter are summarized in the final section.

Geographical distribution of FDI

In general the inflow of FDI to the host countries may be explained by three arguments. The size of the market in any industry and rapid growth and diversification of domestic expenditure are the key features of *market-seeking* arguments; large production and deposits of mineral commodities and increasing demand and exploration requirements are considered as the key ingredients of *resource-seeking* arguments; and low unit labour costs and relocation of labour-intensive industries are considered as the contributor to *efficiency-seeking* arguments. All these three arguments may be applicable in the case of China.

Table 4.1 identifies the number of projects and the principal sources of FDI according to four broad categories in China during the period 1979–2000. It also shows the contractual value of FDI and its actual value according to the sources. China is the host of many countries in terms of FDI inflows during the period 1979–2000. The top ten neighbours dominate in the total share in number of projects (82 per cent), contractual values (73 per cent) as well as actual values (75 per cent). EU total and North America total are more or less close to each other. The previous chapter has already explained the role of neighbourhood and of ethnic Chinese for FDI in China.

Interestingly, Hong Kong plays a significant role in this context. A lot of companies investing in China do it from their 'regional' headquarters in Hong Kong. UNCTAD (2002) believes that much of Hong Kong's investment destined for China is 'transit FDI'. They are temporarily parked in Hong Kong before being invested in East Asian economies including China.[2] For example, in 2000, 855 foreign companies had their regional headquarters in Hong Kong, of which 212 were from the USA, 127 from Japan, and about 200 from EU countries (Apoteker, 2002).[3]

Economic activities have always had a tendency to cluster geographically. Incentive mechanisms, markets and factors of production, specialized skills and suppliers, and institutions guide firms to make an ideal investment decision. Table 4.2 shows the geographical distribution of FDI inflow to China over the period 1996–2000. It appears that on an average about 88 per cent (in terms of actual realized value) of the total investments are located in the coastal region. More specifically, five of them together (Guangdong, Jiangsu, Fujian, Shanghai municipality and Shangdong)[4] received more than 65 per cent of the total investment.

52

Table 4.1 FDI in China classified according to the sources of funds: 1979–2000
(US$100m)

Country/region	No. of projects	Ratio (%)	Contractual value	Ratio (%)	Actual inputs	Ratio (%)
Total	363 885	100.00	6 760.97	100.00	3 483.46	100.00
10 countries/ region in Asia Total	*297 334*	*81.71*	*4 923.55*	*72.82*	*2 616.25*	*75.10*
Hong Kong	192 023	52.77	3 279.18	48.50	1 702.97	48.89
Macao	6 851	1.88	96.57	1.43	39.84	1.14
Taiwan	46 624	12.81	478.16	7.07	261.60	7.51
Japan	20 383	5.60	388.14	5.74	278.01	7.98
Philippines	1 369	0.38	25.64	0.38	10.30	0.30
Thailand	2 880	0.79	49.73	0.74	19.93	0.57
Malaysia	2031	0.56	49.35	0.73	22.05	0.63
Singapore	9 122	2.51	353.80	5.23	169.92	4.88
Indonesia	760	0.21	15.91	0.24	8.37	0.24
Republic of Korea	15 291	4.20	187.06	2.77	103.26	2.96
EU Total	*11 384*	*3.13*	*504.28*	*7.46*	*260.50*	*7.48*
Germany	2421	0.67	122.35	1.81	58.53	1.68
France	1 720	0.47	57.48	0.85	44.35	1.27
Italy	1 495	0.41	27.11	0.40	18.32	0.53
Holland	824	0.23	74.84	1.11	29.90	0.86
Belgium	340	0.09	8.02	0.12	4.17	0.12
Luxembourg	58	0.02	3.12	0.05	0.64	0.02
UK	2 815	0.77	169.75	2.51	87.48	2.51
Ireland	34	0.01	0.89	0.01	0.20	0.01
Denmark	173	0.05	12.10	0.18	3.49	0.10
Finland	118	0.03	4.48	0.07	2.15	0.06
Sweden	418	0.11	9.73	0.14	6.26	0.18
Austria	423	0.12	5.15	0.08	2.23	0.06
Greece	29	0.01	0.57	0.01	0.15	0.00
Spain	464	0.13	7.88	0.12	2.28	0.07
Portugal	52	0.01	0.79	0.01	0.33	0.01
North America Total	*36 100*	*9.92*	*685.44*	*10.14*	*323.61*	*9.29*
Canada	4 789	1.32	79.34	1.17	23.29	0.67
US	31 311	8.60	606.11	8.96	300.32	8.62
Free Islands Total	*3 822*	*1.05*	*356.97*	*5.28*	*157.20*	*4.51*
Virgin Islands	3 188	0.88	279.26	4.13	132.28	3.80
Cayman Islands	312	0.09	56.14	0.83	15.57	0.45
Western Samoa	322	0.09	21.57	0.32	9.35	0.27

Source: Based on *China Economic News*, various issues.

Table 4.2 Geographical distribution of FDI inflow to China (%)

Region	1996	1998	2000
Coastal region			
Beijing	3.71	4.79	4.17
Tianjin	5.14	4.67	2.89
Hebei	1.98	3.15	1.68
Liaoning	4.15	5.31	5.07
Shanghai	9.41	8.10	7.84
Jiangsu	12.44	14.64	15.93
Zhejiang	3.63	2.96	4.00
Fujian	9.75	9.30	8.51
Shangdong	6.29	6.03	7.37
Guangdong	28.07	28.78	27.97
Guangxi	1.58	1.96	1.30
Hainan	1.88	1.58	1.07
Subtotal	*88.04*	*91.28*	*87.80*
Central Region			
Shanxi	0.33	0.54	0.56
Inner Mongolia	0.17	0.20	0.26
Jilin	1.08	0.90	0.84
Heilongjiang	1.35	1.16	0.75
Anhui	1.21	0.61	0.79
Jiangxi	0.72	1.03	0.56
Henan	1.25	1.36	1.40
Hubai	1.63	2.29	2.34
Hunan	1.78	1.81	1.68
Subtotal	*9.52*	*9.90*	*9.97*
West Region			
Chongqing	n.a.	0.95	0.61
Sichuan	1.05	0.82	1.08
Guizhou	0.07	0.10	0.06
Yunan	0.16	0.32	0.32
Shaanxi	0.78	0.66	0.72
Gansu	0.21	0.09	0.15
Qinghai	n.a.	n.a.	n.a.
Ningxia	0.01	0.04	0.04
Xingjiang	0.15	0.05	0.05
Subtotal	*2.45*	*3.03*	*3.03*
Total	*100.00*	*100.00*	*100.00*

Note: n.a.: not available.

Source: Based on *China Economic News*, various issues.

However, an extreme divergence is revealed when figures are compared across provinces in the coastal region over the years 1996, 1998 and 2000. In contrast the central region and the west region received only 9 and 3 per cent of the total investment respectively.

Such uneven distribution may be due to two factors: first, the coastal region is the most developed area in China and, second, the region was taken as a model to allow FDI in China in the 1980s. This observation may have certain limitations when figures are compared across regions over the years 1996, 1998 and 2000. This can be observed by a marginal decline in FDI share of major destinations such as Shanghai, Fujian, Tianjin, Hainan, and Guangdong.[5]

Shanghai seems to be an interesting case in this context. It has been driven by a desire to reclaim its pre-communist era status as a regional financial capital and a cosmopolitan haven for international capitalists eager to penetrate the Chinese market. The expansion of the city has been massive since the 1990s. For example, Pudong was just an expanse of marshy land, villages and old factories. This area has now transformed into the city's new financial district.[6] It is a stunning conglomeration of soaring office towers and high-tech factories that has attracted tens of billions of dollars in foreign investment. In 2003, it sucked in just under $6 billion, more than a tenth of the total for the entire country (The Economist, 2004). In the next few years, changes in Shanghai – whose GDP, according to official figures, grew last year by a sizzling 11.8 per cent[7] are expected to be dramatic. Regarding financial services, the mayor of Shanghai has already formulated a grand plan to develop Shanghai into a national financial and trading centre by 2010. Shanghai has locational advantage over Hong Kong, as it is the economic capital of the Yangtze valley, which accounts for half of China's industrial output. Multinational corporations providing support services vital to the emergence of Shanghai as China's financial centre have reportedly already moved into the city (Chai and Kwong, 1996).

Forms of FDI

It is useful to mention the various forms of FDI in China[8] here. For example, *Chinese–foreign joint equity ventures* – a limited liability venture formed between foreign companies, enterprises and other economic organizations or individuals, and Chinese companies, enterprises or other economic organizations. The parties to the venture shall jointly invest in the venture, jointly manage the venture, and share the profits, risks and losses of the venture according to the share they hold in the registered capital of the venture; *Chinese–foreign joint contractual venture* – formed by contract between foreign enterprises, other economic organizations or individuals and Chinese enterprises or other economic organizations. Terms, distribution of profits, share of risks and losses, investment return, and mode of management of the parties to the venture as well as the division of residual property when the cooperation terminates shall be specified in the joint venture contract; *Wholly foreign-owned enterprise* – solely funded by foreign companies, other economic organizations and individuals. Profits of the enterprise belong to the foreign investors; *Foreign invested joint stock limited company* – incorporated entity whose capital is divided into shares of equal value and whose shareholders assume liabilities of the company according to the number of shares purchased and at least 25 per cent of whose registered capital is purchased and held by foreign shareholders. The company assumes liability for the debt of the company with all its properties. It may be set up by means of initiation or fund raising; *Foreign invested financial institution* – to conduct financial business and Solely foreign funded financial institution or Chinese–foreign joint equity financial institution with Chinese legal person status (incorporated entity) inside China; *Compensation trade* – foreign investors will be responsible for providing equipment and technology and commit to purchase a certain amount of exported products from the Chinese side. The money for importing the equipment and technology provided can be paid back in stages. Money borrowed to import the equipment and technology can be paid back in the form of other products in addition to the products produced with the imported equipment and technology upon agreement between the parties concerned; *Processing and assembling* – for processing with supplied materials and according to supplied samples and assembling with supplied components. The foreign parties are responsible for providing technology, equipment, components and raw and accompanying materials and import the processed and assembled products. The Chinese parties will collect processing or assembling fees. When the equipment is sold to the Chinese parties, the money for purchasing the equipment will be paid from the processing fees in stages; *International leasing* – a special way to raise funds – to be specific, obtaining the right to use foreign advanced equipment by payment of rent. Rent is paid according to the lease agreement. When the lease term expires the enterprise may purchase the leased equipment. The foreign parties or the lessor may also provide technical services, raw materials, fuels, components, and so on; *BOT or Build–Operate–Transfer* – in a typical BOT project, a government signs a contract with a project company sponsored by a private sector foreign investor. The project company is responsible for fund raising and building of infrastructure projects. The project company owns, operates and maintains the facilities, recovers the investment and obtains reasonable profits through collecting utilization fees or service fees during the contract period. When the term of the contract expires, the ownership of the facilities will be transferred to the government free of charge. BOT is mainly used to develop toll roads, power generation plants, railways, waste water processing facilities, subways (urban railways) and other infrastructure; *TOT or Transfer–Operate–Transfer* – here, the undertaking unit, that is the Chinese party, transfers a project that has been finished and is in operation, such as a toll road or power station, to a foreign company to operate. The foreign operator will pay for the transfer in a single upfront payment based on its calculation of the cash flow of the project during the term of the concession. The foreign operator is entitled to collect reasonable service fees, utilization fees and other fees from the users of the facility during the operational period. After the operational period, the foreign operator will transfer the project back to the Chinese party; *Purchase of shares* – acts of purchasing shares issued by Chinese companies and listed overseas, as well as stocks issued to overseas investors and listed inside China through stock exchanges in Shenzhen and Shanghai overseas stock exchanges by foreign investors and individuals, incorporated entities and other organizations in HKSAR, Macao and 'Taiwan province', and by Chinese citizens having permanent overseas residence and investors; *Transfer of enterprise property right* – act of selling or purchasing the property rights of state owned enterprises according to laws. Foreign incorporated entities, individuals or other organizations are entitled to the right of purchasing the property rights of the state owned enterprises according to competent regulations. Once the enterprises are purchased, they will be entitled to the preferential policies extended to foreign funded enterprises.

Performances of foreign invested enterprises and domestic firms

It may be useful to discuss the different types of FDI and their magnitudes in the Chinese economy. Table 4.3 shows foreign investment under different categories in China as on January 2001. It appears that solely foreign funded enterprises (or foreign-invested enterprises or FIEs) are rising in China compared to other forms of investment. This dominance of solely foreign-funded enterprises is further highlighted in Figure 4.1, which is a graphical representation of the data in Table 4.3. Several explanations may be cited in order to justify this interesting observation. A firm's performance may be explained by three broad categories of literature: (i) the industrial organization literature relates firm performance to factors that determine the structure of the market within which the firm operates; (ii) the transaction cost literature emphasizes the imperfections of market-based transactions in influencing the allocation of resources and thus the performance of firms; and (iii) the theory of organization literature points out the dependence of a firm's performance on its organizational structure, including ownership arrangement and corporate governance.

Table 4.3 Foreign investment under different categories in China: Jan. 2001 (US$100m)

Forms of investment	No. of projects		Contracted foreign investment		Foreign investment used in the period	
	Total	Change over 2000 same period (±%)	Total	Change over 2000 same period (±%)	Total	Change over 2000 same period (±%)
Total	*1 629*	*14.32*	*49.26*	*37.62*	*23.30*	*21.10*
1. FDI	*1 629*	*14.32*	*48.56*	*40.59*	*22.21*	*21.23*
Sino-foreign joint equity ventures	573	7.30	10.16	16.64	6.79	1.19
Sino-foreign joint cooperative ventures	90	−26.83	4.24	−20.30	2.11	−19.16
Solely foreign funded enterprises	964	25.68	33.20	62.67	12.81	42.49
Foreign-funded stock companies	1	–	0.97	–	0.01	–
Cooperative development	1	–	0.49	–	–	–
Others	–	–	–	–	–	–
2. Other foreign investment	–	–	0.70	−44.88	1.09	18.48
Issuing stocks abroad	–	–	–	–	–	–
International leasing	–	–	–	–	–	–
Compensation trade	–	–	–	–	–	–
Processing and assembling	–	–	0.70	−44.88	1.09	18.48

Foreign investment approved in the period

Source: Based on *China Economic News*, various issues.

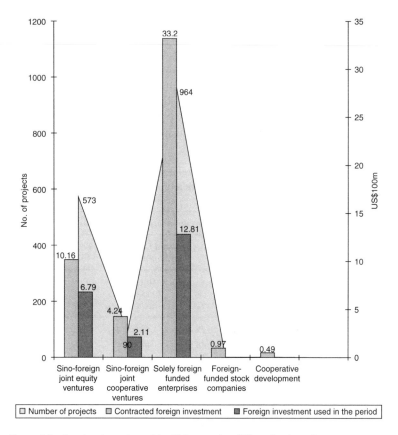

Figure 4.1   Foreign investment in China under different categories
Source: Based on Table 4.3.

Cheng and Wu (2000), in the context of China, argued that as an FIE is a profit-seeking firm in the Chinese market, one would expect its performance to depend on the above factors. From the perspective of market structure, the performance of FIEs may depend on the economies of scale and scope, R&D intensity and advertising intensity because they may lower the cost of production or create barriers to entry. Other things being equal, FIEs that succeed in entering an imperfectly competitive market with high barriers to entry are expected to perform better, and FIEs in industries that are in China's comparative advantages can compete more successfully in the world market.

As regards transaction cost considerations, Dunning (1988) has proposed an 'eclectic' ownership–location–internalization (OLI) model to explain a firm's rationale to invest in a foreign country. Teece *et al.* (1994) argued that a foreign firm (FIE) faces significantly higher transaction costs than its local competitor due to differences in language, culture, legal system and the level of economic development between the host and home countries. Thus it is natural that a foreign firm may possess large advantages in technology and management, etc. in order to overcome transaction cost related disadvantages. On the whole, cultural and geographical proximity may be considered as the local firms' competitive advantages and the intangible assets, managerial and organizational capabilities may be considered as the said local firms' competitive disadvantages which in turn favour the foreign firms. Luo (1998) stressed that the duration of operation and prior experience in international operations may affect the performances of foreign firms. The longer an FIE's operation, the more experience it has accumulated, and thus the better will be its objective performance.

The theory of organization helps to understand why at the initial stage of investment many foreign firms prefer to take the form of joint ventures. Whether a joint venture operates successfully depends on its ownership structure and management arrangement, i.e. the allocation of control rights and benefits among the venture partners. Other things being equal, a joint venture will be more successful if the partner with a more critical contribution at the margin has more control rights and enjoys more benefits than others. Sometimes government policy may contribute to the firm's performance. For example, the government may encourage export-oriented FIEs to improve China's current account balance through exports; it may limit foreign ownership to promote joint ventures as a vehicle of technology transfer.

Cheng and Wu's (op. cit.) findings are interesting in determining the performance of FIEs in China. According to their study, for example, the duration of operation was a consistently positive factor in the success of the FIEs not only in terms of profitability, but also in terms of subjective performance. In addition, FIEs in industries consistent with China's comparative advantages also performed well. Indeed, FIEs owned by Hong Kong investors did not perform any better than FIEs owned by other foreign investors. Finally, FIEs located in Guangzhou and its vicinity performed better than those located in the SEZs.

In general, for both foreign and Chinese investors, wholly owned ventures are, on average, more profitable than alliances. Interestingly, in 2002, alliances in China attracted roughly half of China's record US$55 billion in new foreign direct investment, and many companies expect to pursue more alliances. Kenevan and Pei (2003) explained that it's not just because they remain the sole way to invest in the life insurance, securities, and telecommunications sectors. They perform in other sectors as well, provided the alliances are carefully chosen and skilfully run. Thus they can be just as financially rewarding as wholly owned businesses.

Private enterprises in Zhejiang

One of the most prosperous regions in China is Zhejiang. It is a region of hilly terrain. The new entrepreneurs often start out as traders. One can see that every Chinese person hawking bric-a-brac on the streets of European and North American cities, seems to be from Wenzhou of Ningbo natives. Likewise, every Zhejiang millionaire started out as a salesman. The China Economic Quarterly portrayed an interesting story on Mao Lixiang, Chairman of Ningbo Fotile Kitchenware (Studwell, 2003). To quote:

> He started out as an accountant in a revolutionary brigade unit. After the Cultural Revolution he spent a decade selling television parts. Then he settled on selling and making ignition guns for gas cookers. Soon his home town of Cixi, a satellite of Ningbo, knew him as the 'ignition gun king'. He also came to understand the domestic market for kitchen equipment and started Fotile Kitchenware to make cooking ranges and extractor hoods – launching this business just as housing privatization took off.

Today, as might be expected of a salesman, Mr Mao oversees 3,500 employees of whom 2,500 are in sales, spread among 46 offices around the country. All the management, product, development and manufacturing are handled by the remaining 1,000. With Zhejiang all the rage, Mr Mao has lately been teaching business at Tsinghua University (p. 39). In 2002, the region contributed about US $29.4 billion to China's huge exports (Table 4.4).

Table 4.4   Exports by province: 2002

Province	US$bn
Guangdong	118.5
Jiangsu	38.5
Shanghai	32.1
Zhejiang	29.4
Shandong	21.1

Source: Based on *China Economic Quarterly*, 2003, Q3, p. 38.

Zhejiang entrepreneurs are aware of their specialization. People in this region prefer to manufacture different products, which explain a typical comparative advantage. For example, Datang manufactures socks; Qiaotou is famous for buttons; Shengzhou does ties; Shaoxing does textiles and dyes; Wenzhou concentrates on lighters, pens and low wage electrical equipment; part of the Ninghai are dedicated to electric hand tools, stationery, and pressing and stamping machines; Cixi is an ideal place to manufacture kitchen equipment. The manufacturing centres in Zhejiang not only meet local demand – some of them have become global players in certain product categories. Datang, for example, manufactures 8 billion pairs of socks a year from 8,000 factories. This accounts for one-third of all socks sold annually in the world and two-thirds of those bought in China (Studwell, ibid., p. 39). Tables 4.5–4.7 depict some interesting features of Zhejiang.

FDI and trade

FDI constitutes a major factor in the growth of China's export of manufactured goods. Since the mid-1980s, China's manufacturing sector has benefited from foreign investment. Over the years foreign capital has increased in different sectors. As a result, this capital has spurred the growth of export of goods to China from other countries, where the investors are based. Similarly, it has also created opportunities for Chinese products to get into transnational companies' global sales networks.

Table 4.5 Private paradise: members of 500 largest private Chinese companies' list,* by province

Province	Nos
Zhejiang	205
Sichuan*	40
Jiangsu	33
Shandong	32
Shanghai	22

Note: * Including Chongging Companies ranked by an index comprising revenue, net profit, taxes paid, net assets and number of employees

Source: *Based on China Economic Quarterly*, 2003, Q3, p. 38.

Table 4.6 Richer by half: members of Xincaifu magazine's list of the richest 400 Chinese, by province

Province	Nos
Zhejiang	62
Guangdong	48
Shanghai	36
Beijing	30
Jiangsu	25
Sichuan	20
Liaoning	19
Fuzian	16

Note: Figures refer to the location of the principal company headquarters.

Source: Based on China Economic Quarterly, 2003, Q3, p. 39.

Table 4.7 Millionaire's club – East Zhejiang's richest men

Name	Principal Co.	Location	Main activities	Est. Wealth Rmb m
Hu Chengzhong	Delixi	Wenzhou	Industrial equipment	3 000
Zheng Jianjiang	Sanxing Group	Ningbo	Electricity meters	1 200
Ye Xiangyao	Changcheng Group	Wenzhou	Appliances	1 150
Xu Wanmao	Huamao Group	Ningbo	Education materials	870
Hu Xiangen	Cixing Group	Ningbo	Ball bearings, engines	740
Gao Tianle	Tengen Group	Wenzhou	Electrical components	720
Zhou Cimei	Huaxiang Group	Ningbo	Auto parts	680
Chen Senjie	Sunlight Group	Shangyu	Lamps	610
Zheng Shengtao	Sunlead Group	Wenzhou	Machinery, real estates	550
Su Zengfu	Supor Group	Taizhou	Cookware	500

Source: Based on China Economic Quarterly, 2003, Q3, p. 41.

Some of the facts may be cited here in order to understand the role of foreign capital in enhancing trade. In general, it is observed that a very large share of FDI in China is in manufacturing and real estate. Recent data shows that an estimated 50 per cent of the total foreign investment is in export-oriented activities and mostly from Asian investors having relocated low value added/labour intensive factories. Interestingly, most US and EU investors are targeting the domestic market.

In 2000, for example, *foreign-funded enterprises* contributed 48 per cent of the total value of China's exports, and their share in the total value of China's export of high-tech products – mainly communication/electronic products – was as high as 87 per cent. Foreign capital has helped China to upgrade the technological and managerial level of its manufacturing industry, enhance its capacity for export of non-traditional products, and improve the quality of the industry's products.

Figures 4.2–4.4 and Tables 4.8–4.11 highlight some interesting features of China's foreign trade. It is imperative to mention here that

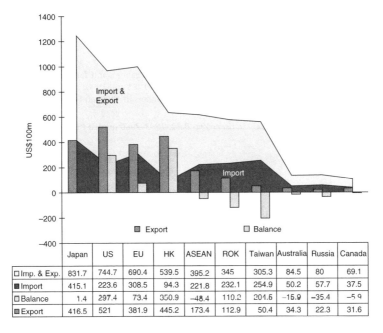

	Japan	US	EU	HK	ASEAN	ROK	Taiwan	Australia	Russia	Canada
☐ Imp. & Exp.	831.7	744.7	690.4	539.5	395.2	345	305.3	84.5	80	69.1
▪ Import	415.1	223.6	308.5	94.3	221.8	232.1	254.9	50.2	57.7	37.5
☐ Balance	1.4	297.4	73.4	350.9	−48.4	110.2	204.6	−15.9	−35.4	−5.9
▪ Export	416.5	521	381.9	445.2	173.4	112.9	50.4	34.3	22.3	31.6

Figure 4.2 Imports and exports of major trade partners of China*

Note: *Refers to year 2000.

Source: Based on *China Customs Statistics Year Book, 1993–2000* quoted in Zhihai and Yumin (2002).

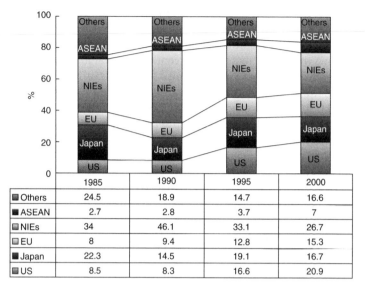

	1985	1990	1995	2000
■ Others	24.5	18.9	14.7	16.6
■ ASEAN	2.7	2.8	3.7	7
■ NIEs	34	46.1	33.1	26.7
■ EU	8	9.4	12.8	15.3
■ Japan	22.3	14.5	19.1	16.7
■ US	8.5	8.3	16.6	20.9

Figure 4.3   China's destination of exports: 1985–2000

Notes:
[a] ASEAN figures refer to 10 member countries.
[b] The NIEs include Hong Kong, the Republic of Korea, Singapore, and Taiwan. China had no direct trade with the Republic of Korea or Taiwan in 1985 and 1990.
[c] There were nine members in the EU in 1985; 12 members in 1990; and 15 members in 1995 and 2000.

Source: Based on *China Customs Statistics Year Book, 1993–2000* quoted in Zhihai and Yumin (2002).

foreign-funded enterprises tend to focus on labour-intensive undertakings, even though FDI has contributed to the increase in China's export of non-traditional products. Available studies have highlighted the fact that foreign-funded enterprises prefer to focus on export of plastic articles, furniture, textiles and garments, stationery, metres and instruments. This suggests that the technologies and the equipment brought in by foreign investors suit the needs of the Chinese market. Besides, the export of products produced by foreign-funded enterprises depends very much on their relatively low prices,

Zhihai and Yumin's study (2002) reveals that China's trade in labour-intensive and low-tech products has enjoyed a constantly growing surplus while the proportion of these products to China's total exports

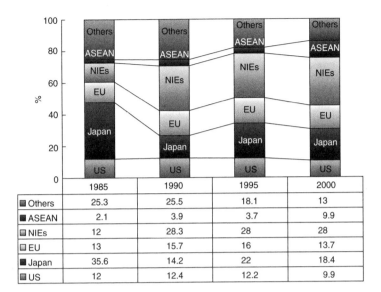

	1985	1990	1995	2000
■ Others	25.3	25.5	18.1	13
■ ASEAN	2.1	3.9	3.7	9.9
■ NIEs	12	28.3	28	28
■ EU	13	15.7	16	13.7
■ Japan	35.6	14.2	22	18.4
■ US	12	12.4	12.2	9.9

Figure 4.4 China's origin of imports: 1985–2000

Notes:
[a] ASEAN figures refer to 10 member countries.
[b] The NIEs include Hong Kong, the Republic of Korea, Singapore, and Taiwan. China had no direct trade with the Republic of Korea or Taiwan in 1985 and 1990.
[c] There were nine members in the EU in 1985; 12 members in 1990; and 15 members in 1995 and 2000.

Source: Based on *China Customs Statistics Year Book, 1993–2000* quoted in Zhihai and Yumin (2002).

Table 4.8 Composition of China's exports (%)

Items	1990	1995	2000
Primary commodities	25.90	14.9	10.9
Manufactures	74.10	85.1	89.1
Labour/resource-intensive products[a]	57.80	50.9	41.9
Low-tech products[a]	11.50	11.0	9.2
Medium-tech products[a]	10.50	13.2	17.5
High-tech products[a]	20.18	24.8	31.4

Notes
[a] These percentages, which are of total exports of manufactures, do not always add up to 100 owing to rounding.

Source: Based on *China Customs Statistics Year Book, 1993–2000* quoted in Zhihai and Yumin (2002).

Table 4.9 Composition of China's imports (%)

Items	1990	1995	2000
Primary commodities	14.4	16.4	20.7[a]
Manufactures	85.6	83.6	79.0[a]
Labor/resource-intensive products[b]	14.0	18.0	14.0
Low-tech products[b]	18.8	9.5	7.3
Medium-tech products[b]	34.6	38.0	35.6
High-tech products[b]	32.6	34.3	43.0

Notes
[a] These percentages, which are of composition of China's imports, do not add up to 100 owing to rounding.
[b] These percentages, which are of total exports of manufactures, do not always add up to 100 owing to rounding.

Source: Based on *China Customs Statistics Year Book, 1993–2000* quoted in Zhihai and Yumin (2002).

Table 4.10 China's top import commodities: Jan. 2001

Import item	Unit	Vol.	Value (US$1,000)	Change over 1999 same period (±%) Vol.	Value
Mechanical and electric equipment (including those separately listed in the list)	–	–	7745 889	–	14.6
High tech products (including those separately listed in the list)	–	–	3947 132	–	24.1
Crude oil	10 000 t	370	796 332	−17.8	−5.6
Primary type of plastic	10 000 t	97	791 354	7.8	1.6
Integrated circuit and micro–electronic devices	10 000 t	154 576	995 852	−0.3	32.7
Steel	10 000 t	115	606 989	−0.3	−1.8
Auto–data processing equipment and components	set	4712 266	317 114	−18.3	−8.2
Oil products	10 000 t	167	321 849	4.1	18.0
Paper and paper board (uncut)	10 000 t	30	167 852	−35.2	−33.4
Copper	t	73 772	179 380	−21.6	−17.6
On–off and protective circuit devices	–	–	223 012	–	8.1
Measuring, testing and analysing self–control instruments and devices	–	–	227 714	–	8.9

Continued

Table 4.10 Continued

Import item	Unit	Vol.	Value (US$1,000)	Change over 1999 same period (±%) Vol.	Value
Synthetic fibre filament fabrics	10 000 m	15 371	125 200	−26.2	−36.4
Paper pulp	10 000 t	25	139 985	−12.2	−11.1
Auto components	–	–	107 533	–	−25.2
Machinery woven cotton fabrics	10 000 m	8 780	108 449	−32.1	−30.4
Iron ore	10 000 t	642	172 141	10.5	20.2
Transformer, rectifier, inducer and parts	–	–	127 069	–	−17.5
Components and accessories of recorders and video machines	t	22 110	113 705	−16.7	−22.3
Aluminum	t	82 529	160 525	4.9	5.5
LPG and other hydrocarbon	10 000 t	33	117 093	−35.2	−11.5
Machine tools for metal processing	set	5 934	146 702	−41.4	3.9
Fertilizers	10 000 t	79	116 412	−2.3	−1.8
Log	10 000 cu.m	95	105 333	4.8	−14.4
Ox hide and horse hide	t	45 698	107 403	−5.9	−15.8
Textile machinery	–	–	158 416	–	19.6
Printed circuit	t	345 009	102 588	−10.7	−2.7
Components and accessories of wire telephone and telegraph	t	1 037	130 919	−34.5	16.2
Wire and cable	t	19 236	87 031	−26.6	−14.5
Knitted or crocheted fabrics	t	22 312	72 711	−18.9	−21.1
Machinery for rubber or plastic processing	–	–	131 161	–	32.7
P–phthalic acid	t	157 239	72 071	14.1	1.7
Motors and generators	10 000 sets	7 817	79 644	−13.0	14.8
Synthesized fibre yarn	t	40 017	75 110	−18.7	−14.4
Plastic products	t	18 197	65 925	−22.7	−17.1
Auto and auto chassis	t	3 983	103 540	68.5	40.8
Printing and binding machinery	–	–	71 765	–	−22.1
Synthetic fibre for cotton industry	10 000 t	6	63 302	−21.1	−21.7
Pharmaceuticals	t	2 713	73 674	11.4	7.3
Timber	cu. m	251 159	64 104	−6.3	−13.4
Soybean	10 000 t	38	82 365	26.9	33.7
Medical instruments and devices	–	–	88 973	–	23.8
Mechanical lifting transporting, loading/unloading equipment and parts	–	–	99 040	–	49.5

Continued

68

Table 4.10 Continued

Import Item	Unit	Vol.	Value (US$1,000)	Change over 1999 same period (±%) Vol.	Value
Air craft	unit	27	225 319	800.0	460.7
Vessels	unit	41	352 859	−4.7	2 712.5
Bloom and coarse forging	10 000 t	69	137 283	365.3	301.4
Waste copper	t	204 461	82 126	11.1	50.6
Waster steel	10 000 t	61	71 459	207.6	279.5
Cotton yarn	t	30 417	65 010	−1.5	5.8

Notes: cu. m = metre; t = ton.

Source: Based on *China Economic News*, various issues.

Table 4.11   China's Top 50 export commodities: Jan. 2001

Export item	Unit	Vol.	Value (US$1,000)	Change over 1999 same period (±%) Vol.	Value
Mechanical and electric equipment (including those separately listed in the list)	–	–	7755 198	–	10.6
Garments and clothing accessories	–	–	2337 925	–	−13.8
High tech products (including those separately listed in the list)	–	–	2977 883	–	42.1
Textiles yarn, fabrics and their products	–	–	1015 943	–	−5.7
Shoes	–	–	737 917	–	−12.1
Auto data processing equipment and spare parts	10 000 sets	3 513	815 743	−9.0	21.4
Input or output parts	10 000 sets	2 290	427 886	−13.9	2.0
Plastic products	t	247 071	340 808	−9.9	−11.9
Toys	–	–	317 205	–	−14.6
Components of automatic data processing equipment	t	36 168	383 736	−8.6	3.0
Travelling articles, bags and suitcases	–	–	278 632	–	−9.6
Furniture	–	–	286 952	–	−1.7
Containers	unit	54 393	96 705	−43.2	−53.0
Recorders, radio-recorders & audio system with CKD	10 000 sets	1 112	151 955	−26.0	−15.2
Aquatic products	10 000 t	8	165 640	−8.6	1.8
Precious metals or jewels inlaid with precious metals	–	–	80 531	–	−36.1

ContinuedContinued

Table 4.11 Continued

Export item	Unit	Vol.	Value (US$1,000)	Change over 1999 same period (±%) Vol.	Value
Telephone (including wireless telephones)	10 000 sets	882	81 888	−37.4	−44.9
Motors and generators	10 000 sets	17 225	123 872	−6.4	−7.5
Integrated circuits and micro electronic drives	10 000 units	44 819	275 437	48.3	92.3
Radio–recorders & audio systems with CKD	t	24 195	108 019	−19.9	−18.9
Oil products	10 000 t	56	140 144	23.0	39.7
Vessels	unit	11 170	291 571	317.3	93.7
Pharmaceuticals	t	12 820	126 502	−12.8	−4.0
Steel	10 000 t	35	132 430	2.2	4.1
Lamps, illuminators & the like	–	–	125 004	–	−9.3
Parts and components of TV, radio & other wireless communication equipment	t	9 641	221 311	−27.3	86.1
Wires and cables	t	33 195	102 526	−18.2	−12.7
On–off and circuit protector	–	121 309	87 710	1.3	–
Cereal and cereal power	10 000 t	75	123 276	78.9	26.9
Static converters	10 000 units	5 669	107 868	6.4	4.9
Vegetables	10 000 t	19	118 109	23.6	7.7
Printed circuits	t	233 018	91 480	6.4	21.7
TV sets, including CKD	10 000 sets	131	203 537	0.9	22.8
Hand or vehicle wireless telephone	set	1826 972	99 662	152.0	201.7
Coal	10 000 t	357	61 184	37.0	42.5
Watches	10 000 units	6 601	68 081	−21.6	−26.8
Mattress, bed–cloth, etc.	–	–	75 836	–	−7.9
Hand and machine tools	t	36 026	96 962	−0.7	0.5
Radio–recorders and audio system	set	1803 180	76 786	13.4	24.0
Auto parts	–	–	64 102	–	12.5
Diode, transistor or similar semiconductor	10 000 units	374 965	63 268	−2.4	2.5
Loud speakers	10 000 unit	8 437	68 636	−25.6	−8.6
Transformers	10 000 unit	17 064	61 961	−24.1	−1.3
Cameras	10 000 unit	476	51 973	10.6	−5.9
Tires	10 000 pieces	608	59 24/	−15.9	−5.9
Storage batteries	10 000 units	4 031	89 216	−24.6	−14.2
Coke and semi–coke	10 000 t	129	52 921	−6.6	16.9
Electric fans	10 000 sets	847	141 312	13.4	12.6
Crude oil 723.2	10 000 t	66	61 868	3 156.8	3
Duplicator	unit	104,484	–	0	14.9

Note: t = ton.

Source: Based on *China Economic News*, various issues.

has kept declining. Medium and high-tech products form a growing proportion of China's total exports, but the deficit for China's trade of these products has been increasing. The growing deficit in China's trade of medium and high-tech products and the increasingly significant proportion of these products to China's total exports can be attributed to two factors: (i) The medium and high-tech products imported by China are of high quality and their prices are therefore high. In contrast, products of the same categories exported by China are of inferior quality and their prices, therefore, are relatively low; (ii) China, more often has had to increase its medium and high tech exports by using products made with imported intermediary products or parts or accessories. It is interesting to note that processing trade for production of labour-intensive products is meant to provide access to foreign companies' sales channels. In undertaking processing trade for production of medium and high-tech products, China has to depend on technological innovations accomplished abroad. As a consequence, China's trade terms for high-tech products are worse than those for labour-intensive products.

In the final analysis *foreign-funded enterprises* operating in China are attracted by the country's relatively cheap labour resources,[9] and for that reason to engage in processing trade. This is bound to influence not only the quantity and value of China's imports but also import prices. For example in 2000, *foreign-funded enterprises* were responsible for 50 per cent of China's total imports, an amount greater than their share of China's total exports.

It is in this context to be mentioned here that China's access to WTO may have both positive and negative effects. The major contributory factors appear to be stabilization of rules, finance and services. Sectorwise, major winners are estimated to be garments, textile, leather products, food products and chemicals. Major losers, however, appear to be automobile, agriculture, electronics, mechanical engineering and refined petroleum.

High-tech product and foreign firms

In recent time a lot of attention has been paid to the status of technology adoption and their relevance in the context of Chinese firms. Perhaps the anxieties of rich countries and Chinese ambitions are inflated in this aspect. Research shows that the Chinese technology base remains far smaller than those of the developed economies, and most technology-intensive manufacturing is actually managed by foreign firms (Rosen, 2004). One of the arguments against China is that it has

Table 4.12 China's imports and exports of high-tech products: 1995–2002

	1995	1996	1997	1998	1999	2000	2001	2002
Exports, US$bn	10.1	12.7	16.3	20.3	24.7	37.0	46.5	67.7
% of all exports	6.8	8.4	8.9	11.0	12.7	14.9	17.5	20.8
Imports, US$bn	21.8	22.5	23.9	29.2	37.6	52.5	64.1	82.7
% of all imports	16.5	16.2	16.8	20.8	22.7	23.3	26.3	28.0
Balance, US$bn	−11.7	−9.8	−7.6	−8.9	−12.9	−15.5	−17.7	−15.0

Source: Based on Department of Science and Technology, Ministry of Commerce quoted in *China Economic Quarterly*, Vol. 8, No. 1, 1Q, 5 Mar. 2004.

seized only those opportunities in the global technology value chain where low labour costs matter the most. The trouble is that the structure of its capital infrastructure is too weak to transform modern technology and it may take years to develop.

By and large, a major share of Chinese production remains low-tech and labour-intensive. Of US$525 billion in Chinese exports in 2002, US$68 billion worth, or 21 per cent was listed as 'high-tech'.[10] Table 4.12 portrays the Chinese definition of 'high-tech products' and their trade balance. Needless to mention here that China's high-tech exports are predominantly produced by foreign managed or foreign owned firms.

Table 4.13 shows China's top technology imports and exports and Figure 4.5 reveals exports and imports of high-tech products by type of enterprise during January–August 2003. It appears that the country continued to rely on import of high-tech inputs as China's manufacturing output reflects giant strides in using basic technology. In other words, foreign partners are the necessary contributors for serious high-tech production in China. For the period January to August 2003, China imported US$71.6 billion and exported US$62.1 billion of high-tech products. More interestingly, fully 50 per cent of Chinese technology imports and 60 per cent of technology exports were done by wholly foreign-owned enterprises (WFOEs). These numbers show the dominant position of foreigners, and specially enterprises under full foreign control in China's technology trade. The role of both private enterprises and SOEs is marginal in this respect. This observation may have an important bearing in the long run, if China at all intends to climb up the technology ladder.

It is possible to examine the differences in access to technology for foreign and domestic firms in China with the help of certain parameters of technological advantage (Rosen, ibid.). It appears that the foreign

Table 4.13   China's top technology imports
and exports: Jan.–July 2003 (US$bn)

	Amount
Imports	
General ICs*	7.4
Electronic components	3.9
ICs 0.18–0.35 microns	3.9
ICs < 0.18 microns	3.5
Composite ICs	2.4
Mobile phone components	2.4
Misc machinery	1.9
Car phone components	1.8
ICs > 0.35 microns	1.7
Hard disk drives	1.4
Exports	
Electronic components	7.6
Digital data-processors	5.0
Car phone components	3.5
Liquid crystal displays	3.2
Mobile phone components	2.1
DVD players	1.5
CRT displays	1.5
Digital cameras	1.3
CD-ROM disks	1.2
Laser Jet printers	1.1

Note: * ICs: Integrated circuits.

Source: Based on Department of Science and
Technology, Ministry of Commerce quoted in *China
Economic Quarterly*, Vol. 8, No. 1, 1Q, 2004.

firms have distinct advantages in all parameters as compared to the domestic firms (Table 4.14). This further corroborates our earlier observation that China has applied its abundant factor – labour in achieving its comparative advantage.

It is useful to focus on how successful economies move through the different stages of technological evolution with the help of Figure 4.6. Economies can get to stage 3 of the seven stages as China has, without factors like intellectual property rights (IPR) protection, a sound financial system, or reliable brand-name businesses. The early climb up the ladder entails labour-intensive export processing, mostly in light industry and in goods that can be transplanted and produced by foreign investors (Hachigian and Wu, 2003).

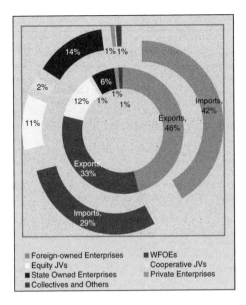

Figure 4.5 China's exports and imports of high-tech products by type of enterprise: Jan.–Aug. 2003

Source: Based on Department of Science and Technology, Ministry of Commerce quoted in *China Economic Quarterly*, Vol. 8, No. 1, 1Q, 2004.

Perhaps China's dream to become a major player in the world semiconductor industry may be unfulfilled without Taiwan's help. Tables 4.15–4.17 provide a glimpse of the world scenario in the integrated circuit (IC) technology. Yeh (2003) has identified three major features of China's semiconductor landscape, which are likely to remain stable through the end of the decade:

1. Demand for semiconductors is high and growing fast, but is supplied overwhelmingly by imports. Import reliance is particularly strong in high-end applications such as personal computer and mobile phone processors.
2. Domestic chip production is accelerating but remains concentrated at the low end of the value chain.
3. Major Chinese chip production facilities, and the technology that they license, are almost exclusively controlled by foreign firms.

Recently, Taiwan has decided to withdraw its ban on mainland semiconductor investment. Consequently, Taiwanese foundries are moving

74

Table 4.14 Technological capacity of domestic Chinese and foreign-invested firms

Technological advantage	Domestic firms	Foreign-invested firms
Supportive advantage	Poor	Excellent
Patent base*	195 per year for Chinese firms (1 125 since 1963)	87 610 per year for US patent receivers (1.9 m since 1963)
Available skilled labour	Good	Better (FIEs more attractive employers)
Management base	Poor	Excellent
Established customers for tech	Poor	Excellent
Brand permits higher margin	Poor	Excellent
Access to R&D subsidies	Good for some, not for private	N/A
Policy bias	Good for some, not for private	N/A
Secured role in cluster	Poor	Often very good
Service sector support	Poor	Excellent
IPR protection/recourse	Poor	Better (can bring pressure)

Notes: * Utility patents filed with the US patent and Trademark Office through 2001.
These scores characterize the overall environment for domestic firms in China versus foreign multinational firms doing business in China. A few top Chinese firms transcended these general weaknesses but the descriptions in this table are more typical.

Source: Based on Rosen, Daniel (2004), *China Economic Quarterly*, Vol. 8, No. 1, 1Q, 2004.

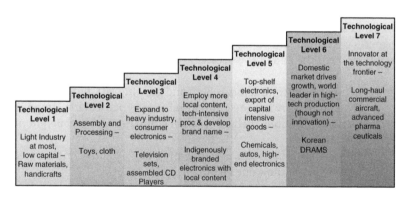

Figure 4.6 The seven stages of technology evolution

Note: China lies between stages 3 and 4.

Source: Based on Hachigian and Wu (2003) modified by Daniel H. Rosen, See http://www.rand.org/publications/MR/MR1719/

Table 4.15 Global IC sales by company origin: 2002 (% of total)

Country	% of total
US	50
Japan	22
Europe	10
Rest of world	18

Source: Based on IC Insights, Deutsche Bank quoted in *China Economic Quarterly*, Q3, 2003, p. 28.

Table 4.16 Global IC manufacturing capacity by region: 2003

Country	% of total
Taiwan	27
US	19
China	15
Europe	10
Southeast Asia	10
Japan	8
South Korea	7
Other	4

Source: Based on IC Insights, Deutsche Bank quoted in *China Economic Quarterly*, Q3, 2003, p. 28.

Table 4.17 Top world IC companies, by revenue: 2002

Companies	US$bn
Intel	23.7
Samsung Electronics	8.8
Toshiba	6.4
Texas Instruments	6.4
ST Microelectronics	6.4
Infineon Technologies	5.4
NEC	5.3
Motorola	4.8
Philips Semiconductors	4.4
Hitachi	4.2

Source: Based on IC Insights, Deutsche Bank quoted in *China Economic Quarterly*, Q3, 2003, p. 28.

low-end and mid-range production to the mainland. Many Taiwanese industry veterans are employed as managers of mainland fabs, and Taiwanese capital has been playing a contributory role in financing new fabs.

R&D

The various aspects of R&D are shown in Tables 4.18–4.21. It is possible to derive certain observations based on the data provided in the tables. It appears that China's R&D intensity (R&D expenditure as a percentage of GDP) has nearly doubled from 0.6 per cent in 1966 to 1.1 per cent in 2000. However, it is still behind most of the Organization for Economic

Table 4.18   China's gross expenditure on R&D: 1995–2001

	1995	1996	1997	1998	1999	2000	2001
Amount (Rmb bn)	34.9	40.5	50.9	55.1	67.9	89.6	104.3
Annual growth, (%)	−0.6	16.0	25.7	8.3	23.2	32.0	59.6
R&D as a share of GDP (%)	0.60	0.60	0.64	0.69	0.83	1.01	1.09

Source: Based on China Statistical Yearbook on Science and Technology, 2002 quoted in *China Economic Quarterly*, Q4, 2003, p. 36.

Table 4.19   R&D intensity for selected countries: 2001

Country	R&D expenditure as % of GDP
Sweden	4.2
Japan	3.1
South Korea	3.0
United States	2.9
Germany	2.5
OECD average	2.3
Taiwan	2.1
Russia	1.2
China	1.1
Brazil	1.0
India	0.9

Source: Based on OECD Science, Technology and Industry Scoreboard, 2003 quoted in *China Economic Quarterly*, Q4, 2003, p. 36.

Table 4.20 R&D expenditure by country: 2001 (US$bn, PPP basis)

Country	US$bn, PPP basis
United States	282.3
Japan	103.8
China	59.8
Germany	53.9
France (av. 1997–99)	35.1
United Kingdom	29.4
Korea	22.3
India	19.4
Canada	17.4
Italy (av. 1997–2000)	15.5
Brazil (2000)	13.7

Source: Based on OECD Science, Technology and Industry Scoreboard, 2003 quoted in China Economic Quarterly, Q4, 2003, p. 36.

Table 4.21 China's R&D expenditure by type of institution, 1995–2001 (% to total)

	1995	1996	1997	1998	1999	2000	2001
Large/medium enterprises	41	40	37	36	37	39	42
R&D institutions	42	43	41	43	38	29	28
Higher education	12	12	11	10	9	9	10
Other	5	6	11	12	15	23	20

Note: Percentages may not add up to 100 because of rounding.

Source: Based on China Statistical Yearbook on Science and Technology 2002 quoted in China Economic Quarterly, Q4, 2003, p. 38.

Co-operation and Development (OECD) economies, although appears favourable when compared to other developing economies. Interestingly, China is among the top three countries in the world in terms of R&D intensity on purchasing power parity (PPP) basis.

China Economic Quarterly (Q3, 2003) made an interesting observation in the context of the role of foreign companies in disseminating knowledge in the economy. To quote:

Most so-called foreign R&D centres are glorified training facilities for local staff, and the training generally relates to management and sales rather than technology. Even the centres doing actual R&D work do so at a very low level. Many of the products advertised by R&D centres in China are software upgrades or systems integration solutions (p. 37).

Cheung and Lin (2003) had an opposite view in this context. They did not find any evidence of 'a crowding out effect'[11] of FDI. Indeed, the 'crowding out effect' is either absent or it exists in China but is dominated by the positive spillover effects of FDI at the provincial level.

It is interesting to note that enterprises remained a dominant source of funding R&D in China during 1995–2001, *vis-à-vis* other sources such as government, bank loans and others (Figure 4.7). Analysing R&D expenditure by user category, the role of big companies and universities has remained stable over several years. Incidentally, Chinese R&D has become even more focused on development as compared to basic and applied research (Figure 4.8). In other words it is only engaged in developing commercial applications for existing technologies, rather than creating new technologies.

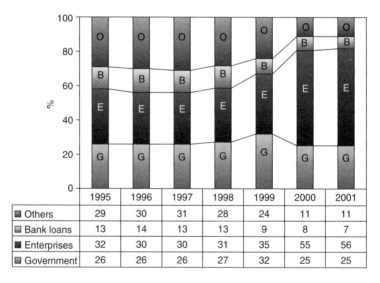

	1995	1996	1997	1998	1999	2000	2001
■ Others	29	30	31	28	24	11	11
▨ Bank loans	13	14	13	13	9	8	7
■ Enterprises	32	30	30	31	35	55	56
▨ Government	26	26	26	27	32	25	25

Figure 4.7   Sources of funding science and technology China: 1995–2001

Note: Percentages may not add up to 100 because of rounding.
Year-wise figures are referring to percentage to total except the last row.
S&T refers to Science and Technology.

Source: Based on *China Statistical Yearbook on Science and Technology* (2002) quoted in *China Economic Quarterly*, Q4, 2003, p. 38.

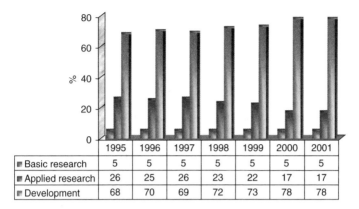

	1995	1996	1997	1998	1999	2000	2001
▪ Basic research	5	5	5	5	5	5	5
▪ Applied research	26	25	26	23	22	17	17
▪ Development	68	70	69	72	73	78	78

Figure 4.8　China's R&D expenditure by type of research: 1995–2001

Note: Percentages may not add up to 100 because of rounding.

Source: Based on *China Statistical Yearbook on Science and Technology* (2002) quoted in *China Economic Quarterly*, Q4, 2003, p. 38.

Spillover effect

Some of the key Chinese macro-economic indicators are revealed in Tables 4.22–4.24. Certain observations may be derived in this context. It appears that until the most recent period, spillover or 'transmission effects' from FDI to the domestic economy remained limited, despite a significant contribution to output and growth. The country has to create 12–15 million jobs every year just to keep pace with its population growth (*The Economist*, 2004). It has to provide opportunities for the 800 million people living in rural areas. This rural population has been left behind by the current prosperity in select areas, and a third of these are under– or unemployed. Many problems are accumulated in the urban centres as well. For example, about 100–150 million migrant workers in the cities do not have job security, no long-term housing, no health care and they need at least a functioning pension system.

There are arguments and counter arguments among the economists about worries that the economy is overheating. In the urban centres bubbles are beginning to form in property, steel, cars, and power generation is running up against capacity constrains. One problem appears to be over investment. For a solution the state owned banks have introduced easy credit. It has however created more bad debts and fewer new jobs. According to *The Economist* (2004), 'nine-tenths of manufactured

80

Table 4.22 Key economic ratios – China: 1982–2002

	1982	1992	2001	2002
GDP (US$bn)	221.5	454.6	1 167.1	1 232.7
Gross Domestic Investment/GDP	33.2	36.2	38.5	41.0
Export of goods and services/GDP	8.9	19.5	25.5	29.5
Gross domestic savings/GDP	34.8	37.7	40.9	44.0
Gross national savings/GDP	35.1	38.0	40.0	43.8
Current account balance /GDP	2.4	1.9	1.5	2.9
Interest payments/GDP	0.2	0.6	0.5	0.5
Total debt/GDP	3.8	15.9	14.6	12.6
Total debt service/exports	8.0	8.6	7.7	6.1

Source: Based on http://www.worldbank.org/data/countrydata/aag/chn_aag.pdf, The World Bank, Washington, DC.

Table 4.23 Structure of the Chinese economy: 1982–2002 (% of GDP)

	1982	1992	2001	2002
Agriculture	33.3	21.8	15.8	14.5
Industry	45.0	43.9	50.1	51.7
Manufacturing	37.3	33.1	34.2	44.5
Services	21.7	34.3	34.1	33.7
Private consumption	50.7	49.2	45.7	42.5
General government consumption	14.5	13.1	13.4	13.5
Imports of goods and services	7.3	18.0	23.1	26.5

Source: Based on http://www.worldbank.org/data/countrydata/aag/chn_aag.pdf, World Bank Washington, DC.

Table 4.24 China's demographic and other leading Indicators: 1995 and 2002

Variables	1995	2002
Population, mid-year (m)	1 204.9	1 281.0
Poverty (% of population below US$1 a day)	n.a.	16.1
Adult literacy rate (% age 15 and over)	81.9	86.4
Urban population (% of total population)	31.4	37.6
GNI per capita (US$)	520.0	940.0
GDP per capita (PPP, US$)	2 520.0	4 900.0
GDP growth (1990–95 and 1995–2002 (%))	12.4	7.9

Note: n.a.: not available.
Source: Based on http://www.worldbank.org/data/countrydata/aag/chn_aag.pdf, World Bank, Washington DC.

goods are in oversupply, yet investment in fixed assets last year grew by 30 per cent and contributed 47 per cent of GDP'.

Many state-owned enterprises (SOEs) are not globally competitive. Yet they are continued to maintain patronage and employment than to generate profits. Huang (2000) argued that conventional explanations of the motivating forces behind FDI flows into China are 'absolutely wrong'. In essence, he views a high FDI to domestic investment ratio as symptomatic of systematic imperfections within the Chinese economy, and not the result of a 'booming economy'. As the government systematically discriminates against private domestic firms, they lack access to loans, retained earnings, and the retention of foreign exchange. Such a system provides privileges to the loss-making SOEs sector, while effectively suppressing economic growth in the private sector. Foreign firms, therefore, serve not only as a source of financial intermediation and liquid capital but also restructure the defunct SOE sector through acquisitions.

Major challenges for the Chinese economy thus appear to be unbalanced development across regions and limited spillover effects. The country lacks the basic conditions for developing capitalism such as law, respect for property rights and free markets.

Summary

The findings of the chapter reveal that the inflows of FDI in China may be explained by market-seeking, resource-seeking and efficiency-seeking arguments. The behaviour of different foreign investors is different according to their origin. Hong Kong-based investors may have been motivated by resource-seeking arguments. In contrast, for US-based investors it may be explained by market-seeking arguments. Interestingly, Hong Kong plays a dominant role as a source of FDI inflow to China. A lot of companies investing in China do it from their 'regional' headquarters in Hong Kong.

The coastal region is the most preferred destination of FDI. More specifically five of the provinces together (Guangdong, Jiangsu, Fujian, Shanghai and Shangdong) received more than 65 per cent of the total investment during 1996–2000. Indeed, Shanghai alone sucked in about US$6 billion of FDI in 2000, more than a tenth of the total for the entire country. There are various forms of FDI existing in China such as: Chinese–foreign joint equity ventures, Chinese–foreign joint contractual venture, Wholly foreign-owned enterprise, Foreign invested joint stock limited company, Foreign invested financial institution, Compensation trade, International leasing, Build-Operate-Transfer,

Transfer-Operate-Transfer, Purchase of Shares and Transfer of enterprise property right.

The study finds that solely FIEs are rising in China compared to other forms of investment. It appears that the duration of operation has been a consistently positive factor in the success of the FIEs not only in terms of profitability but also in terms of subjective performance. In addition, FIEs are in industries consistent with China's comparative advantages. The study has examined the differences in access to technology for foreign and domestic firms in China with the help of certain parameters of technological advantage. It appears that the foreign firms have advantages in all parameters over the domestic firms. Thus it is likely that China has applied its abundant factor – labour – in achieving the comparative advantage.

As regards R&D, it is only engaged in developing commercial applications for existing technologies, rather than creating new technologies. On the whole, the spillover effect of FDI in China is very slow. It remains to be seen as to how China will succeed with its massive rural unemployment in the long run.

5
Foreign Investment: India

Introduction

It is often argued that free trade is better than restricted trade, which in turn is better than no trade at all. This argument may not always apply to the FDI made by MNCs in the respective host countries. Sometimes, the interests of the MNCs are in conflict with those of the host country. An MNC is primarily interested in global profit maximization, which may not necessarily lead to greater investment and employment generation in the host country. Nevertheless, there is room for bargaining to bring about Pareto-improvement, which can be evidenced by gradual removal of restrictions on foreign investment in developing countries by the respective governments, to attract FDI.

It was in the 1970s and early 1980s a basic premise of developing country policy to regulate entry and expansion of MNCs. It was felt that the MNCs frequently engendered a series of undesired effects in developing countries seen from the latter's point of view. Evidence from many developing countries highlights the importance of regulation of the activities of MNCs in order to extract the greatest possible benefit for the economic development of the host country. On the one hand, MNCs can provide enormous financial resources for investment in the host country. They are able not only to generate resources internally[1] but also have privileged access to international capital markets. Other benefits include technology transfer, access to distribution and marketing networks and generation of employment, boosting export-intensity (especially when most of the developing countries are pursuing export-led growth strategies and are in the pursuit of reaping dynamic comparative advantage through manufactured exports), gains through different technological and organizational skills to control complex tasks, furnishing intangible assets (for example established brand names, advertising, R&D facilities, and so on) in the host country. Having expertise in the facets of product development and international marketing, MNCs can take advantage of inter-country differences in costs of production and produce goods with internationally reputed brand names and trademarks.

Alternatively, MNC activities may also come at a cost to the host country. The actual inflow of capital may not be very large; it depends on the extent to which domestic capital markets are used to raise finance for the project. Transfer of technology may not only be limited, it may not even be appropriate to the factor endowment of the host country. If highly capital-intensive technology is employed in a labour-abundant country, employment generation effects could be meager. The MNCs, most of the time are able to resist protectionist pressures at home and so may generate an increase in exports from the host country. Nonetheless, there is also the possibility of encumbrance to exports. MNCs conduct international operations on a global scale and the allocation of markets among their subsidiaries is related essentially to earning of global profitability and, of course, competitiveness or efficiency. If exports from participating in value-added activities in the host country are perceived to be uncompetitive *vis-à-vis* existing profitable operations in other locations and subsidiaries, then there may be corporate control on production of affiliates – especially for goods embodying high technology and quality – and consequently exports may be discouraged. It is very much relevant for any study on FDI to consider the competitiveness of industries in the host country. Although within the limited scope and dimension of our study the competitiveness of the Indian industrial sector is not studied, we must mention that participation in foreign production by an MNC is governed by competitive cost considerations in particular activities in an economy. It is the incentive for creating comparative advantage through trade and investment flows that attracts them to a particular location and in a production activity.

It is well known in the literature that there is no single or unique measure of competitiveness or efficiency. Very often the indicators of export performance such as export orientation and/or export market share in the importing countries are used as measures of competitiveness (which in turn depend on both price competitiveness and non-price factors like product-image, quality, marketing knowledge, adaptation of products according to demand, and so on). Although, export market share is the most commonly used measure as it takes into consideration the performance of individual countries as well as specific sectors, it is subject to qualifications. As far as the Indian experience of 'competitiveness' is concerned, a study has evidenced that in spite of a reversal in India's competitiveness in world markets between 1950 and 1980, there is a recent upswing in India's exports which have grown faster than world exports (including primary commodities).[2] The domestic market size and demand pull factors have, as it has been sometimes argued, prevented India's economy to achieve its export potentialities through cross-border trade and investment flows; other aspects such as firm-specific factors (cost, conscious product differentiation, quality, technology, and R&D), efficacy of policy variables, general economic and institutional factors are also important for making firms internationally competitive. Contribution of FDI in the economic activities of India and in the development of its competitiveness is an area that needs to be explored.

On the whole, the growing importance of FDI in production and international operations can in no way be ignored in a liberalized paradigm when every country in a broad swing of the pendulum has moved from a restrictive regime to a frictionless trading world. In spite of there being no unifying theoretical framework postulating a 'general theory' of FDI (as different theoretical as well as empirical studies have addressed different questions by making different choice of variables in their analytical framework), a complete understanding of this phenomenon is useful. Only then can the inevitability of FDI be realized.

A major focus of this chapter is to investigate the nature of FDI flows into India, specifically in the post-reform period. The rest of this chapter is organized as follows. The next section traces the evolution of India's policy towards FDI from independence to the present. The subsequent sections track the geographic distribution of FDI in India; discuss FDI and export in the Indian context; and the relationship between FDI and R&D. The penultimate section analyses the spillover effect and the final section provides the summary.

Evolution of government policies[3]

It is imperative to spell out the highlights of the government policies toward FDI in India in three phases. The period from 1948 to the mid-1960s can be identified as one of cautious promotion; the period from the mid-1960s to the 1970s as restrictive; and the 1980s, which set the trend towards liberalization. In the 1990s the policy has been liberalized further and made more open and transparent.

Phase I – cautious invitation: 1948–65

Given India's experience with colonialism, it is not surprising that at the time of independence Mahatma Gandhi was eager that India became self-reliant in the invention and production of as many goods and services as possible. These sentiments were also reflected in the government of India's First Industrial Policy Resolution of 1948, which declared that FDI would be regulated to ensure that majority ownership and effective control of firms remained in Indian hands. Nevertheless, the first Prime Minister Pandit Jawaharlal Nehru's Foreign Investment Policy Statement of 1949 revealed no indication of regulating FDI. The political turmoil associated with partition was inhibiting nervous domestic investors from starting many new enterprises; so foreign investment was seen as necessary for supplementing domestic capital and technology. Furthermore, needing hard currency as a result of the foreign exchange crisis of 1957, the Indian government actually began to encourage FDI by lowering corporate taxes on income and royalties, signing an agreement with the United States regarding currency convertibility, sending missions to advertise India to potential investors, and setting up the Indian Investment Centre with foreign branches to facilitate investment in India. In the period after 1957, substantial foreign investment flowed in and MNCs came to control one-fifth of India's corporate assets.[4] Throughout this period, FDI was seen as a means to acquire not only foreign capital but also superior foreign technology. Hence, most collaborations consisted of foreign firms acquiring assets in Indian firms in exchange of the foreign firms' provision of capital and improved technology to the domestic firms.

Phase II – the restrictive phase: 1966–79

A foreign exchange crisis in 1966 created a desire to reduce all flows of funds abroad. Among other things, it was felt that remittance of dividends, profits, royalties and technology licensing fees had to be severely curtailed. This crisis, coupled with India's long-standing goal of self-reliance, was used to justify the adoption of the closed door policy.

The restrictions on FDI began in 1966 when the government broke down industries into three categories: (1) industries in which the government believed indigenous technological capabilities were sufficient so that no FDI was permitted at all; (2) industries for which technology purchase (TP) licenses were permitted but no FDI was allowed; and (3) industries in which indigenous capabilities were particularly lacking so that both FDI and licences were permitted.

Even if a firm was in an industry eligible for TP, an industry in either group (2) or (3) above, the firm would still have to get approval for its specific technology contract from a wide range of review boards. Any of these boards could reject the contract on the basis of the cost of the technology, the availability of local substitutes, the technology's appropriateness, or the impacts that the technology import would have on the development of indigenous R&D capabilities. Furthermore, there were restrictions on the terms of the contracts themselves. Royalties were limited to 3–5 per cent of sales and were subject to a 40 per cent tax. The maximum life of the contract was reduced from 10 to 5 years, and renewals were difficult to obtain. Technology sellers were forbidden to include restrictions on the Indian firms' export of goods produced with the licensed technology unless the seller had affiliates in the country to which the Indian firm desired to export. The seller's trademark could not be used within India. Similarly, there were to be no restrictions on the Indian firms' rights to sublicense the technology.

Unlike the previous period, there was an effort made during this era to unbundle foreign technology and financing. Whenever possible, technology was to be acquired directly through licensing contracts rather than as part of a package deal involving both technology and foreign capital. In this manner it was hoped that Indian firms would acquire only necessary foreign technology and in such a way that domestic ownership of the firms would be promoted. By 1977, only 10 per cent of the technology licensing agreements involved any foreign equity participation.

In 1968 the Foreign Investment Board was set up to deal with all cases of foreign investment or collaboration which did not involve more than 40 per cent foreign equity and where the total investment in share capital was less than Rs40 million. Cases in excess of these limits were referred to a Cabinet Committee. The passage of the Foreign Exchange Regulation Act (FERA) in 1973 significantly tightened the scope of the FDI regime. Its stated objective was to facilitate the achievement of self-sufficiency and Indian control, instead of foreign domination in the economy.[5] FERA required companies to dilute their foreign equity participation to 40 per cent or less. Exceptions permitting foreign participation between 51–74 per cent were made for companies, which were in industries considered critical or strategic; companies which were manufacturing with sophisticated technologies; or which were predominantly engaged in exporting. Many multinationals responded to FERA by simply choosing to pull out of India, and of the 881 which stayed, only 150 of them were permitted to retain greater than 40 per cent foreign equity. Outflow of foreign exchange as a result of dividends, profits and royalties was, therefore, instrumental in government attitude that prompted the adoption of more restrictive policy during this period.

Phase III – gradual liberalization: 1980 to the present

It is well documented that the presence of overarching controls resulted in the failure of India to significantly step up the volume and proportion of manufactured exports because producing for the domestic market was more profitable than for the world market.[6] This led to an erosion of international competitiveness, growing technological obsolescence, quality degradation and a high cost structure. India's lackluster export performance and the crisis brought about by the Oil Producing and Exporting Countries (OPEC) oil shocks provided a stimulus to greater liberalization. During the period, the government announced its Industrial Policy Statements of 1980 and 1982. There was a loosening of the industrial capacity licensing regulations and the restrictions on imports of goods. The government intended to ratify the situation by: (a) emphasizing the modernization of plant and equipment through liberalized imports of capital goods and technology (b) exposing Indian industry to competition by gradually reducing import restrictions and tariffs and (c) assigning a greater role to MNCs in the promotion of manufactured exports by encouraging them to set up export oriented units.[7] More flexibility on the 40 per cent ceiling for FDI was introduced, and 100 per cent foreign ownership was allowed in export processing zones. The restrictions on technology licensing agreements were also relaxed. As a result of these changes the number of contracts approved annually almost trebled in the 1980s as compared to the 1970s.

In spite of these reforms, the foreign exchange crisis persisted and the Indian government introduced a dramatic set of changes in its New Industrial Policy of July 1991. Import barriers for goods were lowered further, and capacity licensing was abolished for about 80 per cent of the Indian industry. Foreign equity participation ceiling was raised from 40 to 51 per cent in a wide range of industries and the bureaucratic procedures for FDI were simplified. Technology licensing controls were loosened so that contracts received automatic approval in priority sectors as long as royalty payments did not exceed 5 per cent of domestic sales or 8 per cent of export sales. In the first six months of the New Industrial Policy, 505 Trading Partner (TP) agreements were approved, as compared with an annual average of 270 and 730 in the 1970s and 1980s respectively.

India now permits direct foreign investment in virtually every sector of the economy, other than the industries reserved for a few sectors.

While majority foreign investment (up to 51 per cent) is freely allowed in most industries, foreign equity up to 100 per cent is encouraged in export oriented units, the power sector and electronics and software technology parks. Depending on the merits of the proposal, 100 per cent foreign equity may also be permitted in other industries. Automatic permission is given to foreign technology agreements in high priority industries up to a lump sum payment of Rs10 million, 5 per cent royalty for domestic sales and 8 per cent for exports, subject to a total payment of 8 per cent of sales over a 10 year period from the date of agreement or 7 years from commencement of production. No permission is needed for hiring of foreign technicians or foreign testing of indigenously developed technologies. In addition, in certain specified industries reserved for the small scale sector, foreign equity is now permitted.

Import of technology may be considered even in industries where foreign collaboration is not considered necessary, under certain circumstances, namely (i) if the technology is too closely held and is not available for use by the entrepreneurs on competitive terms; (ii) if the technology is required for updating existing technology to meet higher domestic requirements or to become competitive in export market; and (iii) for manufacture of items with substantial export potential backed by buy-back guarantees. The import of components, raw materials and intermediate goods and payment of know-how fees and royalties will be governed by the general policy applicable to other domestic units. Other foreign equity proposals, including proposals involving 51 per cent equity but that do not meet any or all of the criteria mentioned above, will continue to require clearance.

The details of foreign collaboration approvals in India are given in Table 5.1 and a summarized pictorial representation of the same is presented in Figure 5.1. India has had basically two routes for FDI inflows. The first is the Reserve Bank of India (RBI) route. This is transparent because the guidelines are clear. If the project satisfies the guidelines, the approvals are practically automatic. But barely 5–10 per cent of the approvals come under this category (see Table 5.1). The other route is the Secretariat for Industrial Assistance (SIA) or the Foreign Investment Promotion Board (FIPB) route. Foreign investors are welcome to make proposals that do not meet the transparent guidelines. Such proposals are considered on a case by case basis and are cleared through the SIA/FIPB route. The FIPB has not lived up to its reputation and there has been severe criticism over the length of time and consistency in clearing projects. Its flexibility is perhaps also its weakness.

Table 5.1 Foreign collaboration approvals in India: 1991 (Aug.)–2004 (Mar.)

	Total (1991–2004)	2004	2003	2002	2001	2000
1	*2*	*3*	*4*	*5*	*6*	*7*
1. Total no. of foreign collaboration approvals by						
(i) SIA	4 699	27	230	420	207	197
(ii) RBI	9 457	242	898	1 010	1 132	551
(iii) FIPB	11 647	198	746	843	931	1 396
Total	25 803*	467	1 874	2 273	2 270	2 144
2. Number of FC approvals involving foreign investment						
(i) SIA	1 657	4	92	298	131	65
(ii) RBI	4 880	222	715	825	920	265
(iii) FIPB	11 438	198	746	843	931	1 396
Total	17 975*	424	1 553	1 966	1 982	1 726
3. Total of foreign investment (Rsbn)						
(i) SIA	1 366.67	13.33	68.89	224.44	175.56	42.22
(ii) RBI	5 051.11	80.00	293.33	617.78	522.22	348.89
(iii) FIPB	58 568.89	260.00	982.22	1 633.33	5 275.56	7 837.78
Total	64 988.89*	355.56	1 342.22	2 475.56	5 971.11	8 231.11
Total in US$ bn	78.3					

Notes: * includes 100 proposals approved by FIPB for American Depository Receipts (ADRs), Global Depository Receipts (GDRs)/Foreign Currency Convertible Bonds (FCCBs) involving an investment of Rs490.81bn; US$1 = Rs45 (July 2004).

Source: Based on *Economic and Political Weekly*, 3 July 2004, p. 2939.

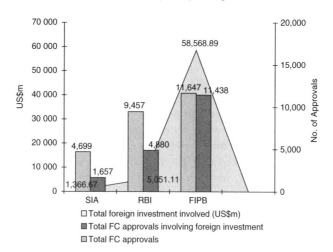

Figure 5.1 Foreign collaboration approvals in India – Aug. 1991–Mar. 2004
Source: Based on Table 5.1.

As a result of the declining importance of the RBI automatic route over the years, most of the proposals are being handled by the FIPB. Naturally, this has led to delays in project approval and hence implementation, because subsequently the investor needs clearances at the state government level as well. A shot in the arm to the entire process of entry could be provided by expanding the ambit of RBI's automatic approval route. Since the guidelines are clearly laid down for foreign investment inflows that come in through this category, increasing both the scope and the equity ceiling would go a long way in improving the transparency and the efficacy of the approval process.

FDI inflows in the post-reform period (1991–2004)

Table 5.2 considers the actual inflows of FDI in the post reform period while Figure 5.2 plots the foreign investment approvals and actuals. The actual FDI inflow is recorded under five broad heads: (i) RBI's automatic approval route for equity holding up to 51 per cent, (ii) Foreign Investment Board's discretionary approval route for larger projects with equity holding greater than 51 per cent, (iii) acquisition of shares route (since 1996), (iv) RBI's non-resident Indian (NRI) schemes, and (v) foreign currency convertible bonds American Depositary Receipt/Global Depositary Receipt (ADR/GDR) route. The aggregate amount of inflows since 1991 to date (May 2004) has been about US$36 billion. The composition of actual inflow of FDI and NRI investment in India is also

Table 5.2 Actual inflow of FDI and NRI investment (US$m)

1	*Total (1991–2004)*	*2004*	*2003*	*2002*	*2001*	*2000*
	2	3	4	5	6	7
Govt's approval	14 561.33	211.33	954.67	1 546.22	2 142.00	1 409.56
RBI's approval	3 554.00	173.11	520.00	867.33	720.22	376.00
Amount of inflows in acquisition of shares	4 842.89	289.78	650.67	1 169.56	658.22	457.33
Various NRI schemes	1 857.56	–	–	2.44	50.89	77.56
ADRs/GDRs/FCCBs	6 254.00	63.11	596.44	686.67	552.67	1 552.89
Total	31 069.78	737.33	2 721.78	4 272.22	4 124.00	3 873.33
Stock swapped	57.11	–	38.44	18.67	–	–
Closing balance	2 031.78	390.89	418.00	439.33	157.11	425.11
Grand total	33 158.67	1 128.22	3 178.22	4 730.22	4 281.11	4 298.44
Grand total (US$bn)	36.62					

Note: US$1 = Rs45 (July 2004).

Source: Based on *Economic and Political Weekly*, 3 July 2004, p. 2939.

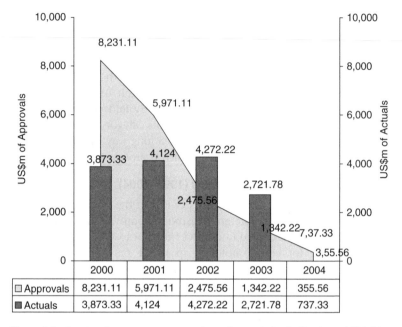

Figure 5.2   Foreign investment approvals and actuals in India: Aug. 1991–Mar. 2004

Note: US$1 = Rs45 (July 2004).

Source: *Economic and Political Weekly*, 3 July 2004, p. 2939.

shown in Figure 5.3. A glance at the table reveals that most of the actual direct investment has been channelized through the SIA/Foreign Investment Promotion Board (FIPB) route. RBI'S automatic approval route has declined in importance in the post-reform period despite an expansion of the scope of this channel.

There is much to argue with the current practice of estimating a ratio for actuals to approvals. Approvals occur at a point in time, whereas actuals over a time period. Hence, it is eminently possible that during a 'good' year the ratio could exceed 100 per cent (if we look at approvals and actuals only in that particular year). Therefore, we caution against the use of a summary statistic like actual to approval ratio to infer about project implementation. This is not to detract from the fact that FDI inflows to India have been sluggish due to long gestation period for projects involving huge investment outlays.[8]

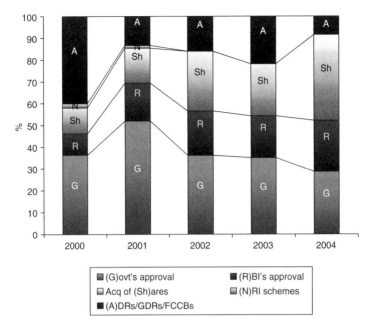

Figure 5.3 Actual inflow of FDI and NRI investment in India
Source: Based on Table 5.2.

Geographical distribution of FDI

The cumulative approvals appeared to be US$78.3 billion during 1991–2004 (March) of which US$36.62 billion of foreign investment was actually made (Tables 5.1 and 5.2). It is clear from Table 5.3 and Figure 5.4 that USA has been the most important investor throughout this period, contributing about 20 per cent during 1991–2004 (March). While Mauritius and UK have become important investors, FDI from Japan and South Korea haven't lagged behind. During the same period, the share of NRIs was only about 4 per cent of the total approved investment.

The US is also one of the largest investors in terms of actual FDI inflow into India. US FDI inflow was about US$3 billion between 1991 and July 2001 whereas the total FDI inflow to India for this period was about US$19 billion. The FDI inflows from the US constitute about 16 per cent of the total actual inflow in to the economy. The overall US FDI inflow-approval ratio is 19 per cent. Sector-wise break-up of US FDI are: fuel

Table 5.3 FDI in India classified according to sources of funds: 1991–2004 (Mar.)

Country/region	Investment (US$m)	%
North America total	*14 889.33*	*22.9*
USA	12 958.89	19.9
Canada	640.22	1.0
Bermuda	139.33	0.2
Cayman Island	864.00	1.3
Panama	142.89	0.2
Other West Indian Islands	144.00	0.2
Africa total	*8 408.44*	*12.9*
Mauritius	7 982.89	12.3
South Africa	425.56	0.7
EU total	*14 378.22*	*22.1*
UK	5 292.00	8.1
Netherlands	2 128.89	3.3
Germany	2 092.00	3.2
France	1 465.33	2.3
Italy	1 069.78	1.7
Belgium	1 019.33	1.6
Switzerland	700.00	1.1
Sweden	459.11	0.7
Denmark	151.78	0.2
Asia total	*10 600.44*	*16.3*
Malaysia	1 354.89	2.1
Singapore	1 254.00	1.9
Saudi Arabia	181.78	0.3
South Korea	2 197.78	3.4
Israel	944.89	1.5
Japan	2 615.11	4.0
Thailand	550.22	0.9
Hong Kong	526.89	0.8
United Arab Emirates	201.78	0.3
China	165.11	0.3
Oman	144.22	0.2
Kuwait	133.56	0.2
Indonesia	117.11	0.2
Taiwan	110.44	0.2
Qatar	102.67	0.2
Australia	*1 514.44*	*2.3*
NRI	*2 524.67*	*3.9*
Euro issues	*10 906.89*	*16.8*
All others	*1 767.56*	*2.7*
Total	*64 989.56*	*100.0*

Notes: Euro issue represents proposals for GDR and FCCB; US$1 = Rs45 (July, 2004).

Source: Based on recomputed from SIA Newsletter, April, 2004, Secretariat for Industrial Assistance, Department of Industrial Policy and Promotion, Ministry of Commerce and Industry, Government of India.

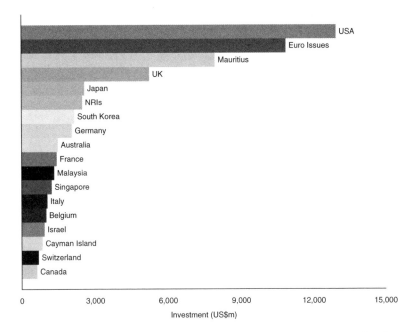

Figure 5.4 Sources of FDI in India: 1991–2004 (all sources with 1% total FDI or higher)

Source: Based on Table 5.3.

(power and oil refinery) 39 per cent; food-processing industries 11 per cent; telecommunications 10 per cent; service sector (financial and non-financial service) 9 per cent; electrical equipment (computer software and electronics) 8 per cent.[9]

The US is the leading investor in India in portfolio investment also. Out of the 538 Foreign Institutional Investors (FIIs) registered with Securities and Exchange Board of India (SEBI), 220 are from the United States. As of February 2001, an investment of nearly US$7 billion out of a total of US$13 billion by FIIs in the Indian capital market was from the United States. This accounts for about 47 per cent of the net investments made by the FIIs since 1993.

Table 5.4 reveals the state-wise distribution of FDI approvals. Gujarat, Maharashtra and Delhi appear to be the major destinations of foreign investors. In fact these three states during the past ten years have been growing at the rate of Asian 'tiger' economies in their better days. Southern states such as Tamil Nadu, Karnataka and Andhra Pradesh are

96

Table 5.4   State-wise flow of FDI approvals: 1991–2004 (Mar.)

State	No. of Approvals	Amount Approved (Rs crore)	Amount Approved (US m $*)	% to total Amount
1	2	3	4	5
Northern Region	*4 216*	*45 967*	*10 214.89*	*15.7*
Delhi	2 638	35 251	7 833.56	12.1
Haryana	858	3 870	860.00	1.3
Rajasthan	341	3 033	674.00	1.0
Punjab	199	2 434	540.89	0.8
Himachal Pradesh	98	1 174	260.89	0.4
Chandigarh	77	196	43.56	0.1
Jammu and Kashmir	5	8	1.78	neg
North-Eastern region	*35*	*77*	*17.11*	*neg*
Eastern region	*947*	*18 444*	*4 098.67*	*6.3*
West Bengal	670	9 317	2 070.44	3.2
Orissa	140	8 229	1 828.67	2.8
Jharkhand	80	145	32.22	neg
Bihar	49	740	164.44	0.3
Andaman and Nicobar Islands	8	14	3.11	neg
Central region	*1 138*	*14 947*	*3 321.56*	*5.1*
Uttar Pradesh	798	4 917	1 092.67	1.7
Madhya Pradesh	242	9 271	2 060.22	3.2
Uttaranchal	51	126	28.00	neg
Chattisgarh	47	633	140.67	0.2
Western region	*6 380*	*71 122*	*15 804.89*	*24.3*
Maharashtra	4 816	51 115	11 358.89	17.5
Gujarat	1 204	18 837	4 186.00	6.4
Goa	245	990	220.00	0.3
Dadra and Nagar Haveli	72	124	27.56	neg
Daman and Diu	43	55	12.22	neg
Southern region	*6 755*	*65 794*	*14 620.89*	*22.5*
Tamil Nadu	2 607	25 072	5 571.56	8.6
Karnataka	2 467	24 138	5 364.00	8.3
Andhra Pradesh	1 226	13 745	3 054.44	4.7
Kerala	325	1 552	344.89	0.5
Pondicherry	129	1 286	285.78	0.4
Lakshadweep	1	1	0.22	neg
State not indicated	*6 011*	*76 008*	*16 890.67*	*26.0*
Total	*25 482*	*292 358*	*64 968.44*	*100*

Note: *US$1=Rs45 (July 2004); 1 crore = 10m.
Source: Based on *Economic and Political Weekly*, 3 July 2004.

equally competitive now in this context. On most measures the investors have shown a preference for states that possess a well-developed infrastructure and governance. Other factors determining the attractiveness of a state in courting FDI are: availability of manpower, power supply, raw material availability, transportation facility, appropriate incentives for industry, water supply, availability of finance and tax holidays and subsidies. In addition, the most important considerations on the part of investors are transparency in dealings, quick approvals, sound infrastructure and consistency in policy.

It is in this context to be mentioned here that Gujarat and Maharashtra, two western states, notched up the fastest growth between 1991 and 1998, whereas growth rates in half the 14 biggest states actually declined (*The Economist*, 21 May 2001). On a per-head basis the difference is even starker. Some states where growth is slow, including the two biggest, Uttar Pradesh and Bihar, also have fastest growing populations.

Table 5.5 shows FDI inflows (approvals) in selected industry groups both in levels of FDI received and as a percentage of the total inflow – while Figure 5.5 provides a summarized visual representation of the same. The general trend seems to be the growing importance of technology-intensive and capital-intensive manufacturing in approvals. It appears that basic industries contribute about 45 per cent of the total industries approved. This is indicative of a change in the structure of production toward a more capital- and skill-intensive one as compared to the traditional labour-intensive production. The inflows in the services sector account for roughly 31 per cent of all FDI. We feel that there is potential for increasing the share of services in total FDI, especially after the deregulation of the financial services sector.

The above data reveals that much of the investment during the period has gone into the infrastructure and industrial sectors. The notion that bulk of FDI has gone to the consumer goods sector is not borne out by the data.

Forms of FDI

In an ideal condition, FDI inflow should get reflected in (i) formation of new firms and factories, (ii) increase in foreign equity holding in the existing firms, and (iii) M&As of existing firms and factories (or parts of them).[10]

As regards fully owned private limited companies of foreign firms, published data reveals very little information about their investment

98

Table 5.5   Industry-wise break-up of foreign collaboration approvals

Name of industry	No. approvals Tech	Fin	amount approved (Rs crore)	amount approved US$m $*	% to total amount
1	2	3	4	5	6
Basic goods industries	1 240	1 326	81 109	18 024.22	44.7
Ferrous metals	202	138	7 274.8	1 616.62	4.0
Non-ferrous metals	29	31	770.8	171.29	0.4
Special alloys	36	20	144.9	32.20	0.1
Mining services	6	16	1 776.6	394.80	1.0
Misc. (metallurgy)	22	39	1 182.6	262.80	0.7
Power	13	134	28 539.9	6 342.20	15.7
Power (other)	3	33	4 874.5	1 083.22	2.7
Oil refinery	86	102	18 422.9	4 093.98	10.2
Oil Refinery (Other)	21	20	3912	869.33	2.2
Others (fuels)	39	75	2 030.4	451.20	1.1
Fertilisers	52	6	246.9	54.87	0.1
Chemicals	698	666	11 230.2	2 495.60	6.2
Cement and gypsum	33	46	702.6	156.13	0.4
Capital goods industries	2 666	2 212	14 757.6	3 279.47	8.1
Boilers and steam plants	40	29	118	26.22	0.1
Prime movers	38	22	91.3	20.29	0.1
Electrical equipment	779	575	4 045.9	899.09	2.2
Electronics	127	220	2 165.2	481.16	1.2
Computer hardware	0	2	0.2	0.04	neg
Others (S/W) (electrical)	13	21	63	14.00	neg
Transportation industry (Misc.)	419	333	3 938	875.11	2.2
Industrial machinery	736	425	1 958.4	435.20	1.1
Machine tools	76	84	278.5	61.89	0.2
Agricultural machinery	27	9	434.1	96.47	0.2
Earth moving machinery	31	19	83.3	18.51	neg
Misc (Mech. and engineering)	247	333	1 120	248.89	0.6
Medical surgical appliances	24	42	241.8	53.73	0.1
Industrial instruments	90	67	116.6	25.91	0.1
Scientific instruments	14	26	61.4	13.64	neg
Mathematical, surveying and drawing	1	4	38.4	8.53	neg
Defence industries	4	1	3.5	0.78	neg
Intermediate goods industries	207	412	3 586.8	797.07	2.0
Dyestuff	3	15	106.7	23.71	0.1
Rubber goods	89	81	1 057.5	235.00	0.6
Leather and leather goods and pickers	33	130	274.2	60.93	0.2
Glass	28	50	1 341.7	298.16	0.7
Ceramics	52	128	790.4	175.64	0.4
Timber products	2	8	16.3	3.62	neg
Consumer non-durable industries	687	1 554	17 671.9	3 927.09	9.7
Photographic raw film Paper	10	9	221.5	49.22	0.1
Drugs and pharmaceuticals	171	136	802	178.22	0.4
Textiles	114	433	2 806.9	623.76	1.5

Continued

Table 5.5 Continued

Name of industry	No. approvals Tech	Fin	amount approved (Rs crore)	amount approved US$m $*	% to total amount
1	2	3	4	5	6
Paper and pulp incl. paper products	62	90	2 308.8	513.07	1.3
Sugar	1	6	1 000.8	222.40	0.6
Fermentation industries	17	41	1 125.5	250.11	0.6
Food products	118	490	8 245.1	1 832.24	4.5
Marine products	19	68	85.4	18.98	neg
Vegetable oils and vanaspati	3	32	193.9	43.09	0.1
Soaps, cosmetics and toilet preparation	15	33	336.2	74.71	0.2
Misc (Incl hort/flori/agro/ tea/cig/coir)	157	216	546	121.33	0.3
Consumer durable industries	*30*	*76*	*5 498.2*	*1 221.82*	*3.0*
Comm office and household equipment	27	43	981.8	218.18	0.5
Passenger cars	3	27	4 474.9	994.42	2.5
Diamond/ornament/gold	0	6	41.5	9.22	neg
Services	*432*	*2 605*	*56 763.3*	*12 614.07*	*31.3*
Computer services	68	685	3 241.3	720.29	1.8
Telecommunications	109	369	32 740.9	7 275.76	18.1
Air/sea transport/ports	11	102	2794	620.89	1.5
Consultancy	80	344	1 708.2	379.60	0.9
Financial services	6	235	7144	1 587.56	3.9
Non-financial services	19	232	2 895.2	643.38	1.6
Banking services	0	16	171.1	38.02	0.1
Hospital and diagnostic centres	7	50	552.3	122.73	0.3
Other services	4	21	806.9	179.31	0.4
Hotel and tourism	112	216	3 490.6	775.69	1.9
Trading	16	335	1 218.8	270.84	0.7
Other misc. industries	*456*	*327*	*1 910*	*424.44*	*1.1*
Grand total	*5 718*	*8 512*	*181 296.8*	*40 288.18*	*100.0*

Note: *Using an exchange rate of US$1 = Rs45.00 (July 2004) neg: negligible.

Source: Based on *SIA Newsletter* (2004).

and output (Nagraj, 2003). In this context it may be mentioned here that a significant number of foreign firms have formed their fully owned subsidiaries by acquiring domestic firms. Tables 5.6 to 5.9 and Figures 5.6 and 5.7 reveal an interesting picture in this context.

It is useful to mention that the heights of the economy are commanded by those that lingered on: the public sector, which produces less returns on half of the total capital stock, and traditional family-owned firms many of which are doing no better. Table 5.10 shows an interesting picture in this context. It appears that seven of the ten most valuable companies on the stock market in 1992 had disappeared from that list by March 2001.

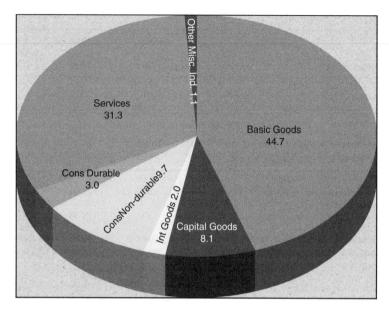

Figure 5.5 Industry-wise break-up of FDI in foreign collaboration approvals: India (%)

Source: Based on Table 5.5.

Table 5.6 Illustrative list of foreign firms not listed in the domestic stock market

Product group	Foreign firms
Automobiles and allied products	GM, Ford, Mercedes Benz, Honda, Hyundai, Fiat, Toyota, Volvo, Yamaha, Cummins, Goodyear
Food and beverages	Coca-cola, Cadbury Schweppes, Kellogg, Heinz, Seagram, Hiram Waker, United Distillers, Perfitti, Wrigley, KFC, McDonalds
Consumer durable goods	Daewoo, Samsung, Sony, General Electric, LG Electronics, Black and Decker, Kimberley Clark
Personal care products	Revlon, L'Oreal, Cussons, Unilevers

Source: Based on Nagraj (2003), p. 1705.

Table 5.7   Illustrative list of units/divisions transferred to foreign firms

Units to be transferred/transferred	Remark
Apar Lighting Division	Transferred to the joint-venture (JV) GE-Apar Ltd
Compressor unit of Kirloskar Brothers	Transferred to Kirloskar Copeland
Compressor unit of SIEL and Kelvinator	Taken over by Tecumseh Venture
Engine valve division of Kirloskar Oil Engines	Proposed to be transferred to a JV with MWP, subsidiary of Mahel Germany.
Halol Plant of Hind Motors	Transferred to a JV with GM of the US
Hinditron Computers	Acquired by Digital Equipment Corp
India Linoleum	Transferred to a JV with DLW of Germany
Premier Auto	Taken over by Fiat
Luxor Pen	Transferred to a JV with Gillette
Electric meters of VXL Ltd	Transferred to VXL Landys Gys Ltd
Motor Cycle division of Escorts	Transferred to Escorts Yamaha Ltd
Oral Care Division of Parle	Acquired by Gillette
Refrigerator division of Godrej & Boyce	Transferred to Godrej-GE appliances
Specialty chemicals div of Max India	Transferred to Max-Atotech
Stabiliser division of Jan Auto	Taken over by NHK Jai suspensions Ltd.
Sugar Machinery div of KCP Ltd	Transferred to FCB-KCP Ltd
Ceat's Two-and three-wheeler tyre plant	Transferred to South Asia Tyres Ltd. with Goodyear

Source: Based on Nagraj (2003), p. 1707.

Table 5.8   An illustrative list of foreign firms moving to de-list from domestic bourses

Sl. no.	Company	Acquirer's current holding %	Offer price (Rs)	Post-offer holding (%)
1.	Cabot	60	100	92
2.	Cadbury	51	500	90
3.	Carrier Aircon	51	100	86
4.	Centak Chemicals	75	200	93
5.	Hoganas	51	100	85
6.	Otis	69	280	79
7.	Philips	51	105	83
8.	Reckitt & Colman	51	250	Yet to open
9.	Sandvik	73	850	89

Source: Based on Business India, 1–14 April (2002), p. 118.

Table 5.9 An illustrative list of foreign companies that issued to themselves shares at a concession

Sl. no.	Company	No. of share allotted (m)	Preferential issue price (Rs)	Market price on allotment date (Rs)	Gain to the company (Rs m)
1.	Colgate	11.3	60	700	7 227.5
2.	Castrol	3.5	110	1 050	3 325.7
3.	Sesa Goa	3.3	120	1 025	2 968.4
4.	Asea Brown Boveri	4.8	60	325	1 260.0
5.	Bata	4.7	35	325	936.7
6.	Coats Viyella	7.5	65	260	1 444.7
7.	Alfa Laval	3.4	73	290	738.8
8.	Nestle	4.8	70	285	1 021.6
9.	Glaxo	4.5	75	255	808.0
10.	Hoechst	2.2	70	370	645.3
11.	Lipton	3.5	105	380	972.4
12.	Proctor & Gamble	4.8	70	285	1 021.6
13.	Proctor & Gamble	1.9	225	340	223.1
14.	Philips	7.7	40	205	340.0
15.	Reckitt & Colman	3.0	100	380	848.4
	Total gain to the foreign firms				24 737.0

Source: Based on Nagraj (2003), p. 1708.

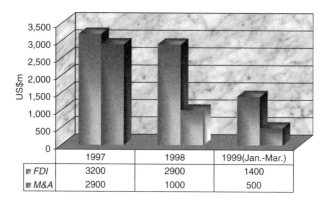

Figure 5.6 M&A in FDI inflows to India
Source: Based an Nagraj (2003), p. 1706.

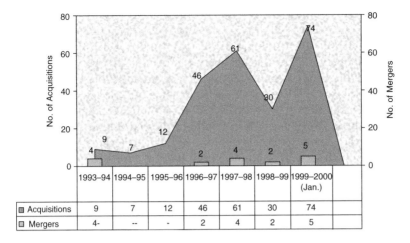

Figure 5.7   Foreign firm related M&A in India
Source: Based on Nagraj (2003), p. 1706.

Table 5.10   Top companies by market capitalization ($bn)

Company	1992	Company	2001(Mar.)
TISCO	2.21	Hindustan Lever	10.3
ITC	1.20	Reliance Industries	8.84
Telco	1.14	Wipro	6.65
Century Textiles	1.13	Infosys Technologies	5.79
Hindustan Lever	0.89	Reliance Petroleum	4.65
Reliance Industries	0.77	ITC	4.29
Grasim	0.74	Oil & Natural Gas	4.05
GSFC	0.73	Indian Oil	2.73
ACC	0.67	State Bank of India	2.26
Colgate	0.57	HCL Technologies	2.22

Source: Based on *Business India* (2002a), p. 156.

Performance of foreign invested enterprises and domestic firms

It is difficult to gather information on the performance of foreign-controlled companies because of certain legal problems. Even the (RBIs) survey of financial performance of foreign controlled companies appears to be silent here.

The literature is thus limited in examining the performance of FDI firms in the Indian context. Kathuria (2000, 2001) made interesting studies to examine a spillover hypothesis for large sized firms. He found that presence of foreign owned firms encouraged local firms to invest in R&D. Interestingly, his results reveal that foreign-owned firms are neither at nor close to the frontier in their respective sectors.

In another study Kathuria (2002) made an attempt to test the productivity spillover of FDI based on a select number of Indian manufacturing firms.[11] His results showed that after liberalization, the productive efficiency of Indian industry had improved. Indeed, the increase in efficiency was greater for the foreign-owned firms. As regards, the non-FDI firms, only the scientific non-FDI firms benefited from the trade liberalization. FDI on the other hand did not have any impact on non-scientific firms.

Strategically, Korean multinationals are more successful in India in the automobile and consumer electronics sectors than their Japanese counterpart. The companies of Korean origin such as Hyundai, LG and Samsung have developed their clusters in India. Park (2004) studied Hyundai Motors India (HMI)[12] to examine the role of industrial clusters in economic activity. He finds that industrial clusters are playing an important role in economic activity.[13] This is particularly true in technology-intensive industries such as IT, automobiles and electronics. Table 5.11 lists the major companies of HMI's industrial clusters in Chennai.

Trade liberalization and productivity performance

It is now open to question as to how the trade liberalization regime influenced the productivity growth. Das (2001) made an attempt to document this aspect in the context of developing economies with particular reference to India. For example, Goldar (1986) used effective rate of protection and estimates of import substitution as indicators of trade policy, whereas Ahluwalia (1991) used a Chenery measure of import substitution to address the issue of determinants of productivity growth. Both the studies found a negative relationship between productivity growth and indicators of trade policy.

Recent studies (Das, 2002), Goldar and Kumari (2002) and Chand and Sen (2002) have addressed the issue of trade-liberalization manufacturing–productivity growth linkage with appropriately defined measures of trade policy reforms. The Das (ibid.) study covers the period 1980–95 and around 72 three-digit industries. Using measures of trade liberalization such as effective rate of protection (ERP) and non-tariff barriers (NTBs), it studied the effect of lowering of tariff and non-tariff barriers on industrial productivity. The results show that lowering of NTBs had a positive impact on the manufacturing as well as intermediate goods sectors'

Table 5.11 HMI's industrial cluster, Chennai (major companies)

Company	Collaboration*	Product or activity	Year	Employee**
Hyundai Motors India (HMI)	Greenfield	Engine, car	1996	2 675(55)
JBM Sungwoo	JBM (50) Sungwoo (31) Mitsubishi (19)	Car body	1997	660(2)
Mando Brake Systems India	Anand (75.8) Mando (24.2)	Brake system	1997	120(1)
Lumax Samlip Industry	Samlip (75.2) Hyundai (4.5) Lumax (20.3)	Lamp, trim	1997	190(2)
Iljin Automotive	Greenfield	Engine parts, TM parts	1997	250(4)
JKM Dalim Automotive	Dynamatic (73) Dalim (27)	Oil pump, Water pump	1997	169(1)
Penta Daewha Auto Parts	Daewha (51) Penta (49)	Oil pump Oil filter	1997	186(1)
PHC Manufacturing	Component Speciality (50) PHC (50)	Door latch Hinge	1997	178(2)
Visteon Automotive India	Visteon (94) Hanla Kongio (6)	Aircon system Cluster	1997	557(4)
Hanil Rear India	Hanil (50) Rear (50)	Seat, interior	1997	250(2)
Changyoun India	Anand (76) Changyoun (24)	Ring-synchro	1997	39(1)
Hwaseung	Hwaseung RNA (74) I-Alpha (26)	Lever, pvc, profile	1997	230(1)
Kyungshin	Kyungshin (50) Mothersn (50)	Wiring harness	1997	645(2)
Samyoung Cable	Greenfield	Battery cable	1997	83(1)
Hwashin	Greenfield	Chassis	1997	163(1)
Dong-A Hwasung	Greenfield	Rubber parts	1997	21(1)
Hyundam Industry	Greenfield	Fuel pump	1997	32(1)
Shinhan Plasto	Greenfield	Crash pad	1997	125(1)

Notes: 'Year' means launched year.
*Figure in brackets indicate ratio of stock ownership;
**figure in brackets indicates number of Korean employees.

Source: Based on Park (2004), p. 3554.

industrial productivity. The study by Goldar and Kumari op. cit. covering the period till 1997/98 shows that a reduction in ERP to industries appeared to have had a favourable effect on productivity growth in Indian industries. However, the observed fall in productivity in the 1990s may be attributable partly to the investment projects. Chand and Sen (2002) showed that a reduction in the price-wage had a positive impact on productivity growth. The study however, covers the period 1973–88 before the onset of major trade liberalization attempts.

Exports and FDI

In the past, exports were generally a residual activity for India. It is now recognized beyond a trace of doubt that exports can contribute usefully to finance India's foreign exchange obligations. This underscores the need for an export policy that may generate high value added exports, improve quality of production and help diversify the export basket. In this area FDI can make a substantial contribution.

It is true that traditionally MNC production was organized for the domestic market. Export-oriented investments were restricted to natural resources. Studies on the determinants of FDI found that factors such as market size were much more important than cost factors for determining such domestic-market oriented investments (UNCTC, 1994). However, an important change has taken place in the last few years. There has been an increase in export oriented investments by MNCs to take advantage of the lower cost of labour. The fall in trade barriers and the improvements in information technology have made it possible for MNCs to locate part of their production in countries like India and other developing countries.

The World Investment Report of 1995 (UNCTAD, 1995) asserts that even labour-intensive, export-oriented FDI is now being restructured, with this activity gradually shifting from the more advanced of the developing countries to the less advanced ones. Over time, the 'flying geese' pattern of development that has taken place in Japan, Korea, and Malaysia can be replicated in India.[14] As labour costs rise in the more advanced Asian countries, it is likely that some export-oriented FDI will be transferred to India. It must be realized that FDI is not motivated by exports in the first round. In the longer run, they may be interested in exports and tap particularly the neighbouring markets in Asia.

India is a very small player in world trade. Figure 5.8 shows the share of Indian exports in world exports. As the figure clearly indicates India's share of world exports has been consistently less than 1 per cent making a marginal presence in the world market.[15]

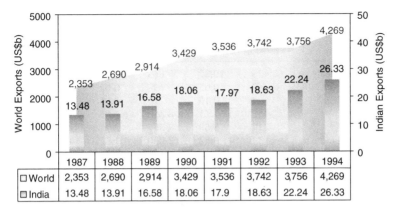

Figure 5.8 World exports and India

Source: Based an DGCIS, *Direction of Trade Statistics and International Finance Statistics* (IMF), 1995.

At a macro level, export was never considered as an engine of growth in the Indian growth model. It was realized to be so only in 1990/91 due to a severe foreign exchange constraint. The Industrial Credit and Investment Corporation of India Ltd (ICICI, 1997) pursued a sample study in order to explore the realities at the beginning of the reform period (1991–96). They took 490 export based companies to examine their contribution to India's exports. It was found that the share of exports of these companies to India's total exports increased from 17.1 per cent in 1991/92 to 19.1 per cent in 1994/95 and then decreased marginally to 18.4 per cent in 1995/96. The sample's share in India's imports rose at a faster rate from 8.1 per cent in the base year to 12.6 per cent in the terminal year. This result may have little bearing as the time period of the study was close to the beginning of the reforms. Since 1991, India has emphasized export as one of her contributors to growth. Table 5.12 and Figure 5.9 show the state-wise distribution of 100 per cent Export Oriented Units (EOUs) in this context.

Using annual data for 1970–98, Sharma (2000) investigated the role of FDI in explaining India's export performance. His results suggest that demand for Indian exports increases when its export prices fall in relation to world prices. Interestingly, foreign investment appears to have statistically no significant impact on India's export performance although the coefficient of FDI variable has a positive sign.

108

Table 5.12   Statewise distribution of 100% EOUs since Aug. 1991

State name	No.	%	Inv (in Rs Crore)	%	Emp (in nos)	%
Andhra Pradesh	425	10.87	9 663	6.54	68 232	10.25
Assam	2	0.05	36	0.02	647	0.10
Bihar	4	0.10	16	0.01	304	0.05
Gujarat	458	11.71	8 356	5.65	58 477	8.78
Haryana	219	5.60	4 397	2.97	32 234	4.84
Himachal Pradesh	32	0.82	2 030	1.37	14 949	2.25
Jammu & Kashmir	3	0.08	39	0.03	422	0.06
Karnataka	423	10.82	5 025	3.40	79 489	11.94
Kerala	74	1.89	907	0.61	9 520	1.43
Madhya Pradesh	118	3.02	9 017	6.10	40 613	6.10
Maharashtra	571	14.60	7 589	5.13	90 025	13.52
Meghalaya	3	0.08	15	0.01	168	0.03
Orissa	41	1.05	8 139	5.51	18 956	2.85
Punjab	131	3.35	3 548	2.40	40 366	6.06
Rajasthan	223	5.70	4 960	3.36	30 186	4.53
Tamil Nadu	608	15.55	60 859	41.17	102 811	15.44
Tripura	2	0.05	4	0.00	153	0.02
Uttar Pradesh	205	5.24	16 746	11.33	35 367	5.31
West Bengal	98	2.51	2 862	1.94	15 828	2.38
Chhattisgarh	28	0.72	455	0.31	2 438	0.37
Jharkhand	3	0.08	7	0.00	61	0.01
Uttaranchal	16	0.41	281	0.19	2 168	0.33
Andaman & Nicobar Islands	3	0.08	2	0.00	108	0.02
Chandigarh	3	0.08	31	0.02	1 099	0.17
Dadra & Nagar Haveli	37	0.95	267	0.18	1 942	0.29
Delhi	106	2.71	1 106	0.75	10 401	1.56
Goa	28	0.72	480	0.32	3 670	0.55
Lakshadweep	1	0.03	3	0.00	34	0.01
Pondicherry	15	0.38	506	0.34	2 627	0.39
Daman & Diu	15	0.38	132	0.09	1 206	0.18
State/UT Not Indicated	16	0.41	329	0.22	1 300	0.20
Total	3 911	100.00	147 807	100.00	665 801	100.00

Notes: 1. The figures are updated on the basis of the information provided by the Department of Commerce. 2. Figures are available up to Dec. 2002 only.

Source: Based on SIA Newsletter (2004).

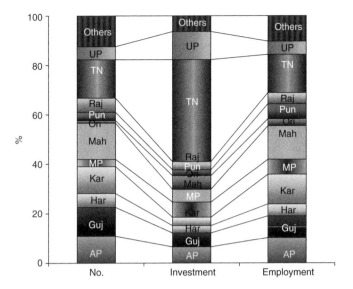

Figure 5.9 State-wise distribution of export oriented units since Aug. 1991
Source: Based on Table 5.12.

The rise of 'knowledge industries' is an important development and it has captured the imagination of India's entrepreneurs. Of these, information technology has been the most successful. It has grown at an average annual rate of over 50 per cent, from almost nothing in 1991 to sales of $8.3 billion in 2000 and employment of around 400,000. It contributes 15 per cent of India's exports. The National Association of Software and Service Companies (NASSCOM), the main trade association for the information technology industry, predicts that by 2008 India will be able to export $50 billion worth of software and allied services, and employ 1.1 million people. According to the same source, the scope of 'IT-enabled services' or 'remote services' is vast. It may expand employment beyond software engineers, potentially to anyone who can speak English.

It is imperative to note the performance of a few companies in this context. Ace Software Exports for example exports more than 90 per cent of its output. These are software products for data processing and web services. This small company purchased technology from abroad in 1996, but has not imported either capital goods or materials (its FDI stake is seven per cent). Its export success depends on its 400 technically skilled computer professionals and its production process does not require large amounts of capital goods.

Kalyani Sharp had high exports (mainly video cassette recorders) in 1997 and 1998, amounting to 52 and 35 per cent of total sales of about $70 million in those years, respectively, because of sales to its Japanese majority owner, the Sharp Corporation. There are some Multinational Enterprise (MNE) affiliates that do not export despite making large imports of capital goods or components. One of these is California Software Co. Ltd. This has a foreign equity stake of 24 per cent from Itochu of Japan and Chemoil of the US. The California location sells e-commerce and Windows-related software to US customers; the Indian company's international business is carried out by its subsidiary abroad rather than by export from India.

Among licensees of foreign technology that do not have direct foreign ownership stakes, perhaps the best known major exporter is Infosys Technologies – which earns about 85 per cent of its total revenue from exports. Infosys Technologies is also a large importer of foreign technology, spending about one-quarter of its revenue on purchases of licences and payment of royalties. Infosys was the first Indian company to list its shares on NASDAQ and the first to draw up its accounts in accordance with American accounting principles. It has opened offices in Toronto, California, Chicago and London. The company with 52,000 employees has some way to go before it catches up with the 'big five' IT consultancies.

Interestingly, quite a few companies/licensees achieved considerable export success without importing substantial amounts of foreign technology. For example, DSQ Software Ltd. deals with client server applications, reengineering, and mainframe maintenance. DSQ Software had an export intensity exceeding 75 per cent of its revenue of $28 million in 1997 despite small technology imports. Almost all of its employees are software engineers. It had two niche markets – Y2K and Enterprise Resource Planning. A significant proportion of its business has been offshore work for foreign clients (e.g. AT&T for whom it is a preferred vendor). It has its own subsidiaries abroad (the result of outward FDI) because it obtains contracts. Accordingly it is possible for the firm to obtain technology transfer by movement of employees in addition to or instead of purchase of licences.

Quite a good number of licensees achieved export success in recent time and half of their revenues accounted for by exports. For example, VXL Instruments Ltd, which supplies computer monitors and components to resellers or as an original equipment manufacturer (OEM) for companies such as IBM, HP, and ICL. The company had only a median level of technology imports, but it also established a European sales and distribution centre. VXL Instruments was established quite a long time ago (for this industry) in 1986 by a team of Indian scientists.

Knowledge exports are not the only major source of Indian exports. Software services are contributing equally to her exports. To quote *The Economist* (2–8 June 2001, p. 19)

The idea of outsourcing back-office work to India is catching on among big first-world companies, led by multinationals such as GE and American Express. Indian companies are offering back-office services to firms that do not want to set up their own Indian operations. Daksh.com near Delhi answers questions from customers of Amazon, the biggest online retailer. In theory India can export just as about any service capable of being carried by fiber-optic cable, from cartoon animation to research and development. NASSCOM guesses that last year 68,000 people were generating 40 billion rupees of revenue in remote services. Some analysts think that India will scoop up clerical work in the developed world, just as China and other East Asian countries commandeered manufacturing.

Siddharthan and Nollen (2000) studied the information technology firms in India. The result shows that the explanation of export performance depends on the firm's foreign collaboration and on the type of technology that it requires from abroad. For affiliates of multinational enterprises, both explicit technology transfer from purchases of licenses and payments of royalties, and tacit knowledge transfer received from foreign ownership contribute to greater export intensity. Interestingly, the domestic firms import raw materials and components as a source of product quality and greater capital intensity. On close examination their results suggest that the motive for direct investment by foreign firms and the existence of subsidiaries abroad by Indian firms affect export performance.

R&D and FDI

In the economics literature, it is well established that industrial innovation in the form of new products and processes has been a major source of US economic growth. The stock of knowledge that firms produce through investments in research and development, and training of workers constitutes an intangible asset base often referred to as intellectual property. This knowledge base or know-how could be an idea or a design for a new product or process, a new molecular entity or a new software package that may be protected under intellectual property rights.

There are however divergent views. Nollen and Brewer (2000) argued that the liberalization of government policies on trade and direct investment changes the international transfer of knowledge by firms, especially in developing countries. Government policy changes, as mandated by the World Trade Organization (WTO) agreements, affect firms' decisions about their mode of business, and mode shifts in turn change the type and amount of knowledge transferred.

As regards MNCs and R&D, they source inventions from any source – from small companies, from other R&D institutions, from national laboratories, and from academic sources and then try and integrate their in-house R&D with all this work from other sources. Incidentally, in the context of India, the country depends for most of the innovations on foreign source. Thus the local R&D intensity may not reflect the innovativeness or technology intensity of the industry. However, the amount spent on R&D in host country, which is usually of adaptive nature, might reflect the level of domestic technological capabilities in adapting/absorbing technology even if it is not really generating it (Kumar, 1989). Historically, the selective policy of the government of India does not normally allow foreign collaboration in industries where certain local technological capabilities have been built up.

Post-1991 policies, FDI and spillover

India's unbalanced growth pattern reveals a clear division across states. Broadly speaking, it has an economically dynamic south and the relatively stagnant north and east. Irrigated India remains lush during months when much of rain-dependent India turns barren. On the whole urban India is richer and more literate than rural India. Interestingly, nearly three-quarters of the population lives in rural areas.

The charge against the post-1991 policies is that it has deepened the above divisions. This is not unusual when the guiding principle for sharing out resources shifts from entitlement to competition. But that doesn't mean that the poor Indians are not benefited. Table 5.13 back up the trickle-down effect in major states. However, the position of the poor would be still better-off if the economy grew faster. Historically the myriad of controls (some of which remain till today) inhibited economic growth and thus failed to implement poverty reduction strategies. Virmani's study (2004) highlighted a rationale for the new paradigm based on a more realistic assessment of what markets and governments can provide and where they fail.

The employment effect in the post-reform period (post-1991) is a research question but the time period is still too small to be evaluated. Majumdar and Sarkar (2004) however, made an attempt to examine the employment elasticity in the organized manufacturing sector during the

Table 5.13   Poverty and literacy rate in major Indian states (% to total population)

State	Poor		Literate	
	1993	1999	1991	2001
Punjab	12	6	59	70
Haryana	25	9	56	69
Kerala	25	13	90	91
Gujarat	24	14	62	70
Rajasthan	27	15	39	61
Andhra Pradesh	22	16	44	61
Karnataka	33	20	56	67
Tamil Nadu	35	21	63	73
Maharashtra	37	25	65	77
West Bengal	36	27	58	69
Uttar Pradesh	41	31	41	57
Madhya Pradesh	43	37	45	64
Bihar	55	43	37	48
Orissa	49	47	49	64
India	*36*	*26*	*52*	*65*

Source: Based on Planning Commission; Census 2001.

periods 1974–80, 1980–86, and 1986–96. The first period (1974–80) had an elasticity close to unity, the second (1980–86) came out with a negative employment elasticity (the period of 'jobless growth'), and the third (1986–96) the 'reform period' was the one when employment started to recover along with an enhanced rate of growth of output – although employment elasticity did not reach the levels of the first period. More strikingly, according to the study, the two major changes in labour market outcomes during the period were (i) the fall in the share of wages; and (ii) the changes in the trade-off towards employment growth rather than wage growth.

That may be a story relating to the organized sector. The people in general seem to be better off. In fact some regions have improved their lot much more than others. The National Council of Applied Economic Research (NCAER), which surveys household incomes and spending on consumer goods, has found a sharp decline in implied poverty rates. The share of households it classifies as 'destitute' dropped from 23 per cent in 1972 to 16 per cent in 1998. More interestingly, the recent employment report reveals that real wages per head in 1993–99 rose by 2.5 per cent a year in rural areas and by 2.7 per cent in cities. Indeed the report found that more people had left the workforce to attend school.

There is a dearth of empirical findings that are consistent with the existence of spillovers from FDI in the Indian context. Theoretically, spillovers from FDI take place when the entry or presence of multinational corporations increases the productivity of domestic firms in a host country and the multinationals do not fully internalize the value of the benefits. There are other possible ways to understand the effects of spillovers: for example, a local firm may improve its efficiency by copying technologies of foreign affiliates operating in the local market either through observation or by hiring workers trained by the affiliates. Other ways as Blomstrom and Ari Kokko (1998) and Javorcik (2004) observed, were due to multinationals' entry and this may lead to more severe competition in the host country market and force local firms to use their existing resources more efficiently or to search for new technologies. The multinationals, however, may have an incentive to prevent technology leakage through formal protection of their intellectual property, trade secrecy, paying higher wages to prevent labour turnover, or locating in countries or industries where domestic firms have limited imitative capacities to begin with (Aitken *et al.*,1996; Sourafel Girma *et al.*, 2001). This observation may point to serious limitation in achieving significant positive horizontal spillovers from FDI. In contrast, there may be the case where multinationals may benefit from transferring knowledge to their local suppliers in case FDI is likely to be vertical. In other words, spillovers are most likely to take place through backward linkages – that is contact between domestic suppliers of intermediate inputs and their multinational clients. Likewise, domestic firms may become more productive as a result of gaining access to new, improved, or less costly intermediate inputs produced by multinationals in upstream sectors (forward linkage channel). The Indian evidence confirms the spillover through vertical FDI linkages. For instance, Sona Steering for Suzuki Motors, suppliers of HMI and IT companies. Local firms are also competitive now in terms of quality, service and other features.

Summary

Historically at the time of independence India followed a self-reliant path for her development. Nationalism perhaps played a contributory role in shaping the policies. Capital – not foreign but domestic capital was considered as useful. Capital in fact may be driven by the incentives mechanism and it may not have any national character. In the Indian context government economic policy was intended to shape the capital by various interventions. Yet, despite significant policy interventions, empirical evidence on the actual economic performance negates the potentialities. In fact, support by state to Indian industries distorted R&D, encouraged import of obsolete technology and discouraged innovation. We have portrayed a few facets in this context.

In the emerging scenario, the survival of a firm is purely determined by its ability to compete. Unfortunately in the Indian context, the government support to the industry was considered as continuous. Indeed, it was not guided by global production function.

The post-liberalization time span is too short to examine the export performance of FDI. Interestingly, the rise of 'knowledge industries' is a new aspect of India's future development. This is the Indian edition of 'leapfrog' where human capital in the high technology sector has acted as a powerful engine of growth. We find that the states (such as Gujarat, Maharashtra), which are relatively well-developed due to manufacturing, have human capital in the low technology sector, less intervention by the state sector and their geographical closeness to prosperous cities. The states which are relatively well-developed due to high technology (computers, software), have created human capital from endogenous factors such as proactive policies and other interventions in order to create an environment. The only outlier is West Bengal. This state is enriched with high-tech human capital but it failed to transform itself due to static policies. It is also a poor performer in the context of human development. Kerala, in contrast, with similar political environment has been able to perform much better in respect of human development.

The spillovers from FDI are a matter of global debate. Thus, India is not free from that. But it is natural to observe productivity spillovers through backward linkages (Original Equipment Manufacturing [OEM] firms) and forward linkages (link between foreign suppliers of intermediate inputs and their domestic customers). The literature, though limited, addresses the key issues in the Indian scenario. For example Kathuria's op. cit. result shows that the productive efficiency and benefits are associated not only with foreign firms but domestic ones have also improved their position.

As regards spillovers in the rural sector, the time period is too short to measure. Even then, the result shows the positive effects in terms of poverty reduction. This aspect is more important if one may endeavor to study at state level. In many cases the myriad of controls inhibited economic growth and thus failed to effectively implement poverty reduction strategies.

6

Foreign Investment: The Caribbean

Introduction

The previous chapter looked at FDI in India. This chapter shows how FDI has affected the small economies in the Caribbean. Most Caribbean countries have pursued an open door policy to FDI from around 1960. This policy was based on the provision of generous tax incentives to foreign investors. Originally, most FDI went to import substitution industries, petroleum and bauxite. Gradually after 1980, FDI in the smaller islands shifted to service industries such as tourism and informatics. The openness of Caribbean economies facilitated the inflow of FDI.

The earliest studies of FDI in the Caribbean were by McIntyre and Watson (1970) and Girvan (1971). The McIntyre and Watson study for the period 1956 – 1967 found that FDI in Trinidad and Tobago was heavily concentrated in the petrochemical industry. Investment income outflows were usually two and a half times the capital inflows. Foreign ownership dominated the economy of Trinidad and Tobago to the extent that profits of foreign-owned businesses as a per cent of corporate business income after tax was over 60 per cent between 1956 and 1962 (McIntyre and Watson, 1970).

Girvan's (1971) study advanced the thesis that foreign capital impeded structural change in the Jamaican economy. Foreign capital in the bauxite industry was the largest single form of investment and of capital inflow in Jamaica between 1950 and 1970. However, the bauxite industry was characterized by an extremely low degree of integration with the rest of the economy. Foreign capital also dominated the financial sector. It is to be mentioned here that the financial system was not geared to stimulate structural change, because bank lending was mainly in the form of credit to finance imported consumer durables, rather than the growing manufacturing sector.

Following the contribution of McIntyre and Watson (1970), Codrington (1987) analysed the pattern of FDI inflows to Barbados between 1977 and 1985, noting that most of those flows went to public utilities, manufacturing and tourism activities. In the case of public utilities, most of the funding was provided by non-resident enterprises with a major controlling interest in the sale of telephone and electricity services. As for manufacturing, the Industrial Development Corporation was established in 1969 to attract FDI and a ten-year tax holiday was granted to manufacturers selling their total output outside of the Caribbean Community (CARICOM). Between 1977 and 1985, foreign ownership was most pronounced in the metals group where 83 per cent of the firms had at least 25 per cent ownership. In the case of tourism, the Hotel Aids Act of 1956, the earliest attempt to develop the tourism industry in Barbados, exempted building materials and equipment for hotels from custom duties and permitted a seven-year tax holiday for some establishments. The formation of the Board of Tourism two years later also provided further stimulus to the industry. By 1970, North American and United Kingdom interest controlled a large proportion of the available capacity. Fifteen years later, just over one-half of the establishments had at least 25 per cent foreign ownership.

Belgrave and Ward (1997) estimated the impact of FDI on the Barbadian economy using the data of 255 firms over the period 1985 to 1995, with specific reference to the manufacturing sector. They looked at the influence of foreign equity on the survival of manufacturing firms, utilizing a binary-choice Probit model. The results showed that the foreign equity variable did not explain firms' survival. Even when the sample was disaggregated by sector, the same result was obtained.

An examination of FDI flows to the Eastern Caribbean was done by Williams and Williams (1998), using pooled data with a macroeconomic model that encompassed investment, savings, imports, exports and growth equations. FDI was found to exert a positive influence on investment, savings and imports. The estimated coefficient of FDI in the export equation was surprisingly negative, considering that most of the flows are channelled into tradable activity in the tourism industry. The FDI growth nexus appeared to be through gross capital formation, particularly private investment.

Campbell (2003) is cautious about the FDI approach in the context of Barbados. He examined the impact of FDI on Barbados' current account from 1970 to 1999, with the use of co-integration regression analysis. The results show that FDI inflows lead to deterioration in the current account balance, both in the long run and the short run. This has serious implications such as the possibility of gains derived from this type of investment eroded by purchases of goods and services from abroad and investment income payments to non-residents. This view may call for further investigation as it was seen in a static labour market.

It is in this context to be mentioned here that foreign direct investment inflows in developing countries have diverse causes and implications. Companies that originated in developed countries have been investing beyond their national boundaries. As a consequence mergers and acquisitions have accounted for a substantial share of FDI in recent years. This is particularly relevant in Caribbean countries where privatization of state-owned assets brought significant benefits across the developing world, including recently in the financial sector.

The outline of this chapter is as follows. The next section discusses the investment climate in the Caribbean. The following sections discuss the types of FDI in Trinidad and Tobago; the characteristics of CARICOM cross-border location activity; the domestic pull and external push factors for investment in the Caribbean, and the structure of the skill development system in the Caribbean, respectively. The final section presents a summary.

Investment climate in the Caribbean

The countries in the CARICOM region have decided to open their economies to foreign investors with three specific objectives: to generate employment opportunities, to increase foreign exchange earnings and to contribute to the development of the technological and productive base of the economy. Incidentally, despite the attractiveness of investment locations, and the closeness to the large US market, the actual volume of investment flows to the region (except for a few Member States) has been rather disappointing as compared with the East-Asian economies. The Caribbean economies cover a small area with relatively few people. In addition, there is a strong microeconomic incentive for the skilled English speaking Caribbean citizens to migrate to the large neighbourhoods such as USA, Canada and England. This aspect may be considered as a powerful factor in explaining the above disappointments. In the penultimate section we reveal some interesting insights in this context.

All CARICOM States have fairly liberal foreign investment policies with very few restrictions on direct investment. Those restrictions if any are primarily administrative and are mainly in the area of foreign exchange control, land acquisition and reservation of certain sectors for domestic operations. The restrictions apply to both intra-CARICOM and third country investors. To a certain extent, these restrictions have impeded the development of trans-regional companies. However, the general view is that the activities of non-CARICOM foreign investors have not been significantly affected by these restrictions.

A legal framework either in the form of specific legislation or as elements of other relevant legislation designed to facilitate the increased investment inflows characterizes the investment policy environment in CARICOM. Some member states have established a specific legal framework to address the needs of investors in the offshore sectors namely in the form of international business legislation. This framework is supported by policy statements for the approval of investments. The arrangements and procedures are administered by government departments or by semi-autonomous agencies set up for the purpose of investment promotion and administration.

There has been a considerable policy change in the region in order to attract FDI. The notable steps are, streamlining the process for investment approvals, establishing export-processing zones, and entering into bilateral investment and double taxation agreements with third countries as well as intra-regionally, in order to strengthen the guarantees given to investors regarding the security of their investments. Table 6.1 shows comparison of investment locations in this respect. It appears that from the investors' point of view the Caribbean economies may be considered as the ideal destination of FDI. But the size of the market is small and the scale-based industries may have difficulty in reaching the minimum efficient economic scales of production.

Interestingly, some countries with a small share of total FDI flows have high FDI-to-GDP and FDI per capita ratios. A few Caribbean economies also reveal similar trends. Figure 6.1 shows this pictorially. We have seen in Chapter 3 that the FDI flows in the Caribbean seem to be less attractive in terms of absolute values when compared to other FDI destinations. However, the FDI-to-GDP ratio is the highest (24 per cent) in case of St. Vincent and the Grenadines. In terms of per capita FDI St. Kitts and Nevis leads the Caribbean with US$950. Barbados portrays a dismal picture, for example, its FDI-to-GDP ratio appears to be only 0.60 per cent. Similarly, her per capita FDI shows only US$52. One may offer several explanations in this context. Barbados, commonly known as Little England with a population of 267,000 is one of the top performers according to the Human Development Indicators. But the current structure of its labour market fails to leverage the growing demand of the service sector with particular reference to financial and information technology services. As a result FDI in this sector is slowing down – also,

Table 6.1   Comparative attractiveness of investment locations

	Barba dos	Antigua and Barbuda	Dominican Republic	Grenada	Jamaica	St. Kitts and Nevis	St Vincent	Trinidad and Tobago
Market access to USA/EEC	1	1	1	1	1	1	1	1
Political stability	1	1	2	3	3	1	1	3
Ambiance security	1	1	2	1	3	1	1	3
Domestic infrastructure (Utilities)	1	2	2	2	2	1	2	1
International transport links	2	2	1	2	2	2	3	1
Investment incentives	2	2	2	2	2	2	2	2
Freezone incentives	3	3	1	3	1	3	3	3
Investor's language compatibility (English)	1	1	3	1	1	1	1	1
Total Score	*12*	*13*	*14*	*15*	*15*	*12*	*15*	*15*

Note: 1: very good; 2: good; 3: not good. Rankings based on professional judgments and perception of investor opinion.

Source: Based on Mathew Stamp PLC.

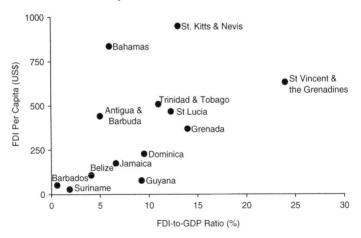

Figure 6.1   Some characteristics of FDI in small Caribbean economies

Source: Based on UNCTAD, *World Investment Report, 2001*; Fuchs and Straubhaar (2001) and UNDP, OECS Human Development Report 2002, Barbados.

the island nation is not at all competitive in manufacturing due to rising labor cost.

Table 6.2 shows the changing structure of the Caribbean economies in accordance with the GDP by sector during 1980, 1990 and 2000. Two distinct trends may be discernible. One, the contribution of services in general to the GDP is rising (excepting Guyana) and on the other hand the contribution of agriculture is declining across all Caribbean economies. Guyana is the only exception in this context. Incidentally the pace of this development is not in accordance with the human development in the region. As economies are moving towards globalization, agriculture is not cost effective and as a consequence, poverty,

Table 6.2 Changing structure of the Caribbean economies: GDP by sector (%)

Country	Sector	1980	1990	2000
Antigua and Barbuda	Agriculture	7.1	4.2	3.9
	Industry	18.1	20.1	19.1
	Of that: Manufacturing	5.3	3.4	2.2
	services	74.8	75.5	77
Bahamas	n.a.	n.a.	n.a.	n.a.
Barbados	Agriculture	9.9	7.4	6.3
	Industry	22.5	19.7	21.0
	Of that: Manufacturing	11.9	10.1	9.0
	services	67.5	72.9	72.8
Belize	Agriculture	27.4	20.7	21.4
	Industry	30.9	25.4	27.0
	Of that: Manufacturing	23.9	14.9	17.4
	services	41.7	53.8	51.6
Dominica	Agriculture	30.7	25	17.4
	Industry	20.9	18.6	23.5
	Of that: Manufacturing	4.8	7.1	8.3
	services	48.4	56.4	59.1
Grenada	Agriculture	24.7	13.4	7.7
	Industry	13.1	18.0	23.9
	Of that: Manufacturing	3.8	6.6	7.6
	services	62.2	68.6	68.3
Guyana	Agriculture	23.4	38.1	35.1
	Industry	35.8	24.9	28.5
	Of that: Manufacturing	12.1	10.3	10.1
	services	40.9	37.0	36.4
Haiti	Agriculture	n.a.	33.3	29.6
	Industry	n.a.	21.8	21.1
	Of that: Manufacturing	n.a.	15.7	7.1
	services	n.a.	45	49.3
Jamaica	Agriculture	8.2	6.5	6.5
	Industry	38.3	43.2	31.3
	Of that: Manufacturing	16.6	19.5	13.4
	services	53.5	50.4	62.2

Continued

122

Table 6.2 Continued

Country	Sector	1980	1990	2000
St Kitts and Nevis	Agriculture	15.9	6.5	3.6
	Industry	26.6	28.9	26
	Of that: Manufacturing	15.2	12.8	10.4
	Services	57.5	64.6	70.4
St Lucia	Agriculture	14.4	14.5	7.9
	Industry	23.6	18.1	19.6
	Of that: Manufacturing	10.5	8.1	5.5
	Services	62	67.3	72.5
St Vincent and the Grenadines	Agriculture	14.3	21.2	9.8
	Industry	26.5	22.9	25.5
	Of that: Manufacturing	10.5	8.5	6.3
	Services	59.2	55.9	64.7
Suriname	Agriculture	9.1	11.2	9.7
	Industry	38.9	27.3	20.4
	Of that: Manufacturing	18.6	13.3	7.8
	Services	52	61.5	69.9
Trinidad and Tobago	Agriculture	2.3	2.5	1.6
	Industry	62.5	46.2	43.2
	Of that: Manufacturing	8.9	8.6	7.7
	Services	35.2	51.2	55.2

Note: n.a.: not available.

Source: Based on www.worldbank.org/data/countrydata/countrydata.html#DataProfiles.

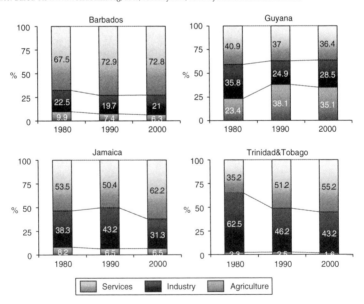

Figure 6.2 Changing structure of some of the Caribbean economies
Source: Based on Table 6.2.

malnourishment are common features of recent time (Banik and Iyare, 2003a, b; Banik, 2004; Banik *et al.*, 2004a, b). The changing structure of a few Caribbean economies is also captured in Figure 6.2.

There is a strong variation in investment across the Caribbean because of the lumpiness of most investments (CARICOM, 2000). For example, about 90 per cent of the equity capital inflows reported for Trinidad and Tobago (US$488.5 million) was associated with the investment in a natural gas facility (Atlantic LNG Plant) by BP Amoco and Repsol. The UNECLAC study showed that in Trinidad and Tobago most FDI was in the form of reinvestment of earnings followed by equity capital. In Jamaica equity capital was the most important form of FDI. In the countries of the Organization of Eastern Caribbean States (OECS) equity capital was followed by land sales before 1995. By 1998 reinvestment appeared to be more important than equity investment in the OECS (see CARICOM, 2000).

The UNECLAC (1995) study also reported the sectoral distribution of FDI for Jamaica and Trinidad and Tobago before 1993. In Jamaica two-thirds of FDI went to the bauxite industry. Other sectors in order of importance were textiles, tourism and the film industry. In Trinidad and Tobago the petroleum related industries attracted 72 per cent of net FDI in 1987, 58 per cent in 1989, 86 per cent in 1991 and 94 per cent in 1993 (UNECLAC, 1995). The study also concluded that most foreign investments in the OECS countries between 1988 and 1993 were geared towards the tourism sector.

Historically, the USA is the main external investor in the Caribbean followed by UK and Canada. There were some alterations during the 1990s in the strategies adopted by transnational investment corporations who did not entirely abandon their traditional ways. First, they pursued greater efficiency with a view to improving their competitiveness in the US market that was being threatened by external competitors (such as the Asian companies). The US companies therefore built new plants mainly in the manufacturing sector (textile and electronics). Similarly, other transnationals invested in the services sector to take advantage of local markets that have a huge growth potential. This has been possible by participating in the privatization processes underway in the region particularly in the electrical, energy, natural gas and telecommunications sectors.

The CARICOM (2000) has analysed the most recent sectoral distribution of FDI. Tourism is the main sectoral recipient of FDI in the Bahamas and Barbados. Financial services, manufacturing and informatics are also important recipients in Barbados. In Jamaica tourism, mining and manufacturing are leading sectors while tourism, agriculture and manu-facturing are the main sectors in the OECS. In Trinidad and Tobago and Guyana, the natural resource-based industries followed by infrastructure are of primary importance.

Forms of FDI

The three forms of FDI are equity capital, reinvested earnings (i.e. profits not distributed as dividends) and intra-company loans (i.e. loans made by a parent to a subsidiary or affiliate). Equity capital can be for a greenfield project in which the foreign investor's funds are used to create or expand physical assets or it can be used to acquire existing assets, as in privatization, or merely effect a merger of two entities. Less direct forms of foreign involvement are of a non-equity nature and include management contracts, franchises and technology licensing.

While countries are keen to attract new capital, they would also want to maximize the rate of investment of earning from existing capital. The rate of reinvestment could be a reflection of not only prospects for the future but, also the degree of satisfaction of the investor with the local business environment and effectiveness of the investment promotion authorities. Despite the obvious disaggregation problem and other data

Table 6.3 Caribbean economies push factors – forms of FDI in Belize, Guyana and Trinidad and Tobago

Country		Forms of FDI/Years	1992	1993	1994	1995	1996	1997	1998	1999
	1.	Equity capital	94.4	72.1	83.9	76.0	78.9	68.1	74.7	90.8
Belize	2.	Re-invested earning	5.6	27.9	16.1	24.0	21.1	31.9	18.4	6.7
	3.	Other (mainly parent loans)	0.0	0.0	0.0	0.0	0.0	0.0	6.9	2.5
	1.	Equity capital	8.1	39.9	10.4	9.8	11.3	11.6	15.5	14.1
	2.	Re-invested earning	5.0	17.8	11.0	21.5	16.3	11.8	7.5	6.4
Guyana	3.	Other (mainly parent loans and privatization)	86.9	42.3	78.6	68.7	72.4	76.6	77.0	79.5
	1.	Equity capital	12.2	24.1	18.4	40.9	52.5	77.4	83.5	n.a.
Trinidad	2.	Re-invested earning	79.6	24.5	36.4	52.3	47.5	12.5	11.7	n.a.
and	3.	Privatization	0.0	45.4	45.2	6.8	0.0	10.4	0.8	n.a.
Tobago	4.	Other (mainly parent loans)	8.2	6.0	0.0	0.0	0.0	−0.3	4.0	n.a.

Notes: n.a.: not available.
All figures are % of the total FDI for the year.

Source: Based on CARICOM (2000), p. 210.

weaknesses, Table 6.3 shows considerable variation in the rate of reinvestment between three natural resources endowed countries – Belize, Guyana and Trinidad and Tobago. During 1992–99, the rate of reinvestment was considerably lower for the first two countries than for the third. In 1997 and 1998, the rate of reinvestment fell dramatically in Trinidad and Tobago but this is partly explained by the huge injection of new capital in those years. In the case of Guyana, the rate of reinvestment has been low for the entire 1992–99 period, partly because there was little foreign investment for a long time prior to 1992 and also because, since then, the foreign capital (mostly loans from the parent firms to those companies engaged in gold and timber production) has gone into projects with a fairly long gestation period and, therefore, only very limited profits were probably available.

For the OECS countries, as Table 6.4 shows, the rate of reinvestment is also modest, but not insignificant. Reinvestment amounted to 25 per cent in at least one of the three years for all of the countries except one, for which the average figure was nearly 20 per cent. For three countries, the figure exceeded 73 per cent in at least one of the years; and one country, in at least two of the three years.

It is noticeable that land sales in the OECS sub-region were greater in value than other equity in at least two of the three years for all of the countries except Dominica. This might be due to the relaxation of the application of the Alien Landholdings Act, as in the case of Guyana. The form of FDI in the OECS countries seemed to reflect a strategy of hedging

Table 6.4 Caribbean economies push factors – forms of FDI into the OECS Sub-Region (1995, 1997 and 1998)

Country/Forms	New Equity			Reinvestment			Land Sales			Other*		
	1995	1997	1998	1995	1997	1998	1995	1997	1998	1995	1997	1998
Antigua and Barbuda	7.4	22.9	52.8	15.8	17.8	26.3	11.0	43.2	9.7	65.8	16.0	11.1
Dominica	69.4	51.5	13.7	10.4	39.5	73.4	1.9	2.0	9.2	18.3	7.0	3.6
Grenada	24.4	44.3	–	17.5	21.3	17.6	47.9	28.7	21	10.2	5.7	61.4
Montserrat	0.6	–	–	22	74.9	74.9	77.4	25.1	25.1	–	–	–
St Kitts and Nevis	10.5	30.5	56	25.6	26.1	18.1	61.6	42.3	25.9	2.3	1.1	–
St Lucia	0.1	2.0	0.3	76	24.8	18.7	12.4	5.0	3.7	11.4	68.1	77.3
St Vincent and the Grenadines	–	–	–	24.1	14.2	26.5	15	12.4	13.1	60.8	73.4	60.4

Notes: All figures are percentages of the total FDI for the year; * mainly loans from parent companies.
Source: Based on CARICOM (2000), p. 211.

against risks and a preference for committing loans, rather than equity. For four of the OECS countries, loans from the parent firm exceeded 60 per cent of the total FDI flows in at least one of the three years, for two countries in at least two years, and for one country, in all three years.

FDI in Trinidad and Tobago

Our analysis in this section concentrates on the details of FDI in Trinidad and Tobago (T&T). This is due to the fact that more detailed data are available for Trinidad and Tobago than for other Caribbean countries. Trinidad and Tobago is an export-propelled economy that depends heavily on petroleum exports.

Trinidad and Tobago seems to be positioned somewhere between the investment and innovation driven stage. Table 6.5 and Figure 6.3 show that a significant amount of FDI has flowed into the T&T economy in the period 1973–2000. These FDI resources are mainly targeted at the petroleum industries of T&T. T&T was the recipient of US$679.5m in 2000 as compared to US$62.5m in 1973. Even more significantly, T&T received US$3,410.6m in the period 1996–2000 as compared to US$3,558.8m in the period 1973–1995. A substantial amount of these investments were in areas of cutting edge technology (Nucor, Cleveland Cliffs or Atlantic LNG (ALNG)). Some of the plants that these FDI helped to establish are amongst the largest of their kind in the world and to date T&T is the world's largest exporter of ammonia and methanol and by May 2003 when trains 2 and 3 of ALNG are fully operational, this country would become the world's fifth largest exporter of LNG. BHP Billiton, an Australian MNC was able to accelerate the development of its Angostura field, the most significant oil find in Trinidad and Tobago in 30 years. Production is expected to commence in 2004. British Petroleum Trinidad and Tobago (BPTT) has also brought more oil on-stream from its Mahogany, Immortelle and Kapok fields, so that by the end of October 2002, T&T produced 145,450 bpd of oil, 26 per cent more than average daily production in 2001 and the highest daily average since 1990.

During 2002, British Petroleum Trinidad and Tobago (BPTT) had a very active exploration and development programme. This resulted in three new discoveries – Rd Mango, Cashima, and Iron Horse. These three discoveries unlocked more than 3 trillion cubic feet (tcf) of natural gas. In addition, EOG found 500 bcf of gas in the Parula field. As of 1 January 2003, Ministry of Energy and Energy Industries (MEEI) revised audit of non-associated gas reserves of T&T stood at 34.8 tcf of gas. The proven component was 20.35 tcf.

Table 6.5 The distribution of FDI inflows to the T&T economy: 1973–2000

| | | US$m | | | | % distribution | | |
| | | *Of which (1)* | *Of which (2)* | | | | *Of which (1)* | *Of which (2)* |
Year	Petroleum industries	Mining exploration & production, refineries petrochemicals (US$m)	Service contractors, marketing & distribution (US$m)	Total all economic activity (US$m)	Year	FDI to petroleum Industries as a % pf all FDI flows	Mining exploration & production, refineries petrochemicals	Service contractors, marketing & distribution
1973	52.65	52.84	−0.19	62.54	1973	84.19	84.50	−0.31
1975	193.14	190.72	2.42	180.55	1975	106.98	105.64	1.34
1980	102.75	97.79	4.96	136.96	1980	75.02	71.40	3.62
1985	35.31	27.06	8.24	49.67	1985	71.08	54.48	16.60
1990	64.10	57.2	6.8	109.4	1990	58.50	52.29	6.22
1995	266.0	253.6	12.4	295.7	1995	89.96	85.76	4.19
1996	334.7	320.6	14.1	356.3	1996	93.94	89.98	3.96
1997	954.2	947.6	6.6	999.6	1997	95.46	94.80	0.66
1998	599.7	585.3	14.4	731.9	1998	81.94	79.97	1.97
1999	467.7	449	18.7	643.3	1999	84.86	69.80	2.91
2000	613.7	613.9	−0.2	679.5	2000	84.89	90.35	−0.03

Source: Based on *Balance of Payments Yearbook of Trinidad and Tobago*, various issues, Central Bank of Trinidad and Tobago, Port of Spain.

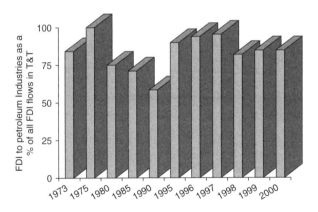

Figure 6.3 FDI petroleum industries as a % of all FDI flows in Trinidad and Tobago economy
Source: Based on Table 6.5.

The share of each of the three components in the interest income remitted from Trinidad and Tobago in various years is shown in Figure 6.4. It is interesting to note that reinvested earnings by the petroleum companies remain a high proportion of investment, although equity capital increased its contribution considerably between 1996 and 1998. It appears that

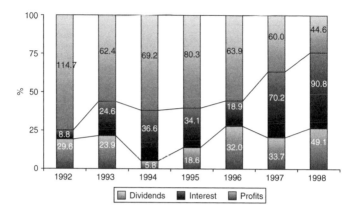

Figure 6.4   Investment income remitted from Trinidad & Tobago towards FDI made (US$m) and its components

Source: Based on Howard and Banik (2001), p. 2775.

repatriated profits contribute the highest proportion of remitted investment income followed by interest and dividend in 1992. In contrast, in 1998, interest payments increased significantly while the other components remained more or less unchanged from the previous year.

Characteristics of CARICOM cross-border location activity

Data on the value of CARICOM cross border investment are not easily available. However, some concrete information exists on the number of branch plants/offices and subsidiaries that have been set up across the Region. This information was available in the companies' annual reports. Of the 39 companies with cross-border operations studied, 33 had their head office in the MDCs. The main source countries were Trinidad and Tobago, Barbados, Jamaica, Guyana, Antigua and Barbuda, St. Vincent and the Grenadines, and St. Lucia, with 16, 10, 6, 4, 1, 1 and 1 locations respectively, in other CARICOM countries.

Most of the CARICOM outflows had the OECS countries as their destination. From the information available, no firm indicated that it had cross border operations in Montserrat and only one firm had a related activity in Suriname, probably because of the very tiny market and constant threat of volcanic activity in the former, and the fairly recent ascension to CARICOM status of the latter.

The preference for investing in the OECS is most likely due to these countries having a somewhat lower level of technological and entrepreneurial endowment and capability than the other countries in the Region while at the same time possessing a medium level per capita income. Besides steady economic progress, the OECS countries have also exhibited a reasonable amount of political stability.

There are certain characteristics that are worth highlighting. First, the cross-border activities tend to be mainly in the financial, light manufacturing and distribution sectors. These are all fairly low technology activities. For example, operations in the financial sector are fairly standard, and easily adopted even when rapid electronic advances are taken into account. The main barrier to entry is, also, not the minimum capital asset requirement, which, in any case, is not considered very high or onerous. The real guide to establishment is, therefore, the ability to fulfill such prudential requirements as reputation and track record for integrity and soundness of operations.

Ownership lines, not only in the financial services sector but in most other sectors, are becoming increasingly blurred as a result of the inter-industry linkages that have emerged, and are still emerging across the region. The core operations and ownership of some firms are at best nebulous and difficult to ascertain. And yet at the same time, these conglomerates are probably a necessary mode for accelerating movement of capital across the Region.

In the manufacturing sector, there is the full range of entry modes, with 100 per cent participation occurring just as frequently as majority ownership (less than 100 per cent) and other forms of minority and subsidiary ownership (less than 50 per cent). Similarly, in the financial sector, both branch (in which home and host operations are aggregated for accounting purposes) and subsidiary (in which accounting is disaggregated and local incorporation is necessary) modes of participation occur. There are also instances of conglomerate formations in which manufacturing and or distribution firms, starting out with their original core operations, have diversified into a variety of other cross-sectoral activities. While this obviously has advantages for the firm concerned, it can also stretch to the limit corporate, managerial and accounting capabilities. It may also cause identification problems for the tax and other administrative authorities. The major regulatory problems, however, occurs when a company operating in the non-financial sector acquires a firm, which is essentially a provider of financial services.

Traditionally, regulators strictly prohibit a financial firm from acquiring a non-financial enterprise but the reverse does not necessarily obtain.

Frequency of entry in the financial sector

Regionally owned commercial banks can be found in a number of the OECS countries, and are mainly branches or subsidiaries of either the Royal Bank of Trinidad and Tobago, or the Republic Bank of Trinidad and Tobago (RBTT). These two largest banks in Trinidad and Tobago are locally owned and are on a regional expansion path. Between the two, they have branches and subsidiaries in seven other Member States and a number of other non-CARICOM Caribbean countries as well. It is interesting that although Trinidad and Tobago investors have profitably acquired a significant amount of assets in the somewhat depressed Jamaican market during the 1990s, no purchases were made of any of the troubled domestic banks. At the same time, however, Citizens Bank Jamaica, one of the troubled banks, had its wholly owned subsidiary operations in Guyana acquired by local investors in the late 1990s.

There are three modes of cross-border entry into the banking sector by Caribbean firms:

- *Acquisition*, where a controlling interest is purchased in an existing firm, as an alternative to setting up a greenfield establishment.
- *The incorporation of a new subsidiary*, as was done in December 1985 by the RBTT Holdings Limited, in setting up a wholly owned entity, The Caribbean Banking Corporation, in St. Vincent and the Grenadines, to provide additional banking services to the OECS sub-region, and also, in the case of the Caribbean Credit Card Corporation, which is owned by banks from the OECS sub-region.
- *Minority equity participation*, as in the case of participation by the indigenous banks of the OECS in the National Commercial Bank of Grenada.

Domestic pull and external push factors and economic impact of FDI

It is often argued that the entry of external capital may lead to greater economic activity and encourage savings, but it may also lead to the appreciation of assets (through the accompanying stock and real estate market booms), which might raise consumption and reduce savings. The effect may be multiplied if the national currency is overvalued and import tariffs are lowered as this facilitates access to imported goods.

The problem may be more acute if the domestic loans are consumption-driven. Obstfeld (1994) asserts that the direction and magnitude of foreign capital is determined by the differences in factor proportions among countries. Foreign capital bridges the gap between capital demand and supply, and allows capital-scarce developing countries to expand their production frontier, increase physical capital per worker and upgrade technology. Empirically, Howard and Banik (2001) studied both external push and domestic pull factors in explaining FDI inflows to the Caribbean. They considered domestic savings rate and exchange rate as external push factors and GNP domestic pull factor in their analysis.

Figure 6.5 shows the gross domestic investment and gross domestic saving as percentage of GDP. It is interesting to note that the gross domestic investment has exceeded the gross domestic saving in most cases due to the contribution of FDI. Thus, it is reasonable to infer that FDI has had both positive direct and indirect effects on the growth of the Caribbean economies [(see also Borensztein, *et al.* (1998)]. Figure 6.6 portrays the impact of FDI on gross domestic capital formation. Trinidad and Tobago, a natural resource based country benefited significantly compared to the other islands. As we have indicated, openness is an important factor that attracts FDI in the Caribbean.

The Caribbean economies are very open, and tend to focus on very few export goods. Table 6.6 depicts the principal exports during the period 1994–98. It appears that the exports items are more or less primary in nature and most of them have lost price competitiveness. Consequently, it has serious socio-economic impact across Caribbean island nations.

Figures 6.7 and 6.8 and Tables 6.7 and 6.8 reveal the nature of openness in the Caribbean. Two extreme pictures may be depicted. First, the importance of USA as a destination of Caribbean exports is declining, but its importance is increasing as a source of Caribbean imports. The analysis shows that aggregate intra-regional imports have been increasing in the More Developed Countries (MDCs) of CARICOM. Imports have risen in Jamaica but have fluctuated in Barbados during the 1990s. There has been a decline in aggregate intra-regional imports for the LDCs of the region. Intra-regional exports as a proportion of total country exports have been increasing for most countries. These trends indicate that there is some merit in the pursuit of economic integration of the Caribbean islands.

Another view is that the flow of goods and services replacing the flow of investment from the United States is greater for the Caribbean

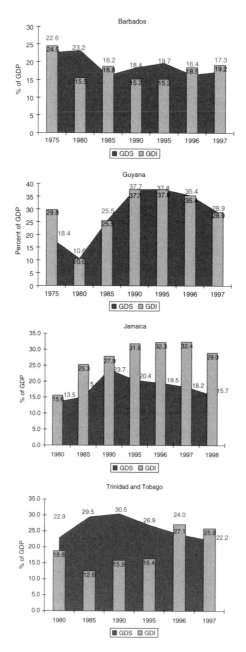

Figure 6.5 Gross Domestic Savings (GDS) and Gross Domestic Investment (GDI) as a % of GDP in a few Caribbean economies

Source: Based on CARICOM (2000), pp. 309–10.

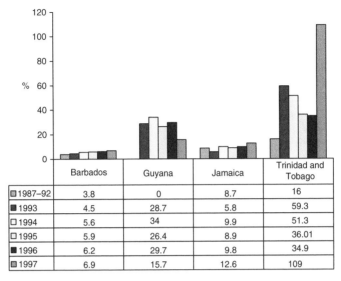

	Barbados	Guyana	Jamaica	Trinidad and Tobago
1987–92	3.8	0	8.7	16
1993	4.5	28.7	5.8	59.3
1994	5.6	34	9.9	51.3
1995	5.9	26.4	8.9	36.01
1996	6.2	29.7	9.8	34.9
1997	6.9	15.7	12.6	109

Figure 6.6   FDI inflows as a % of GDCF * in a few Caribbean economies
Note: * GDCF: Gross Domestic Capital Formation.
Source: Based on UNCTAD, World Development Report 1999.

Table 6.6   Caribbean economies pull factors – principal exports (% to total exports): 1994–98

Country		1994	1995	1996	1997	1998
Bahamas	Food and live animals	31.6	29.1	28.4	26.9	21.1
	Non edible raw materials excluding fuel	16.6	13.8	12.9	13.9	6.2
	Chemical products	11.1	7.4	6.9	13.9	11.7
	Capital goods	11.4	20.3	13.4	12.4	21.6
Barbados	Sugar, molasses and rum	25.4	22.8	19.5	23.6	22.2
	Electronic components	19.4	16.6	12.7	12.3	12.9
	Chemicals	15.2	15.8	12.8	13.4	13.5
Belize	Sugar, molasses and rum	29.1	30.7	30.7	27.5	n.a.
	Citrus	10.7	17.7	17.3	13.4	n.a.
	Bananas	14.7	13.4	16.8	14.6	n.a.
Dominica	Bananas	43.9	33.5	32.5	30.1	24.1
	Soap	25.9	29.5	33	32.1	29.6
Grenada	Spices	21	17.7	24.5	30.8	n.a.
	Seafood	12.6	15.6	15.1	14.2	n.a.
	Cocoa	12	14.3	12.3	7.2	n.a.
Guyana	Sugar, molasses and rum	26	25.3	26.2	22.5	23.6
	Gold	28.6	19.1	18.1	23.5	22.7
	Bauxite and alumina	17.6	16.7	15	15.1	14.2
	Rice	12.4	15.4	16.5	14.2	13.4

Continued

Table 6.6 Continued

Country		1994	1995	1996	1997	1998
Jamaica	Bauxite	49.3	40.1	39.5	42.8	43.2
	Garments	20.8	15.5	14.3	13.1	12
St Kitts and Nevis	Machinery and transport equipment	53.4	47.1	50.4	n.a.	n.a.
	Sugar, molasses and rum	33.8	39.3	36.0	n.a.	n.a.
St Lucia	Bananas	41	40.9	47	39.1	37.2
	Garments	14.3	12.2	6.9	7.3	7.4
St Vincent and the Grenadines	Bananas	30.9	35.3	37.5	31.1	41.5
	Flour	17.4	14	12	18.4	13.9
	Rice	12.3	10.3	10.3	12.5	12.9
Suriname	Bauxite and alumina	72.4	77	76.4	77.1	80.5
	Seafood	9.9	7.1	7.2	8.4	7
	Rice	9.1	7.8	7.7	6.4	4.7
Trinidad and Tobago	Oil and fuels	39.1	45.7	50.3	46	48.5
	Chemicals	26.6	25.1	22.7	24	23.8
	Steel products	8	8.2	7.1	7.3	8.4

Note: n.a.: not available.

Source: Based on International Monetary Fund, Recent Economic Developments, various issues.

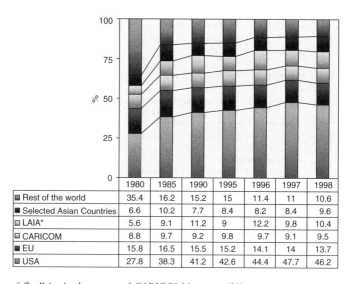

	1980	1985	1990	1995	1996	1997	1998
▨ Rest of the world	35.4	16.2	15.2	15	11.4	11	10.6
■ Selected Asian Countries	6.6	10.2	7.7	8.4	8.2	8.4	9.6
▨ LAIA*	5.6	9.1	11.2	9	12.2	9.8	10.4
▨ CARICOM	8.8	9.7	9.2	9.8	9.7	9.1	9.5
■ EU	15.8	16.5	15.5	15.2	14.1	14	13.7
▨ USA	27.8	38.3	41.2	42.6	44.4	47.7	46.2

Figure 6.7 Principal sources of CARICOM imports (%)

Notes: * Latin American Integration Association.
Selected Asian Countries are China, HongKong, India, Japan, Singapore, South Korea, Taiwan and Thailand.
1990 excludes data for Antigua and Barbuda.
1995 excludes data for Antigua and Barbuda, Guyana and Montserrat.
1996 excludes data for Antigua & Barbuda, Guyana, Montserrat, St Vincent & the Grenadines and Suriname.
1997 excludes data for Antigua Barbuda, Guyana, Montserrat and Suriname.
1998 excludes data for Antigua Barbuda, Dominica, Guyana, Montserrat, St Kitts & Nevis amd Suriname.

Source: A quick reference to some summary data 1980–96 and CARICOM (2000), p. 115.

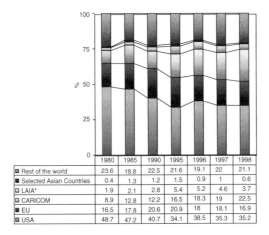

	1980	1985	1990	1995	1996	1997	1998
▨ Rest of the world	23.6	18.8	22.5	21.6	19.1	22	21.1
■ Selected Asian Countries	0.4	1.3	1.2	1.5	0.9	1	0.6
▨ LAIA*	1.9	2.1	2.8	5.4	5.2	4.6	3.7
▨ CARICOM	8.9	12.8	12.2	16.5	18.3	19	22.5
■ EU	16.5	17.8	20.6	20.9	18	18.1	16.9
▨ USA	48.7	47.2	40.7	34.1	38.5	35.3	35.2

Figure 6.8 Principal destinations of CARICOM exports (%)

Notes: *LAIA Latin American integration Association.
Selected Asian Countries are China, Hong Kong, India, Japan, Singapore, South Korea, Taiwan and Thailand.
1990 excludes data for Antigua and Barbuda and Montserrat's re-exports.
1995 excludes data for Antigua and Barbuda and Guyana.
1996 excludes data for Antigua & Barbuda Guyana and Suriname.
1997 excludes data for Antigua & Barbuda Guyana, Montserrat and Suriname.
1998 excludes data for Antigua & Barbuda, Dominica, Guyana, Montserrat, St Kitts & Nevis and Suriname.

Source: A quick reference to some summary data 1980–1996, and CARICOM, (2000), p. 119.

Table 6.7 Percentage distribution of intra-regional imports by country: 1990–1998

CARICOM countries	1990	1991	1992	1993	1994	1995	1996	1997	1998
CARICOM	100.0	100.0	100.0	100.0	100.0	100.0	100.0	100.0	100.0
MDCs	60.2	58.4	56.7	59.5	61.9	70.8	71.6	72.7	74.3
Barbados	21.9	21.0	19.8	19.5	18.5	17.5	16.3	14.5	20.8
Guyana	4.9	6.5	8.6	9.8	10.4	n.a.	n.a.	n.a.	n.a.
Jamaica	17.5	14.0	13.3	20.8	23.4	35.4	37.7	37.0	40.0
Suriname	n.a.	n.a.	n.a.	n.a.	n.a.	6.9	6.5	9.8	n.a.
Trinidad & Tobago	15.8	16.8	15.0	9.4	9.6	11.0	11.1	11.5	13.6
LDCs	39.8	41.6	43.3	40.5	38.1	29.2	28.4	27.3	25.7
Belize	2.6	1.4	2.1	1.9	1.8	1.8	1.4	1.3	1.4
OECS	37.2	40.2	41.2	38.6	36.4	27.4	27.0	26.0	24.3
Antigua & Barbuda	6.9	5.6	6.8	6.0	6.9	n.a.	n.a.	n.a.	n.a.
Dominica	5.0	5.4	5.3	4.3	4.4	4.5	4.2	4.1	n.a.
Grenada	5.1	5.7	5.8	7.1	5.4	5.0	5.3	5.5	7.2
Montserrat	1.6	2.0	1.6	1.2	1.1	n.a.	n.a.	n.a.	n.a.
St Kitts & Nevis	3.2	4.1	3.5	3.7	3.3	3.2	3.4	3.3	2.0
St Lucia	9.7	10.5	11.4	10.6	10.0	9.6	9.0	8.3	9.1
St Vincent & Grena'dines	5.6	6.8	6.7	5.7	5.4	5.1	5.1	4.9	6.1

Notes: *All figures are %s Suriname became a member of the Caribbean Community and Common Market in July 1995. n.a.: not available.

Source: Based on CARICOM (2000), p. 56.

Table 6.8 Intra-regional exports as a % of total exports by country: 1990–98*

CARICOM countries	1990	1991	1992	1993	1994	1995	1996	1997	1998
CARICOM	*12.4*	*12.1*	*12.8*	*15.9*	*14.8*	*16.5*	*17.1*	*17.3*	*22.9*
MDCs	*11.4*	*11.1*	*12.1*	*15.7*	*14.4*	*16.3*	*17.1*	*17.0*	*22.8*
Barbados	30.7	32.7	34.3	38.8	35.5	37.4	35.8	35.4	43.3
Guyana	7.3	n.a.	n.a.	n.a.	6.3	n.a.	n.a.	n.a.	n.a.
Jamaica	6.1	5.5	5.7	5.6	4.8	4.1	3.8	3.3	3.3
Suriname	n.a.	n.a.	n.a.	n.a.	n.a.	2.5	5.1	5.5	n.a.
Trinidad & Tobago	12.7	12.0	13.4	19.8	19.5	23.8	24.4	25.4	31.5
LDCs	*19.8*	*20.0*	*17.7*	*17.3*	*19.4*	*19.1*	*17.0*	*20.1*	*24.6*
Belize	6.6	6.0	4.5	3.8	3.5	3.4	3.0	4.2	7.1
OECS	*24.6*	*25.2*	*22.7*	*22.2*	*28.9*	*29.2*	*25.5*	*32.4*	*37.6*
Antigua & Barbuda	38.4	26.6	14.3	6.0	n.a.	n.a.	n.a.	n.a.	n.a.
Dominica	25.3	26.0	29.6	30.6	36.9	42.3	46.7	51.1	78.3
Grenada	26.4	35.8	28.8	31.4	26.6	29.2	29.1	34.3	25.1
Montserrat	33.8	39.2	54.4	36.4	20.7	5.7	2.2	n.a.	n.a.
St Kitts & Nevis	13.0	12.4	11.8	12.2	13.0	11.5	4.2	3.4	3.3
Saint Lucia	17.1	17.5	12.6	17.4	15.4	16.0	13.4	16.1	19.5
St Vincent & Grenadines	34.3	37.4	41.1	46.2	55.3	62.3	49.6	57.8	49.1

Notes: All figures are %. Suriname became a member of the Caribbean Community and Common Market in July 1995. n.a.: not available

Source: CARICOM (2000), p. 57.

sub-region where labour costs among other things, are not competitive (ECLAC, 2000). In other words, market integration means high intra-island cost of transport. This cost may be one of the significant factors in explaining the impediments. However, a few islands may benefit because of their natural resource base.

The Caribbean system of skill development

In recent time, the inflows of FDI have not been promising in the Caribbean (UN, 2002a). This may be due to the prevailing level of uncertainty on international markets and the fact that the privatization drive in the region is nearing its end. Experts argue that fiscal and other incentives and labour market dynamics are equally important that explains the inflows in the long run. Ireland in recent time is quite successful using corporate tax as a tool to attract new investors. The incentives are available to both foreign and domestic enterprises, the former are able to take greater advantage according to studies (for example CARICOM, 2000) of the concessions because they are export oriented. Table 6.9 reveals a picture in this context.

It is tempting to suggest that the state of material well being of a nation is captured quite accurately in its per capita income: the per head value of final goods and services produced by the people of the country over a given period. Indeed, for long periods of time performance in economic development was judged exclusively by the yardstick of per capita income since economic development at the national level is a conscious goal (Ray, 1998).

One may be a little careful in this context. It is difficult to suggest that economic development be identified, in a definitional sense, with the level or growth of per capita income exclusively. It is more commonly accepted that development is not just about income, although income (and more generally economic wealth) has a great deal to do with it. Development is also the removal of poverty and under-nutrition; it is increase in life expectancy; it is access to sanitation, clean drinking water and health services; it is reduction of infant mortality; it is increased access to knowledge and higher education.

It is imperative to cite the case of the Caribbean island nations in this context. The countries' performance in the overall ranking of Human Development Index may be considered as a significant achievement (Table 6.10). The primary school enrolment rates are high, and the overall literacy rate is more than 97 per cent. Infant mortality, life expectancy, and crude death rates in most countries are now equivalent to those in North America.

Table 6.9 Fiscal and non-fiscal incentives in CARICOM

Fiscal incentives	Countries	Description of policy
1. Harmonization of fiscal incentives to industry	All except Guyana	Tax holiday and duty-free inputs for specified time period for approved firms.
2. International business Corporation Act	Antigua and Barbuda, Barbados, Belize, and Montserrat	Tax holidays and duty exemptions for foreign firms; exemptions from foreign exchange controls and levies.
3. Double taxation agreement	All except Antigua and Barbuda and St Lucia	Agreement to prevent double taxation of income earned CARICOM countries.
4. Free trade zone	Antigua and Barbuda, Belize Jamaica, St Lucia, and Trinidad and Tobago	For exporting firms, exemption from duties in Jamaica, Automatic tax holidays for unlimited period. In St Lucia apply under fiscal incentives act.
5. Export incentives not covered by 1.	Guyana, Barbados, Belize Jamaica St Vincent and the Grenadines, Trinidad and Tobago and	Tax reduction, import consumption duty exemptions; incentives vary.
6. Hotel aids ordinance	All	Tax and duty exemptions not harmonized across States.
7. Modernization of industry programme	Jamaica	Approved firms receive education on import duties and assistance for modernization.

8. Investment allowance	Barbados, Dominica, St Lucia, St Vincent and the Grenadines and Trinidad and Tobago,	Tax reductions for expenditure on plant and machinery.
9. Factory construction	Barbados, Dominica, Jamaica	Tax relief on operating income from leasing of factory or profits from sale of factory.
10. Bauxite and Alumina industry encouragement	Jamaica	5–10 year exemption from customs duty on imports and machinery,
11. Locational incentives	Belize, Jamaica, Trinidad and Tobago,	Tax concessions for firms locating in designated areas,
12. Other fiscal Incentives not covered by 1.	Grenada, St Lucia, St Vincent and the Grenadines, Trinidad and Tobago.	Incentives for small scale sector (St Lucia); duty free import of machinery (Trinidad and Tobago, Grenada).
	Other incentives	
13. Training workers	All	Special wage reduction for Government sponsored training programs, variable across CARICOM,
14. Industry estate	All	Factory shells provided at low rental rates, variable across CARICOM,

Notes: Extracted from CARICOM *Proposals for a Harmonized System of Incentives for Industry, Tourism and Other Services and Agriculture*, Dec. 1993, p. 32 (updated by CARICOM where possible).

Source: Based on CARICOM (2000), p. 268.

Table 6.10 Select development indicators of the Caribbean economies: 2000

Human Development index Rank (by world rank)	Country	population (m)	Life expectancy at birth (years)	Territory students in science, math and engineering as a % of all tertiary students	combined primary, secondary and tertiary gross enrolment ratio (%)	per capita income (ppp US$)	Population below income poverty line according to national poverty line (%)	Audlt literacy rate age 15 and above (%)	
								F	M
31	Barbados	0.3	76.8	21	77	15 494	8	n.a.	n.a.
41	Bahamas	0.3	69.2	n.a.	74	17 012	22	97	95
44	St Kitts and Nevis	0.04	70	n.a.	59	15 799	15	n.a.	n.a.
50	Trinidad and Tobago	1.3	74.3	41	65	8 964	21	92	96
52	Antigua and Barbuda	0.1	70.4	n.a.	69	10 541	12	n.a.	n.a.
58	Belize	0.3	74.0	n.a.	73	5 606	35	75	73
61	Dominica	0.1	73.4	n.a.	65	5 880	33	n.a.	n.a.

66	St Lucia	0.1	73.4	n.a.	70	5 703	25	n.a.	n.a.
74	Suriname	0.4	70.6	n.a.	82	3 799	47	n.a.	n.a.
83	Grenada	0.1	65.3	n.a.	65	7 580	27	n.a.	n.a.
86	Jamaica	2.6	75.3	20	62	3 639	34.2	91	83
91	Saint Vincent and the Grenadines	0.1	69.6	n.a.	58	5 555	17	n.a.	n.a.
94	Dominican Republic	8.4	67.1	25	72	6 033	20.6	84	84
103	Guyana	0.8	63	25	66	3 963	43.2	98	99
146	Haiti	8.1	52.6	n.a.	52	1 467	65	48	52

Notes: n.a.: not available. F: female, M: Male.

Source: Based on United Nations (2002b).

As regards higher education, available data point to significant wastage in the Region's education and training systems. According to a study (CDB, 1998), the chances of progressing from primary school through to tertiary and higher level institutions are quite limited. In addition, the performance of primary and secondary school students is generally weak on national and regional examinations. The poor enrolment at the tertiary and university level may be explained by (a) limited availability of places in some disciplines, especially medicine, natural sciences and technology related disciplines; (b) deficiencies in the secondary level; and (c) unsatisfactory performance and the non-relevance of programmes to the current and projected demands of the market place.

There are many different types of public and private training programmes in the region, which aim to address problems of low skill levels, high youth unemployment, and displacement of workers. Training programmes are important, both to employers and workers, yet they are expensive. Youth training is particularly relevant as unemployment rates among youth are high. Until recently, skill training for unemployed youth rested with government ministries. Government programmes have found it difficult to respond to the changing needs of the labour market, and to provide up-to-date equipment because of bureaucratic and fiscal pressures. In some countries programmes have shifted to the private sector and parastatals (for example, HEART in Jamaica, SERVOL and YTEPP in Trinidad). In addition to vocational skills training, some of these programmes offer basic literacy and numeric training, entrepreneurship, career planning and attitudinal training. Such initiatives hold promise for enabling vulnerable youth to enter the labour market.

Authors (for example, Thurow, 1992; Pantin, 1996) have argued that the level of education is below the performance required to integrate entrants to the labour force. They emphasized the need for a well-educated work force as the key determinant of development in the region. According to them part of the low productivity levels in the region are partly explained by ineffective education.

It is useful to examine the rate of unemployment according to education level across Caribbean economies. Table 6.11 reveals two interesting pictures across island nations. One, there appears to be a strong relationship between the level of education and the unemployment rate. The better-educated youths on the other hand are more or less absorbed in the economy. On the whole Table 6.11 suggests some support for the poor status of skill development programmes.

Over the past decade, there has been a sharp decline in capital expenditure in most economies. A significant proportion of this financing

Table 6.11: Unemployment rate under various categories in the Caribbean economies: 2000

Country	Unemployment rate(%)			Unemployment rate(%) up to secondary education			Unemployment rate (%) above secondary education (tertiary and technical)		
	M	F	Total	M	F	Total	M	F	Total
Barbados	8	11	10	8	15	11	3.5	5.5	5
Bahamas	9	6	10	7	11	9	3	3.5	3
St Kitts and Nevis		n.a.			n.a.			n.a.	
Trinidad and Tobago	9	15	11	9	16	11.5	0.9	3	2
Antigua and Barbuda	6	5.6	6		n.a.			n.a.	
Belize	9	20	13	9	21	13	4	3	4
Dominica	20	27	23		n.a.			n.a.	
St Lucia	13	21	16		n.a.			n.a.	
Suriname	7	17	11	8	18	11.5	3	2.8	3
Grenada	11	21	15		n.a.			n.a.	
Jamaica	10	21	15		n.a.			n.a.	
St Vincent and the Grenadines	18	22	20		n.a.			n.a.	
Guyana	6	14	9		n.a.			n.a.	
Haiti					n.a.			n.a.	

Notes: Col. 3 refers to % of unemployment up to secondary education to total secondary educated labour force. Col. 4 refers to % of unemployment above secondary education to total above secondary educated labour force.
n.a.: not available. M: male; F: female.

Source: Based on data from http://www.ilocarib.org.tt/digest/tt/thi50.html.

now comes from external sources in the form of concessionary loans. Given the current economic climate, access to such funds is likely to become more limited. The high cost of providing tertiary level and university education and the inability of governments to meet even present obligations, compel the region to diversify funding sources. The studies (for example World Bank, 1996) find that real expenditure on education and health have fallen in many island nations over the past decade. As a consequence, physical structures have deteriorated, equipment is lacking, and teaching aids are non-existent in most schools.

Key features of the Caribbean system of skill development

FDI is considered to be capable of making useful contribution to the process of economic development. This is relevant not only in the context of inflows of capital but also of transfer of technology, management skills and marketing know-how to the host countries for realizing a country's export potential. In the Caribbean, like in other developing regions, policies towards multinational corporations have undergone considerable evolution, with the degree of change varying from one country to another. The tendency has been to move from a policy of nationalization and/or state control in the 1960s and 1970s to one of liberalization in the 1980s and privatization and further liberalization in the 1990s. In recent times, there is a policy of pro-active promotion of foreign investment under globalization in the context of increasing competition for such resources. In the Caribbean, this dependence on foreign investment is further accentuated by a persistently low level of savings, significant decline in ODA, and the unattractiveness of the region for international private bank loans and portfolio investment flows, partly because of the relatively high transaction cost in such a small market (CARICOM, 2000). A key condition for foreign investment is the need to meet demands for technically trained manpower. An early step to meet the demand for skilled personnel (not higher skilled personnel) was through the establishment of local training institutions that focused on technical skill development. But this skill under the present conditions may not be appropriate in the region in general and a few island nations in particular. The structure of labour market should also change as the economies move into higher value-added and more technologically advanced products that require general skills (vocational and technical training for occupations such as fitters, electricians, welders) and specialized skills germane to the industries that are growing as a result of foreign investment.

It is to be mentioned here that the size of intra-CARICOM trade is less than 20 per cent of the region's total trade. Thus, to the potential foreign investor, even the integrated regional market remains too small in size. The investment and employment effects of integrating the markets of the region, therefore, have serious limitations (CARICOM, op. cit.). Instead, investors should consider the regional market as a mere pedestal for penetrating the wider international world with the products of the said investments. This is only possible when foreign investors do not face skill shortages in a tight labour market, given that they have some control over the supply of skilled people.

Lochan (2002) in the above context assessed the effectiveness of educational schemes that promote through adequate preparation of the youth cohort (age group: 15–24 years) in the Caribbean. He has examined three institutions in Trinidad and Tobago: John S. Donaldson Technical Institute (JDTI), San Fernando Technical Institute (SFTI) and Servol (Service Volunteered for All); one in Barbados: Samuel Jackman

Prescod Polytechnic (SJPP); and another in Jamaica: Heart Trust NTA. According to the study, in both Trinidad and Tobago and Barbados, the major institutions for technical/vocational training seem to be too structurally inadequate and poorly equipped to operate in today's world. It is useful to cite the example of Singapore in this context due to the fact that Singapore's growth has largely been driven by larger inputs of capital and labour rather than productivity growth (Krugman, 1994). It is often argued (James *et al.*, 1999, for example) that Singapore's acclaimed skills development system may be considered as an example of a concerted national and integrated effort, given its multilevel focus and private sector collaboration. It is successful because it is linked to other national policies (e.g. economic development, technology transfer), and various institutions appear to work together. Kuruvilla *et al.* (2002) have examined several key actors and institutions in this respect. The Ministry of Trade and Industry (MTI) played a key role for broad economic development policies. A range of semi-autonomous agencies have played an active role. For example, the Economic Development Board (EDB) has the primary function of attracting foreign direct investment and foreign investor's demands for the required skilled personnel. Likewise the Productivity and Standards Board (PSB), the Institute of Technical Education (ITE), and other industry-specific bodies such as the Precision Engineering Institute (PEI) have also been working to meet the skill demands of foreign investors. The National Manpower Council (NMC) of Singapore as a second key institution consults MTI and Ministry of Education (MoE), polytechnics and universities in order to prepare the intake and output targets of ITE. The Council for Professional and Technical Education (CPTE) has the overall responsibility for matching the demand for and supply of skills in the economy. Based on existing levels and estimated future needs, this body works together with different parts of the education system (universities, polytechnics and schools) and skills development institutions (ITE, and other industry specific training institutes) to ensure the supply of sufficient number of workers with the desired level of skills for industry requirements. A third key actor is the MoE, which has direct jurisdiction over schools, polytechnics, universities and the ITE.

Summary

The available data on the Caribbean show that FDI is highest in Trinidad and Tobago. For example, our analysis showed that the ratio of exports to GDP was the only economic determinant of FDI in the oil-exporting economy of Trinidad and Tobago. Foreign investors have been attracted to the Caribbean because of the strategic geographical position of these countries, and the prospect of marketing their products to a global market. Our results reveal that the USA is the major export destination of Caribbean export. However the trend is declining. In recent years tourism and infrastructure have attracted FDI in countries such as Guyana, the OECS and Jamaica. The Caribbean countries continue to use an open door FDI policy in the light of structural adjustment programmes aimed at economic liberalization. The dynamics of the labour market may be considered as a powerful ingredient in explaining these facets.

The study reveals that higher education and the skill development strategy of the region lack vision. We showed the institutional aspect of Singapore model and then tried to compare it with the Caribbean economies. The system may play an important role in enhancing long-term growth. Moreover, by making effective use of electronic commerce, especially in the area of services, the Caribbean economies would be able to partly neutralize the advantage typically enjoyed by large economies. But the increasingly skilled and knowledge-intensive nature of the associated activities would require continuous upgrading of education and training. Unfortunately, the existing structure is too weak to transform the economy from low growth to prosperity.

7
Technology Transfer: Case Studies

Introduction

Industrialization is an essential component of the development process. Technology seems to be the principal stimulus and an effective catalyst for this process of industrial growth. It can be argued that spillovers from invention and innovation at the international level generate technological changes, which can be effectively employed by the developing or newly industrializing nations. The process of acquiring technology from a country that has substantially improved technological knowledge is known as technology transfer. The importance of technology transfer has engendered much exploration in the fields of productivity analysis, market operation, corporate learning and overall growth of the economy. In this context, there can emerge two principal ways of utilizing transfer of technology – namely, gradual learning and leapfrogging. In comparison to leapfrogging, gradual learning is incremental, painstaking, long-term and cumulative.

Quite often, the technology transfers and the resultant spillovers result in slow and gradual changes with no appreciable difference in the relative position of the countries participating in the trade or the investment processes along the technology frontier. However, under the regime of globalization and cost competitiveness this may not always be true. Sometimes, the firms in low-knowledge countries leapfrog the standard life cycle and are able to make their final product competitive.

This chapter takes a case study approach to study the process of successful technology transfer – through formal technical collaboration as well as through trade in equipment and raw materials embodying technology. This is based on an analysis of six case study firms. The next section reviews the existing literature of technology transfer and its links with FDI. Based on this foundation our aim is to portray the historical behaviour of technology adopted, absorbed, assimilated as well as developed in one Chinese, three Indian and two Caribbean firms. The firms considered are from different industries but all of them from the manufacturing sector. In this setting, we examine the nature, direction and determinants of technological learning of the firms in the subsequent section. Our purpose is to locate the case material with historical evidence and generate further questions for analysis. The penultimate section presents detailed interpretation and analysis of the cases, and, the final section summarizes the chapter.

Review of literature on technology transfer

Some economists have emphasized that technology should be accumulated through a gradual process of assimilation and learning. However, modern technology analysts suggest that leapfrogging by the developing countries might enable them to catch up in any field. Explanations of international trade assume a constant technology. The basis for trade is attributed to factors like labour productivity, factor endowments, and national demand structures. In a dynamic world, however, technological changes occur in different nations at different rates. Technological innovations commonly result in new methods of producing existing commodities, or in the production of new commodities.

It can be said that technological accumulation takes place through time, beginning with simple activities such as assembling and then gradually moves toward more complex tasks such as process adoption and innovation and eventually R&D. In this context, research on the role and determinants of FDI and other forms of technology transfer and their developmental impact assumes importance as it could be of considerable value to policymakers.

It is often argued that from the standpoint of diffusion of technology, the cost of imitation is smaller than the cost of innovation. This is particularly relevant in those cases where a country that was initially technologically backward would eventually become the innovator. Some researchers argued that the benefits from the backwardness are strong enough to generate not only a convergence effect, but also a tendency for leapfrogging (Brezis *et al.*, 1999). They assumed that the country with the current technological lead has learnt through experience to be highly productive with the existing techniques. The leader's knowledge is assumed not to be accessible by other countries and the returns from experience are diminishing within each country. To quote Barro and Sala-i-Martin (1999):

> Fundamentally new technologies appear occasionally; these new approaches offer potential of higher productivity, but not until substantial learning-by-doing has occurred. As a consequence, the adoption of the new technique may be unattractive for the current leader – who has the option to continue with the old method of production at a currently high level of productivity – but may be worthwhile for a laggard. Since the new technology is more productive in the long run, the follower eventually becomes the leader; hence, the leapfrogging effect (p. 280).

For example, the English passing the Dutch by the 1700s or the United States and Germany overtaking England in the late 1800s.

It is imperative to mention here that knowledge embodied in the form of technology is transferred by multinational corporations (MNCs) to businesses abroad using a variety of mechanisms. First, knowledge can be embodied in imported physical goods that are used to produce products or services. Secondly, a business abroad can purchase knowledge directly from foreign suppliers for a lump-sum payment or by licensing or franchising it and paying a recurring royalty. Thirdly, movement of people, for example, can obtain knowledge from expatriate engineers and managers, from short-term visits of experts from a foreign partner company, or by sending local employees to a foreign supplier or parent company. Finally, knowledge can be acquired from the media, including written documents or oral conversations using telephones, faxes, e-mails, memos, reports, newsletters, and journals.

However, authors have categorised knowledge into different types depending on their method of transfer and cost of transfer (Winter, 1987; Kogut and Zander, 1993; Inkpen, 1995). For example, explicit knowledge is articulated, codified, and tangible. It can be written down or spoken and communicated by formal language in the form of databases, operating manuals and blueprints. These are disembodied and free standing, but explicit knowledge can also be embodied as performance features of products. Indeed, explicit knowledge is relatively easy to transfer by a variety of methods (Nollen and Brewer, 2000). In contrast, tacit knowledge is not fully expressed. It is partly conscious and partly intuitive and is difficult to learn and share with others. It is likely to be part of a larger system of integrated knowledge components. Examples of tacit knowledge are the manual skills of craftsmen and the interpersonal skills of supervisors. In this case basic knowledge level may be considered as an exogenous factor.

During the late 1960s, the standardization of a wide variety of technologies, and hence, increasing competition coupled with the improved bargaining position of host country governments, provided arm's-length licensing of intangible assets as an alternative to FDI. The presence of location advantages and ownership of tangible assets are still necessary conditions for FDI but these advantages needed to be complemented by some incentives for internalization of the markets of intangible assets. Thus transfer of technology either based on intra-firm or through FDI is considered as the most relevant one. The literature on FDI and technology transfer is extensive. See Blumenthal (1979), Teece (1981, 1983), Lall (1983, 2001a), Katrak (1985, 1989), Winter (1987), Siddharthan (1988, 1992), Fikkert (1993), and Hobday (1994, 1995). The findings of some of these studies are discussed later.

Technology is imported either in the form of technology licensing contracts or as a part of an FDI package with technology adapted to the local environment. Both are complex. Two strands of literature have tried to approach this. One has looked at the nature of interface between technology imports and local R&D. The other group of studies has examined the diffusion of imported technology to the rest of the economy through knowledge and productivity spillovers, vertical inter-firm linkages, and employee mobility.

In recent development literature, the contentious issue is the nature of the relationship between technology imports and local in-house R&D. One school of thought describes technology imports and local in-house R&D as substitutes, whereas the other school of thought looks into the relationship as complementary. Blumenthal (op. cit.) argued that the technological level of a country is a function of indigenous R&D, technology imports and the relation between the two. Her empirical exercise for six countries namely Australia, Japan, France, West Germany, Italy and Sweden, led to no firm conclusion. Evidence of complementarity is observed only for three countries, that is Australia, Japan and France. However, no significant relationship was found in the case of the other three countries.

The literature has investigated the relationship between technology imports and in-house R&D in India using firm and industry level observations. Desai (1980) and Lall (op. cit.) have mentioned that Indian R&D is basically adaptive and consequently import of technology would encourage in-house R&D. A number of empirical exercises including Lall (op. cit.), Katrak (ibid.), and Siddharthan (op. cit.), confirmed the complementary relationship between imported technology and local R&D. Kumar (1987) argued that the nature of relationship between imported technology and local R&D is also influenced by the mode of technology import besides other factors. Kumar (1994) examined the effect of technology imports on the probability and intensity of in-house R&D activity for a sample of 291 firms. The data obtained from the RBI survey was analysed in the framework of Probit and Tobit models. The empirical result of Fikkert (1993) depicts that (i) technology imports and R&D have a significant negative relationship; (ii) firms having foreign equity participation have an insignificant direct effect on R&D but they tend to depend significantly more on foreign technology purchases which in turn tend to reduce R&D; and (iii) trade restrictions have induced adaptive R&D. In view of these findings, he concludes that India's closed technology policies with respect to FDI and technology licensing had the desired effect of promoting indigenous R&D.

Lall (op. cit.) has simplified the list of drivers of technological learning in the light of successful countries such as Singapore, Korea and Taiwan. The governments in these economies emphasised the need for building local capabilities (to different extents and in different combinations). Some of them are: trade policy and domestic credit policy to influence resource allocation; infrastructure development; firm size and cluster formation; skill development; technological activity and promotion; FDI attraction, targeting or restriction. However, the present structure of international trade and finance greatly limits the ability of countries to practise the above forms of industrial policy today. But it is possible to focus the supply-side determinants of competitiveness in this context such as skill development, technological activity and FDI.

Acquiring new technology may not be considered a one-time task. The process is continuous in the context of dynamic status of knowledge development, human labour condition, market, institutions and the role of the government. A competitive firm may lose in the long run due to a competitor's upgradation of technology. It is thus argued that countries or firms must move into more advanced technologies in order to remain competitive in a regime of rising costs. Herein lies the government's role that indirectly supports the firms by providing incentives, factors and institutions. Each can suffer from market failure if not integrated.

Case studies of Chinese, Indian and Caribbean firms

Case 1: a case of a Taiwanese OEM Firm in China[1]

This company was formed in 1971 and began its operations with the production of transformers used in black and white television receivers. It has now grown to become Taiwan's largest manufacturer of transformers and switching power supply units for use in personal computers and other information technology related products. As a former employee of a TRW subsidiary in Taiwan, in its initial days, the founder of the company was employing most of its engineers from TRW and General Instruments – two companies best known in Taiwan for transformers and transformer related products. The company began its operations with just NT$100,000 (US$2,500) and 15 employees. It began by supplying transformers to Tatung. Incidentally, Tatung is Taiwan's largest indigenous producer of TV receivers. As Taiwan's TV receiver industry boomed riding the surge in global exports of the 1970s, the company's business also expanded. The multinational companies that were operating in Taiwan such as Philips, RCA and Zenith became part of the customer base of the company.

The size, speed and success of personal computer industry in Taiwan encouraged the company to manufacture PC-related components such as EMI filters and switching power supplies (SPS), both extrapolated from transformer-related technologies. It also acquired the technology to produce computer fans which largely monopolized by Japanese producers at that time. Taiwan's PC industry experienced a boom in the 1980s and this helped the company emerge as a world-class manufacturer of PC electronic components. In addition to local PC manufacture, the company also struck deals with renowned global players such as IBM, HP and Compaq to supply SPS. Interestingly, the company exported about 85 per cent of its total products to the US market.

Just as there were several competing companies in Taiwan, there were also many possible benefits of operating from the highly competitive environment. Still, in 1987, the company decided to invest in Nogales in Mexico, where its products were to be incorporated into IBM's assembly operation in maquilladora (border plants). This decision was actually inspired by its major customer IBM to satisfy the local content requirement for duty-free entry into the US market. This move of the company was primarily strategic to strengthen its alliance with IBM. In fact, Taiwan's wage rates had become comparable to those in Mexico by then and so there wasn't much of a cost reduction motive.

The subsequent decision to invest in Thailand in 1988 significantly reduced the cost of production and preserved the company's price competitiveness as the then Thai wage rates were about one-third the level in Taiwan. Later and largely at its own initiative, the decision to invest in China may be considered as a major expansion drive on the part of the company. The decision has made the company a global player in the electronic components industry. The company undertook experimental production in 1993, first by renting an existing factory in Dongguan, Guangdong Province. It hired around one hundred workers for the endeavour. The experiment succeeded and the company took steps such as acquiring land to build its own plants. In 1999, the company built five successive plants in Dongguan with a total strength of 26,000 workers. These, together with the 9,000 workers in Thailand and the 800 workers in Mexico, made the company the world's largest producer of PC-related transformers and SPS. The total revenue reached US$1.6 billion indicating a world market share of 25 per cent in SPS.

Dongguan has developed in recent time although it was largely farmland in 1993. The most dramatic and biggest expansion came when the company bought land along with some 20 component suppliers from Taiwan. Their initial production capacity was to be fully absorbed and guaranteed by the company. This group provided components and their proximity to the assembly line was essential for production efficiency and flexibility. Interestingly, this group of component suppliers has attracted Taiwan's second largest SPS producer also to invest in the same region. In turn, this attracted more component suppliers in the region due to the presence of additional assemblers. The agglomeration process rolled on and by 1999 there were more than 70 SPS-related component producers in Dongguan including a few local and Hong Kong-based companies. Consequently, the company was able to procure most of its components locally due to the clustering of component producers.

In May 2000, local procurement was accounting for 70 per cent of all component procurement in terms of value, and for 90 per cent in terms of number of items. Some more valuable components such as cores and diodes came from Japan, the US and Europe. In contrast a few also came from Taiwan. Meanwhile, there had been a few small SPS assemblers relocating to Shenzhen, a special economic zone neighbouring Dongguan – with superior infrastructure and fiscal incentives prior to the company's move into Dongguan. Despite all this activity, however, they were too small to prompt the supply chain to follow in their footsteps.

Large firms can also enjoy tremendous advantages in China's labour market. The company, for example, employs mostly out-of-province female workers who are housed in company dormitories with their room and board covered by company expenses. The turnover rate for out-of-province workers is much lower than that of local residents, which normally exceeds 40 per cent a year. There are, however, extra costs incurred for employers of out-of -province workers, in terms of the 'temporary domicile fee' charged on non-local workers by the local governments. The fee is, nevertheless, subject to negotiation and large companies with a large number of non-local workers are in a good position to bargain for a lower levy. It was found that in Guangdong province, the per-capita 'temporary domicile fee' ranged between 10 and 100 renminbi, with local officials holding discretionary power.

China's existing supply of skilled labour is limited. However, the country's higher education system does offer a substantial pool of talent, which can be cultivated and transformed into admirable engineering capabilities. Locating itself in Dongguan, a town that is little-known among China's elite university students, the company has indeed experienced major difficulties in recruiting students from China's premiere institutions such as Peking and Tsinghua universities. It has to turn to the regional universities of Hubei, Hunan, Sichuan and so on, to recruit less privileged, but nevertheless, promising graduates. In order to gain a better position in China's skilled labour market, the company established a research centre in Tianjin's free trade zone, along with a battery plant investment in the same location by way of a consortium with the renowned Japanese battery-maker, Yuasa. The company succeeded in staffing research centre, which is not far from Beijing, with recruits from premier universities such as Peking, Tsinghua and Nankai. The advantage from this is that some of the engineers can then be deployed to the factory sites in Dongguan to undertake process-related research work. The company also takes advantage of its overseas manufacturing facilities and sales offices outside of China to attract young engineers. More than one thousand Chinese engineers, along with 110 Taiwanese expatriates living and working in China, have become the mainstay of the company's research force in China.

The company has not delved into vertical integration, but it did take advantage of its good relations with foreign clients to develop new computer parts, notably colour monitors, as a means of diversification. It is imperative to mention here that the company had no previous experience of manufacturing monitors in Taiwan. However, the related technology was readily available there, since Taiwan supplies over 50 per cent of the world demand for computer monitors. It began its monitor production in Thailand, targeting the subcontracting market, and successfully secured orders from computer manufacturers Dell and Gateway which were operating assembly lines in nearby Malaysia. Monitor production was later extended from Thailand to China where larger facilities were built and more advanced products made. In 2000, the Chinese plant manufactured about 400,000 colour monitors per month to support, among others, Japanese PC-makers such as Sony, Fujitsu and Mitsubishi. This strategy avoids head-on competition with other Taiwanese monitor manufacturers whose main customers are the American brands. Assuming the technology can be sorted out, it still depends on careful selection for new possibilities such as creation of high-skilled but lost-cost labour. The company is so far successful in this endeavour.

Case 2: Sundram Fasteners Ltd – India[2]

Sundram Fasteners (SFL), a part of the TVS group, was the brainchild of Mr Suresh Krishna and started its operations in 1966. SFL is the largest manufacturer and exporter of high-tensile fasteners in India. Its wide product range caters to almost all the vehicle manufacturers in India and many from outside the country. The three main product groups of the company are: (1) fasteners: bolts, screws, nuts, sockets; (2) cold extruded products: cold extrusion is closely allied with cold forging technology in which SFL is a specialist; (3) sintered products: sintering is a process of compacting by using the principles of powder-metallurgy. The company, which started with a meager turnover of Rs0.4 million in 1996, has grown rapidly since then and recorded a turnover of Rs6.89 billion in 2003–04 including Rs1.71 billion of exports.

The first manufacturing plant was set up in Padi, Madras in 1965 and a second fastener plant was opened in Aviyur, a backward village of Ramnad district in Tamil Nadu in 1981. Together, these two units comprise the fasteners division of the company. SFL wanted to manufacture a category of automotive components, which could be manufactured by the process of cold extrusion. Accordingly, SFL commenced its first diversification venture in 1979 by setting up a unit for the manufacture of cold extruded components in Hosur, again a backward district of Tamil Nadu, in technical collaboration with M/S Neumeyer Filespressen Gmbh of Germany. This technical collaboration was only for the transfer of the technology.

In 1983, the company further diversified into powder metal (sintered) products in technical collaboration with Sintermetallwerke Krebsoege GmbH – also in Hosur. As part of its strategic backward integration, SFL acquired an iron powder manufacturing unit in Hyderabad in 1990. A part of the iron powder which was not required for sintering, was sold to welding electrode manufacturers in India. Together, the plants in Hosur and Hyderabad constitute the Hosur division of the company.

In 1992, SFL set up an export oriented unit to manufacture radiator caps, oil filler caps and petrol filler caps. This product category was a chance addition for SFL. SFL was supplying fasteners to the Opel plant of General Motors (GM) in Germany and while the GM technical auditors were interacting with SFL executives during one of their technical audit-related visits, they mentioned that GM was planning to close and sell a radiator caps plant in Britain and enquired if SFL would be interested in making radiator caps for GM. Taking advantage of the liberalized economic environment in India, SFL bought the machinery from the plant in Britain and shipped it to Madras and soon became a 100 per cent supplier of radiator caps to GM. To become a 100 per cent supplier to GM, it is necessary to have total reliability of supplies, zero level of defectives and globally competitive prices. SFL now supplies radiator caps to 27 GM plants located across the globe and won the 'Supplier of the Year' award from GM five years in a row – from 1996 through 2000.

In 1998, exports contributed 1 per cent of the total turnover of the company. Exports grew to 10 per cent in 1993, 20 per cent in 1999 and further to about 25 per cent of the total turnover for the financial year ending March 2000. The automobile sector faced recession during two phases, first during 1992/93 and again in 1997/98. However, the company managed to increase its sales with a slight decline in operating margin by mainly resorting to reduction in costs. It has also managed to use its fixed assets efficiently since inception and as a result the fixed assets turnover has not declined but has marginally increased over the period of twenty years from 1981 to 1999. During 1981, the fixed assets turn over ratio was 1.64, which, in 1999 was 1.88.

Starting with the product profile, the market of high tensile fasteners for SFL can be broadly classified into two categories, 'Standards' and 'Specials'. The characteristics for 'Standards' are low tooling costs and more market in USA. Sundram Fasteners Ltd concentrated its resources into 'Standards' till 1988. 'Specials' is a relatively new area which holds bright prospects in Europe and which needs high investment in tool manufacturing technology. It includes dry wall screws and sockets.

Table 7.1 shows the total market potential of Sundram Fasteners in Europe. Over a thousand manufacturers – of which there are around fifteen key players – supply the European market for fasteners. The major exporters for Europe are Taiwan, Japan, Korea and China.

Table 7.2 shows the major componets of the fasteners market in USA. The American market is expected to grow at the rate of 6 per cent annually. The growth is ascribed mainly to the increase in demand for

Table 7.1 Country-wise details of potential export market for 'specials' fasteners: Europe

Country	Value (US$m)
West Germany	1219
UK	751
France	607
Italy	587
Netherlands	245
Belgium	212
Denmark	120
Eire	74
Greece	53
Spain	318
Portugal	86

Source: Sundram Fasteners Ltd.

Table 7.2 Market share in USA

Sl. no.	Type of consumer	Market share (%)
1	Automotive industry	24
2	Aerospace industry	14
3	Non-electrical machinery	11

Source: Based on data supplied by Sundram Fasteners Ltd.

externally threaded fasteners. There are low prospects for growth in 'Specials' and internally threaded fasteners. The prominent exports to the US market are from Japan, Taiwan, China and Korea. Out of the total market, more than 50 per cent requirements are to be met by imports.

The fasteners market provides certain options for SFL to attain a sustained growth rate in future. They are: (1) growth in the existing line itself; (2) growth though backward integration in areas where the company's core strengths could be utilized; (3) acquisitions and mergers; and (4) diversification into unrelated lines. The company took certain steps proactively, which were considered necessary to ensure its competitiveness in global markets and also to increase its competitiveness and profitability in the domestic arena.

SFL acquired Autolec, a leading manufacturer of oil pumps, fuel pumps, water pumps and other automotive components in 1999. In December 2003, SFL acquired the Cramlington precision forging unit of

Dana Spicer Europe. Even though the plant was making a highly specialized product (bevel gears), its very existence was at stake as parent Dana was not interested in this line of business. SFL acquired it with plans to double the capacity of the plant and to use it as a beachhead to export its own products into Europe.

Later in May 2004, SFL inaugurated its China plant to manufacture fasteners – both standard and special. This plant would be used to meet the domestic demand of fasteners in China as well as to export to other countries.

SFL continued with its strategies persistently which paid off in the long run. It has not only increased its business with General Motors but also broken into other international markets like the German market where it achieved a sizable contract from Daimler Benz AG and the Japanese market where after four years of hard work the company secured orders from Japanese engineering giant Komatsu for track shoe bolts and nuts. It has also secured orders from Cummins US for supply of fasteners. SFL continues as a 100 per cent Indian company with no FDI, but has benefited through technology collaborations as described earlier.

Case 3: Moser Baer India Ltd – India[3]

With an 11 per cent share of the global market, Moser Baer India Limited (MBIL) has emerged as the third largest producer of recordable optical media in the world. Its products are produced in six state-of-the-art manufacturing facilities for discerning global customers spread over 82 countries across six continents of the world. The company has a strong focus on research and development and many of the processes and techniques used have been developed in-house. This also enables the company to constantly innovate and introduce new products and processes.

The products manufactured by the company span the complete range of removable storage media – both optical and magnetic. The company manufactures Compact Discs – both recordable (CD-R) and rewritable (CD-RW); as well as Digital Versatile Discs – again both recordable (DVD-R) and rewritable (DVD-RW), in the optical storage media segment. It also manufactures pre-recorded CD/DVD. It manufactures Compact Cassettes, Micro Floppy Disks (MFD) and Digital Audio Tapes (DAT) in the magnetic storage media category. The emphasis on the quality of its products and services has enabled the company to export over 80 per cent of its production and today it is an OEM supplier to 11 of the top 12 global brands.

MBIL was established as a joint venture in collaboration with Moser Baer AG of Switzerland in 1983 to manufacture time recording devices in India.

As this product did not do very well in the market, the company entered the magnetic removable storage media industry and started the production of 8-inch and later 5.25-inch floppy disks in 1985. Although this business was more successful, the company continued with the production of time recording systems and formally exited only in the mid 1990s. The promoter family purchased the Swiss company's shares in 1986 but continued with the name of the company. The company went public in 1988. The major events in the life of MBIL are summarized in Table 7.3.

Although MBIL was established in New Delhi, its founder and managing director Mr Deepak Puri had moved a few years earlier from Kolkata in West Bengal, where he was running an aluminum conductors and cables business. Like Mr Puri, many other businessmen were also forced out of West Bengal by labour unrest. As an engineering graduate of the Imperial College of Science and Technology, London, Mr Puri has a deep understanding of engineering and technology and has been successfully directing business in the high technology engineering industry.

Soon after ensuring their foothold in the 8/5.25-inch floppy disk market, MBIL commenced production of 3.25-inch floppy disks in 1987. During this period, the Indian manufacturing industry was operating in a protected environment. Import tariff was as high as 200–300 per cent and there were as many as 13 domestic producers (Business India, 2002a). With the government initiating economic reforms in 1991,

Table 7.3 MBIL – milestones

1983	MBIL established as a joint venture between a Swiss and an Indian company to manufacture time recorders and time keeping systems in India
1985	Entered the magnetic storage media industry by manufacturing the 8/5.25-inch floppy disk
1987	Commenced production of 3.5-inch floppy disks
1988	MBIL became a public limited company
1991	5.25-inch disk capacity expanded
1994	3.5-inch disk capacity expanded
Mid-1990s	Exited the time keeping systems industry
	Production capacity reached 120m diskettes
1996	Decided against entering the CD manufacturing business
1997	Decided to enter CD manufacturing
1998	MBI gets ISO 9002 certification
1999	Commenced production of CD-Rs
2000	Commenced production of CD-RWs
2002	Production of cake & jewel boxes
2003	Production of DVD – DVD RWs

MBIL sensed the need to be globally competitive by scaling up volumes and capacities and by cultivating a strong R&D team. Consequently, 5.25-inch floppy disk capacity was expanded in 1991 and 3.25-inch disk in 1994. From 5 million diskettes per year in the 1980s, the production capacity increased to 120 million units by 1996. The sales of the company jumped from Rs91.5 million in 1993/94 to Rs338.4 million in 1994/95 and further to Rs433.8 million in 1995/96 (CMIE, 2004).

Further expansion of production capacity was planned in 1996 – but this was not implemented – as the company realized that newer technologies were likely to affect the future growth of the magnetic media industry. Optical storage and retrieval technology had proved commercially meaningful and the increasing stock of CD writers held a promise for a large market for recordable CDs. However, the large infusion of capital needed to establish manufacturing capacities in CD-Rs was perceived as highly risky and the company decided to do nothing except continuing with the R&D on CD-R products and processes. But the next year, the company decided to establish capacity for manufacturing CDs, as the risk perception had decreased significantly by then. The production of CDs actually started in 1999 and with this MBIL moved to another growth trajectory as can be seen from Table 7.4; it also signified a major strategic shift for the company.

Table 7.4 MBIL – a brief profile (Rs m)

	March 1997	March 1998	March 1999	March 2000	March 2001	March 2002	March 2003
Sales	607.9	718.6	1 012.8	1 547.9	3 360.8	6 805.6	10 855.2
Exports (FOB)	447.0	540.9	831.1	1 362.6	3 117.5	5 882.0	9 269.4
Purchase of fixed assets	279.6	213.6	157.4	2 015.0	3 694.2	5 972.5	7 957.2
Profit before tax	106.2	132.0	204.6	441.5	1 386.0	2 200.4	2 359.8
RM Purchases (Rs m)	388.1	500.7	638.3	810.0	1 913.2	2 740.6	2 895.9
Exports as % of sales	73.53	75.27	82.06	88.03	92.76	86.43	85.39
Imported capital goods as % of purchase of fixed assets	73.28	49.81	5.21	59.94	88.79	75.63	70.84
RM import as % of RM purchases	90.18	79.63	77.25	90.77	97.78	92.58	n.a.

Note: n.a: not available.

Source: Based on CMIE (2004).

As the process of economic reforms was gathering momentum MBIL also slowly started developing the vision of being a world class player in all the products they were manufacturing. The decision to quit the production of time-recording system was also part of this vision as was the decision to expand capacities of 5.25-inch and 3.5-inch floppy disks. They already had a reputation for high quality, and they focused on achieving a 'zero defect' manufacturing. MBIL also committed significant resources on its R&D which had the mandate of developing product and process technologies useful for the company. In an industry where technological obsolescence was high, this meant to be always at the frontier of product technology and having manufacturing processes which would strengthen the competitive advantages of the company. Although MBIL decided not to enter the CD industry in 1996 after having toyed with the idea, they thought the risks had reduced by 1997 and commenced production in 1999 – implying that they had the technology to make CDs all along. The later developments clearly bring out the mindset of a global player.

R&D has emerged as one of the most important drivers of MBIL's success. R&D has enabled the company to be at the forefront of technology and offer unique product and service offerings to its customers and achieve cost reductions through continuous improvements. Development of the company's PC12D process and its subsequent versions has helped the company's products to achieve broad compatibility across a wide spectrum of drives with writing speeds from 1X to 52X along with significant cost reductions. The company developed the fastest CD-R line in the world in cooperation with a major German company in 2002–2003. MBIL has entered into technology co-development agreements with some of the leading technology companies in this industry from Japan and Europe. Its ability to design manufacturing facilities and fabrication equipment – as well as the ability to develop processes which are highly flexible – thereby enabling the company to move quickly between different optical disk formats including customized disks, have been possible because of its strength in R&D.

Having missed the early growth phase of the CD-R product life cycle due to high perceived risks in an industry where margins keep falling as the product matures, MBIL decided to enter the DVD market as early as possible. The production of DVD-R and DVD-RW commenced in 2003.

Besides the PC12D-XT process along with its subsequent modified versions, the company has successfully developed high capacity small form factor disks as well as high-end magnetic and optical media for the professional segment of the market. It has also developed advanced groove geometries that help in reduction of cycle time and cheaper alternatives to replace high cost raw materials. Besides lower labour costs, MBIL has also achieved lower capital and integration costs through indigenous development of dye-coating and raw material recycling technology.

While following an OEM-centric international strategy, MBIL is now trying to strengthen its own brand in the domestic market. This would help the company realize higher margins from the large domestic market as well as spread their business risks. In 2003, MBIL launched its Moser Baer brand of optical media in the domestic market. It has plans of moving up the value chain by leveraging its manufacturing strengths and experience in the field of storage technology to capture 50 per cent of the fast growing Rs4 billion optical media market in India. MBIL also owns the Xydan brand name, has licence to use the Emtec brand name and with the acquisition of CAPCO in Luxembourg acquired the strong European brand MMore.

MBIL is now setting up a manufacturing unit in Germany that would produce up to 17 per cent of its expanded capacity of two billion discs a year. The investment envisaged is US$100 million and the plant is expected to commence commercial production by early 2005. A production facility in the heart of Europe would insulate the company from any future European tariff or non-tariff barrier. However, this is also a pointer to the fact that MBIL has graduated to a stage where it is not dependent on low labour cost processes to gain competitive advantages. In fact, it is confident of competing effectively with other global producers even after producing the discs in Germany.

Moser Baer India Limited is an Indian company managed by Indian promoters and it has not benefited from any direct investment from another foreign optical media producer – although the company has investment from many foreign institutional investors and private equity firms like the International Finance Corporation (IFC), Warburg Pincus and Electra Partners.

Case 4: Sona Koyo Steering Systems Limited – India[4]

Sona Koyo Steering Systems Limited is the largest manufacturer of steering gears in India with a market share of 50 per cent. Its product range includes manual and power steering systems; rigid, tilt and collapsible steering columns; axle assemblies and propeller shafts for the automobile industry. Besides being a large domestic player, it has entered the export market in a big way after setting up its 100 per cent export-oriented unit in 2004 and has plans of earning 20 per cent of its revenues from exports and overseas sales by 2007 going up to 45 per cent by 2010. In a way, the progress of Sona Koyo represents that of the Indian automobile industry in recent times.

The automobile industry in India which had over the years settled at a low-volume, low-innovation, low-competition equilibrium experienced a severe jolt with the entry of Maruti Udyog Limited in 1983. Maruti was set up as a joint venture between the government of India and Suzuki Motors of Japan. Initially Maruti was importing all its critical parts and components from their Japanese technical partner but they had massive plans for indigenization. Sona Steering Systems Ltd was set up in 1985 during this phase of indigenization to manufacture manual steering gear assemblies and steering column assemblies in technical collaboration with Koyo Seiko Co. Ltd of Osaka, Japan. Dr Surinder Kapur, who was running a reasonably successful company called Bharat Gears from Mumbai till then, was the promoter of Sona, but Maruti also picked up a 10 per cent stake in the equity of Sona Steering – thus giving Sona the status of one of its joint ventures. Sona Steering established its manufacturing plant in Gurgaon, in close proximity of the Maruti plant.

Koyo Seiko, the technical collaborator of Sona Steering is a leading global producer of auto steering assemblies and ball bearings and is affiliated with Toyota Motor through a 24.9 per cent stake. Koyo Seiko is Japan's largest and the world's second largest maker of steering systems for automobiles with a 23 per cent global market share. The world's first electric power steering system (EPS) was developed by Koyo Seiko. It is also the fourth largest producer of ball bearings in the world. Its engineering and manufacturing capabilities range from super large bearings with outer diameters of seven meters to miniature bearings with inner diameters as small as one millimeter. Koyo Seiko has also utilized its technical base established through these main products to develop other products as well – including factory automation products, various precision instruments, heat treatment furnaces, electronic devices, and others.

Koyo Seiko was established in 1921. Along with its group subsidiaries it has 34 plants in America – both North and South, Europe and Asia. The group sales were US$4.78 billion for the year ending 31 March 2004 out of which automotive sales contributed US$4.18 billion. Koyo Seiko supplies to Toyota and other Japanese car manufacturers. It supplies regularly to foreign car makers such as Audi, Citroen, Peugeot, Renault and Volkswagen and has also supplied to BMW, Daimler-Chrysler and Saturn.

Koyo Seiko's major competitive strength lies in targeted R&D, high product quality and low cost production. The primary R&D is undertaken at their Engineering and Technical Centre located in Japan. This facility is supported by two centres in Europe and two in the US. One of the two centres in each location specifically focuses on steering systems. Koyo Seiko hopes to benefit from the growing demand for EPS systems, which are more energy efficient than hydraulic systems and allows manufacturers to programme features on them. Koyo Seiko's management has stated that they will work to improve the company's profitability by networking their overseas production bases in an efficient manner. Such a networking may benefit Sona through getting large export orders particularly for manual steering assemblies.

With such a strong technical collaborator, Sona Steering thrived in its initial years riding piggyback on the success of Maruti. As Maruti increased its market share in the growing but protected Indian automobile market, Sona Steering's sales also rose. However, Maruti continued as it's only large customer. For each steering assembly, Maruti paid Sona the unit cost plus a nominal profit. After the Indian government announced its policy of economic liberalization in 1991 and the automobile sector was opened up in the mid-1990s, Sona also had to upgrade its product mix and look beyond Maruti. Till 1999, Sona mostly made manual steering systems for different categories of Maruti vehicles. But over the years it has extended its product range to include power steering gear assemblies – both hydraulic and electric, propeller shaft assemblies, rear axle assemblies and its sub-assemblies.

The automobile sector in India witnessed quick changes in the mid-1990s. As many new foreign car makers entered the market, the protective environment of the earlier decade gave way to fierce competition from both domestic and foreign competitors. However, this also provided an opportunity to companies like Sona Steering to expand their base. Given the nature of its products, the company gets the bulk of its revenues from the original equipment market. In 1998 the company established its second plant in Chennai to cater to the requirements of carmakers in southern India.

In the beginning Koyo Seiko was only a technical collaborator, but in 1992 they also picked up a small equity stake in Sona. As the need for fresh infusion of technology rose, Koyo Seiko also hiked its stake from 8 to 21 per cent in 1998. With the increase in the financial commitment of the foreign partner, the company also changed its name to Sona Koyo Steering systems Limited, to reflect the new reality.

Sona Steering had established itself as a high quality producer right from its early days. This reputation helped it in increasing its production and sales year after year. With rising demand it increased its capacity in both Gurgaon and Chennai plants and in October, 2004 it established a 100 per cent export oriented unit in Sriperumbudur near Chennai to cater to the demand from its overseas customers, namely Koyo Seiko who are also their technical collaborator and financial partner. This facility is expected to become a production hub in the global production network of Koyo Seiko. Although Sona Koyo expected an export revenue of US$4 million in the first twelve months from this unit, the company has set an export target of US$45 million in five years time.

Sona Koyo has also set up a state-of-the-art power steering facility recently and is currently manufacturing these for Maruti Esteem and Mitsubishi Lancer. With a 45 per cent market share, Sona Koyo is the largest domestic producer of steering systems followed by the Rane Group of Chennai with a 35 per cent share.

As it caters to the OEM market, Sona Koyo realized that growth in volumes would be its key driver of earnings as there would be limited scope for improvement in profitability. In fact like others in the auto ancillary industry it finds itself unable to revise its price to completely offset any increase in input cost. Therefore, it had to learn the skills required to continuously improve its business and manufacturing processes to achieve lower costs and better quality simultaneously. Even now Sona Koyo largely depends on its technical collaborator Koyo Seiko for its product and process technology but it has gone a long way in not only absorbing and assimilating that technology but also in improving it – particularly the shop floor implementation of the same – through continuous improvement.

Although Sona Koyo enjoyed a good reputation for the quality of its products, it embarked on its Total Quality Management (TQM) programme in 1996. The chairman and other members of the top management communicated the future needs of the company to all its employees. This communication helped to impress upon everyone the necessity to improve their processes through TQM in order to weather the future uncertainties of business. Gradually the employees, who had earlier questioned the need for TQM when the company was already doing well, began to appreciate the value of TQM. Where previously reactive counter-measures were taken after receiving customer complaints, proactive actions were taken in the changed scenario. The company started monitoring its cost of poor quality and production operators started doing routine preventive maintenance, earlier being done by maintenance personnel alone. Target setting was gradually based on action plans, rather than being based on subjective assumptions. This was soon followed by enthusiastic promotion of Total Productive

Maintenance (TPM). Lead time for new product development also reduced from 12.3 to 5.7 months.

Sona Koyo identified its core competency areas and decided to do away with the non-core activities. Outbound logistics was outsourced as was the management and control of the receiving, storage and issue functions. Procurement of steel bars was done away with as all the machining vendors directly bought steel from the steel mill and supplied forgings and cut length blanks to the company. Sona Koyo now undertakes collaborative efforts with its suppliers in the areas of product development, quality improvement initiatives, cost control measures and supply related issues. The company has installed an i-Supplier portal through which the scheduling and monitoring of all components is done. Suppliers can also get the status of their bills and the portal is also being used for online buying of maintenance, hardware and consumable items like bearings, cables, electric panels and Galvanized Iron (GI) pipes. Sona Koyo has also outsourced to its 3PL service providers several activities such as milk run collections of parts from local suppliers and pick up, transport, storage and delivery of parts to its Chennai plants on a Just-In-Time basis.

All employees at Sona Koyo were involved in group Kaizen activities. Significant improvements had taken place in quality-related business processes. Operations at Sona Koyo had strong support from TPM and TQM techniques – the resulting effects being corroborated by the drastic improvement in profitability and quality of its products. Involvement of all the employees in these techniques contributed to lasting operating results. Subsequently in 2003 Sona Koyo emerged as the first steering systems making company in the world to win the coveted Deming Application Prize.

The Prize acted as a shot in the arm for everyone at Sona Koyo and strengthened its brand equity. The company no longer felt the need to establish its credentials to the global auto majors looking out for low-cost world class suppliers. It thought it could plan to leverage the Deming Prize to scale up its export plans. Accordingly, it had to revise its investment and product development plans and established its 100 per cent Export Oriented Units (EOU). The GM certification also helped as did the new production network concept of Koyo Seiko around the same time, utilizing cost-competitive units elsewhere as production hubs.

R&D expenses are only 0.8 per cent of net sales at Sona Koyo. This is low by international standards but Sona Koyo has the advantage of getting technical assistance from its partner Koyo Seiko. Sales of new products, developed not more than three years ago, accounted for about one-third of total sales at Sona Koyo. Even as late as 1999/2000, Sona Koyo depended on Maruti for 97 per cent of its sales. This has come down to about 57 per cent by 2003–04 and is likely to fall further in future years as the management has adopted the strategy of derisking the business through geographical and customer diversification. It hopes to move up the value chain through a shift in its product mix towards more power steering systems which have double the margin of manual steering systems. In exports, it expects to benefit from a similar move by Koyo Seiko as it vacates the production of manual steering systems to produce more of EPS in favour of other low-cost producers. Net sales of the company increased from Rs1800 million in 1999–2000 to Rs2354 million in 2003–04 and is expected to touch Rs5000 million by 2006–07 based on company projections. Sales increased by 31.3 per cent over the previous year in 2003–04 while post-tax earnings rose 87 per cent in the same period. Exports contributed 0 per cent of net sales in 1999/2000 and only 2 per cent in 2003/04, but are expected to contribute 20 per cent of net sales by 2006/07. Manual and power steering systems contributed to 30 and 20 per cent of net sales respectively in 1999/2000. This changed to 25 and 30 per cent in 2003/04 and is projected to further change to 15–20 per cent and 45–50 per cent by 2006–07.

Sona Koyo intends to continue adding to its capacity in line with increasing demand of its products. It also plans to enhance its design and development capabilities in future. The acquisition of 21 per cent equity stake in Fuji Autotech France Sas in October 2004 has also provided Sona Koyo with a toehold in Europe. The company, through Koyo Seiko has already secured export orders worth US$35 million for manual steering gears to be executed over a five-year period. It has also been identified as the sole supplier of manual steering gear for Toyota's new vehicle to be launched globally.

Case 5: Lenstec Inc. – Barbados[5]

Lenstec's parent company is headquartered in St. Petersburg, Florida, and commenced operations in 1991. The company developed and sold technology for production of high quality intraocular lenses to organizations in Africa, Asia (India, Nepal, Indonesia) and several other developing economies. In 1996, Lenstec Inc. made a strategic decision to move away from technology transfer and into direct production of the finished product. The company opened a facility in Barbados to manufacture and distribute a precision product, namely high-quality intraocular lenses for surgical replacement of cataracts in human eyes. Several factors encouraged the company to move to Barbados. These included an educated workforce and fiscal incentives offered by the government of Barbados. The company in the tiny island nation overcame the perception that a precision product could not be produced in Barbados by focusing on quality and service. In the medical device industry, high quality is a given – a company must produce a high quality product to survive – but to thrive the company had to compete on other bases. Lenstec elected to compete on service and currently exports its product to every region of the globe. It is able to service orders from markets in Europe faster than many European companies are able to and it has done this by focusing on an internal imperative for speed and accuracy of delivery, and by utilizing external factors such as the excellent courier service available from Barbados to Europe.

Lenstec, which employs 85 people, achieved revenues of about US$6.5 million in 2003 (compared to US$5 million in 2002), 99 per cent of which was generated from exports to more than 30 countries, including all of Western Europe, Eastern Europe, the Middle East, Asia, and Africa as shown in Table 7.5. Lenstec devoted a lot of effort to technical training with in-house specialists, but also realized that a well-functioning customer service could provide the company with another competitive edge. Alcon is the major competitor in this product category and their

Table 7.5   Lenstec in the global market: 2003 (no. of lenses)

Country/region	Total sold	% of total
Africa	2 757	1.21
Asia	30 734	13.50
Caribbean	4 684	2.05
Eastern Europe	18 298	8.05
Latin America	10 358	4.55
Middle East	24 039	10.56
North America	27 628	12.14
Germany	53 157	23.36
France	14 043	6.17
Italy	29 194	12.83
Spain	300	0.16
UK	8 448	3.71
Rest of the Western Europe	3 894	1.71
Total	*227 534*	*100.00*

Source: Based on data supplied by Lenstec, Barbados.

major manufacturing unit is based in Texas. Lenstec's advantage is that there are not many competitors in the developing economies, as the product may not be considered as price elastic. Lenstec is able to compete effectively by:

1. being a niche player and not directly competing head-to-head with Alcon;
2. continuously striving to move towards products at the technological barriers of ophthalmology;
3. basing its R&D activities in the US, but with input from all members of the management team in US, Barbados and the company's direct sales branch in UK. The company terms R&D as 'Reconnaissance and Development', which mirrors the way the company stays close to, and involved in, clinical developments in ophthalmology;
4. being a low-cost manufacturer by virtue of basing its manufacturing facility in a relatively high productivity jurisdiction, but one that does not carry with it a connotation of third-world quality standards.

The obstacles to exporting that Lenstec faced included non-tariff restrictions in importing countries, principally regulatory requirements; lack of access to working capital and capital for expansion, and the absence of a network of distributors.

To enable it to grow, Lenstec reinvested all its revenues and also sold a stake in the firm to Japan's largest ophthalmology company, Santen. These funds were used to:

1. increase production capacity
2. develop, commission and commercialize new production technologies
3. develop and commercialize new intraocular lens types
4. market the company's products and in turn build an international distribution network.

The sale of equity to Santen helped to increase distribution of the company's products, by assuring a long-term source of demand from its Japanese stakeholder/investor. The persistence of Lenstec's sales team and it's world-class products have also done much to improve distribution.

Lenstec Inc. measures its success as an exporter by the rapid expansion of its sales and workforce. The company is now considered a major employer in the quality jobs sector in the Caribbean and competes with companies from the United States and Europe.

Case 6: Doyle Offshore Sails Ltd – Barbados

Doyle Offshore Sails Ltd, of St. Philip, Barbados, founded in 1987, manufactures sails for sailboats and tarpaulins in an area where there is plenty of water, but no sail making industry. The company's principal business is the manufacture of sails for cruising boats ranging from 20 feet to 70 feet in length. This category accounts for about 95 per cent of the company's products. Besides sails, the company also supplies a small number of racing boats for the local and regional sailing regatta markets. In addition to sails, Doyle Offshore also makes canvas awnings on a customized basis, and water-proof tarpaulins for the Bridgetown Port.

The company produces a range of canvas shopping bags in two sizes, the motivation for this being a desire to assist with a reduction in the use of non-biodegradable plastics in the supermarket and other retail trades. Doyle Offshore also carries out repairs to sails and other canvas products for third-party customers.

Doyle Offshore Sails Ltd is an independent company and is the Caribbean licensee of Doyle Sailmakers Inc. of Marblehead, Massachusetts in the United States which in turn is the world's second largest sail making group, encompassing sails for racing and cruising. Doyle Offshore has affiliates throughout the Caribbean, located in Trinidad and Tobago, Grenada, St. Vincent, St. Lucia, Antigua, St. Maarten, St. Thomas, USVI, Puerto Rico and the Republic of Panama, all of whom it supplies with sails manufactured in Barbados. Some shipments have also been made to the South Pacific and Hawaii.

According to Mr Andy Watts, the Managing Director of the company:

> In the early 1980s when we were considering setting up a new company in the Caribbean, we were interested in an area where we could obtain trainable staff supported with high quality local infrastructure and stable government. These were elements we were sure were needed to ensure the success of our company.[6]

Historically, sail making was completely new in the Caribbean in general and Barbados in particular. The product was initially thought to be inferior to a North American product. It was really a challenge to the company to establish its credibility. Over the years the company has been able to hire local staff for its production line and train them to possess the necessary skill to offer the customers a top quality product. This required training from the very basics and providing other related incentives to the work force as sailmaking was foreign to the average Caribbean citizen. However, the current demand for their products has validated both the original concept of the viability of a sailmaking unit and the success of the training imparted to its workers.

The company's main competition comes from South Africa, Sri Lanka, Hong Kong, mainland China and Taiwan. The market for sails is an intensely competitive one, with lead times, product customization, price, quality, and on-time delivery ranking as major competitive factors. The company feels that Doyle Offshore has a significant advantage over the competition in product customization. The other contributory factor in explaining the success is the product quality within an appropriate time-frame demanded by the industry. Another beneficial decision was aligning itself with the name Doyle, known the world over for quality sails, and displaying the name at boat shows.

The company's organizational structure comprises a Managing Director, a Production Manager, a Floor Manager, 3 Assistant Supervisors and some 39 sail makers or production floor workers, making up a total of 45 full-time staff members. Some 98 per cent of the company's products are exported to the Caribbean (CARICOM), USA, Canada, Europe, Puerto Rico, USVI and St. Maarten among others.

Doyle Offshore Sails Limited is essentially a large format apparel-type operation. It has all of the compartments of a standard garment manufacturing entity but everything is a lot larger and a lot more heavy-duty. The canvas or plastic raw material itself is more bulky, thicker and stronger and requires large working surface areas for assembly into the finished product, sails.

Given the extensive amount of floor space required, Doyle Offshore actually occupies three buildings, comprising a total of 21,000 square feet. The company currently has 15 heavy-duty sewing machines, specially designed for the sail making business. Several of the machines are of the Swiss and German Adler types, which have been customized by Jentschmann, and fitted with the necessary pneumatic controls by Ontario Sewing Automation of Ontario Sewing Machine Company. Most of the machines are around 14 years old and capacity utilization during the past three years has ranged from 70 to 85 per cent.

The cutting table where the raw material is first laid out has a surface area two to three times that of a standard garment factory. The heavy-duty sewing machines and their operators are countersunk in 'cut-outs' in the concrete floor of the factory to facilitate the use of the floor itself as the working surface for the assembly operations. In addition, all of the sewing machines are highly specialized and outfitted to handle the canvas and other tough fabrics from which the sails and other components are made.

Doyle Offshore makes a profit every year. Market share declined some-what in 2001 due to the fall out from the events of September 11th in the USA. However, the company still made a profit in 2001. Labour accounts for about 9–10 per cent of total costs and is relatively constant. Although market share is currently stable, customer satisfaction ranks high. Product costs are very competitive and this is reflected in very positive financial performance in terms of cash flows and net return on assets. The company's performance over the past two years has been stable, with little change in sales turnover, number of employees, profitability, prod-uct range, number of customers or number of suppliers. Over the past five years, sales have been in the region of Bds\$3 million.

Doyle Offshore recognizes the importance of building the finest, most durable and technologically advanced sails possible. The company's prin-cipal products, sails, are bulky and are virtually all exported. In addition, the average life expectancy of a sail is 10 years. The company acknowl-edges, therefore, that there is no room for returns or rejects by the customer and this is reflected in the maxim 'get it right first time' adopted by the company. Doyle Offshore's performance on quality vision, product reliability and internal defect levels are all at Best Practice levels and supplier partnerships for raw materials are strong and well established. In order to achieve a good final product, the company upholds the internal customer concept, whereby each production line station is the customer of the preceding line station, and must receive high quality work in progress from that station. This concept is engendered through in-house training.

A great advantage of building sails in the Caribbean, besides first hand knowledge of the conditions the sails are used in, is the ability to pro-duce sails at considerably lower prices. Doyle Offshore's loft in Tortola is the largest in the Northern Caribbean while the loft in Barbados, where all the sails are made, is one of the largest in the world. The low cost of building sails in Barbados coupled with free trade agreements with most other countries allow Doyle Offshore to give their customers the very best sails at savings of 20–40 per cent.

As all their major competitors are in low labour cost areas, it was neces-sary for Doyle Offshore to focus their efforts on efficiency of production. To this end they have employed the use of computer aided design tech-nology. This has streamlined their product to meet the demands of their market.

Discussion

Cases 1–4 suggest a simple framework for analysing the nature, direction and determinants of latecomer technological learning in China, and

India. Cases 5–6 are Caribbean-specific export-driven firms. The nature and role of FDI in either technology development or technology transfer is also quite different in the six cases. A detailed analysis of the six cases using a common framework and with special focus on latecomer technological learning is presented in this section.

From simple to complex learning and R&D

The firms in cases 1–4 supply to OEM customers but case 3 also deals with an Indian firm that transformed into a global player based on its in-house R&D process innovations. The cases also represent technological accumulation through time, beginning with simple activities such as manufacturing according to parent firm's requirement and gradually toward more complex tasks such as process adaptation and eventually R&D. On the marketing side, the cases reflect the transition from OEM to Own Design Manufacturing (ODM) and for the case 3 firm to Own Brand Manufacturing (OBM). It appears that learning develops in sequence, shifting from production to engineering to innovation capabilities. For all these case firms the scale of demand created by large customers at the initial stage was critical to the survival of the firms. It appears that in many cases MNCs overcame rising cost problems by relocating production through FDI or (as in the case of case 2 and case 4 firms) through outsourcing production to lower cost countries such as India.

As demonstrated by the case 3 firm, a strict linear progression need not occur through time. R&D may begin fairly early on and there may be feedback between early and later stages. It suggests however, that there is a general tendency for firms to begin with simple tasks and accumulate capabilities systematically in a path-dependent, cumulative manner, with skills and knowledge gradually building on each other.

Cases 5–6 are Caribbean specific. FDI is an important way of accessing foreign resources. The host country resources that are in short supply but essential to maintain the competitive advantages are clearly most valuable. But this is only possible by careful selection of firms and their long run sustainability in a globalized world.

Implications for traditional innovation models

The path of technology frontier may be depicted with help of the above cases. It is defined here simply as the position where new product or process innovations take place. This is a moving frontier occupied by leading firms at any given time. Through time, the latecomers gradually narrow the technology gap between themselves and the leaders. By the

1990s, some latecomers reach the frontier in at least some product lines. In all the above cases, substantial investments in process implementation and process innovations have been made to compete with the international leaders. At the frontier, standard innovation models will begin to apply as R&D becomes an early and central part of the innovation process and follower dynamics begin.

Our cases reverse traditional models of innovation based on leadership or followership and generally place R&D at the centre of innovation. For latecomers the key to competitiveness runs contrary to theories which stress R&D or place R&D at the beginning of the innovation process. R&D generally occurs (if at all) in the later stages of a catch-up learning path, which begins with simple tasks such as labour intensive assembly for established products, in line with Vernon's (1966) life cycle model.

The cases should not be considered as leading to a generalised model of innovation, but rather a specific model which attempts to capture the historical catching up. The ideas may well not apply to other types of industry, which do not exhibit the key features of the above cases, including fast export growth and the possibility of an extensive division of labour across national boundaries.

Although R&D may not be central to latecomer firm strategies, innovation is essential for catching up to occur. Latecomer innovation focuses on engineering effort to improve production processes and reduce manufacturing costs (at least in the initial stages). Later, innovation occurs as firms learn to make incremental changes to product designs and eventually introduce their own new designs. This type of behind-the-frontier innovation is probably a necessary condition for latecomer firms to narrow the technology gap between themselves and market leaders. In the absence of relatively fast innovation, firms would merely keep up rather than catch up.

Latecomer innovation is triggered by profit opportunities provided by fast growing export markets. At the early stage, the small size of local markets forces companies to export. Firms initially compete with each other for export orders on cost and speed of delivery. Over time they compete on quality, reliability and own design capabilities. Local competition and imitation generate continuous process improvements and the rethinking of business and technology strategies. Channels such as OEM and subcontracting relay export market requirements directly to the latecomers. The case of Sundram Fasteners is an ideal case in this context.

Not all firms need to innovate in the above manner. New start-up firms may jump in at advanced levels, missing out the early stages. As the absorptive capacity of the economy increases new start-ups may bypass earlier phases. Spin offs from older firms, diversifications from other sectors, and new experimental start-ups all constitute the growing industrial base. There is no automatic process by which technology accumulation occurs. On the contrary, firms learn to innovate by their own efforts and investments in technology, build up new competencies and catch up with market leaders.

The OEM-based firms, Sundram Fasteners and Moser Baer suggest that process and product technology are closely linked and that feedback occurs from one to the other during the catching up process. While early entrants tend to concentrate on assembly and absorbing basic manufacturing skills, in the later stages the distinction between product and process innovation becomes more blurred. Improving the production process often requires knowledge of product design and reliability as well as skills in production processes. During the 1980s the ability to precisely specify product designs to enable manufacturing efficiency (design for manufacturing) became a key competitive factor in electronics. The locus of overall technological capability tends to shift cumulatively from operational skills to process improvements, to product innovation capabilities and eventually to development and research abilities. The Moser Baer case highlights the importance of R&D in catching up and then in maintaining the leadership position.

As regards the Caribbean cases, the host country has to provide competitive immobile assets – skills, infrastructure, services, supply networks and institutions to complement the mobile assets of MNCs.

Understanding exports and learning

In the simple cases, learning occurs not only at the technological level but also at the marketing level. Firms learn to package, distribute and market their goods. Some establish marketing departments at home and then in the advanced countries. Marketing know-how enables firms to diversify their customer base and to increase their growth opportunities and, like technology, involves substantial investments in skills and organization. Advanced latecomers ultimately establish their own brand abroad and may advertise directly to customers.

In other cases there may be concrete connections between market and technology. The channels for learning technological and marketing skills may be one and the same, as with OEM/ODM. To increase sale of production capacity to key customers, joint engineering work may be needed as shown in the case studies. Later on, to bring new products to the market, firms may need to make long-term investments in R&D.

To sum up, in the simple model, exports pull forward the technology of latecomer firms, enabling them to overcome the lack of user-product links enjoyed by leaders and followers. Through OEM and other channels, export demand acts as a focusing device for learning and forces the pace of progress. Local competition stimulates innovation, more latecomers imitate successful exporters, and gradually a relocation of production to a developing economy occurs. As regards the Caribbean, it is useful to target products having high income elasticity of demand for exports, maximize technological 'spreads' effects, or establish a foothold in important new technologies.

Shop floor learning and Innovation in business and manufacturing processes

Case firms 2–4 have produced excellent shop floor results. All of them are primarily catering to their OEM customers, which has helped them in restricting their marketing expenses to manageable levels. The second and the fourth case firms went to the world market after establishing themselves in the domestic one while Moser Baer entered the Indian market after establishing its credentials as a global OEM supplier – but as an OBM. However, all of them excelled in absorbing and assimilating the technology initially obtained from either the technical collaborator (as in case 2 and case 4 firms) or from their equipment and raw material suppliers (as in case 3 firm). The shop floor improvements and other small process innovations established each one of them as high quality, price competitive and dependable suppliers and helped them in developing scalable business models which could be ramped up as the market grew. All the case firms seem to have internalized the value of continuous learning to survive in the dynamic environment. Among the three Indian case firms, Sona Koyo has also developed a symbiotic relationship with their foreign partner wherein the basic product and process technology is supplied by Koyo Seiko while Sona Koyo implements the same on the shop floor meticulously and also with improvements. Finally, Koyo Seiko has also emerged as an overseas customer for Sona Koyo.

FDI and learning

The diversity of firms covered in the case studies also highlights the marginal role of FDI in the transfer as well as development of technology. It appears that the transfer of 'core' technology by a foreign firm is usually associated with licensing. It appears that Sundram Fasteners was induced to produce the radiator caps by GM and the equipment and product details were provided by GM to SFL without any associated FDI. This could be because radiator caps design as well as their production did not constitute any core technology for GM and in fact GM soon exited the production of radiator caps.

MBIL developed its expertise gradually – first trying its hand in floppy diskettes and gradually moving to CDs and DVDs as the firm established its credentials with its customers. Sustained investments in R&D also contributed to the confidence of the firm in launching new products (optical storage media, for example) using new process technologies.

Another insight that can be gained through these cases is that firms producing final goods for consumption can leapfrog through technology spillovers from FDI – like the two Caribbean case firms – even in the absence of large domestic markets. OEM firms producing intermediate goods may gain technology spillovers from their importers and may not depend only on FDI even in the early stages of their catching up. Also, in a globalized economy technology spillovers may occur through trade in final goods as well as trade in intermediate goods and through FDI – thus enabling firms to accelerate the catching up.

Summary

In this chapter we argue that traditional models of innovation have not always been validated. It revealed that the balance between local and foreign sources of technology is closely entwined. Likewise, foreign channels are an essential feature of fast catch-up growth.

Our analysis shows that most latecomers are still distinct from followers and leaders. Although some have made the transition to follower and leader in some areas, many are highly dependent on OEM and subcontracting for access to markets and technology. Through the 1990s and into the next century a variety of strategic options face the latecomer firms. As more of them approach the innovation frontier, they may require new strategies to acquire technology and to overcome remaining weaknesses. They may wish to take on characteristics of followers and leaders by increasing their R&D expenditures and improving their brand image aboard. Alternatively they may wish to expand their basic OEM activities into neighbouring low-cost areas. They may even decide to pursue a mixture of both strategies.

The evidence suggests that there is no easy or automatic transition from latecomer to leader or follower. Indeed, products are grown extremely rapidly and successfully on the basis of subcontracting, OEM and ODM. Once some basic capabilities are developed, it is relatively easy for such a firm to shift to the production of new products based on those capabilities. This could be seen in the case of SFL when they entered the production of radiator caps, which was an entirely new line of products. Similarly, once they developed the capability to produce manual steering assemblies, Sona Koyo did not find it very difficult to produce power steering assemblies given the technological support of their technical collaborator.

A transition to leadership and followership on a broad front would require radical changes not only in the way latecomer firms operate but also in the environment in which they compete. For example, firms would have to develop strong marketing capabilities and invest heavily in creating brand images acceptable to worldwide consumers. Similarly, they would have to create a strong research culture within their companies and considerably increase their investments in basic and applied research to generate significant new innovations. Manufacturing firms would also need the support of a much stronger local capital goods sector and software industry than exists in selected Asian economies.

The Caribbean cases reveal that the careful and strategic selection of firms were not wasted or abused despite the privileges granted to them. Their choices also reflected strategic rather than economic priorities.

8
Summary and Conclusions

This book has examined various facets of FDI inflows in the developing economies of China, India and the Caribbean. Two of these are large economies by any definition and the third is a collection of many small economies and together, they provide a perspective as well as a contrast unmatched by any other similar collection. Interestingly, the FDI inflows in these economies have witnessed significant increases despite all the wheezing about the declining trend in global FDI inflows in recent time. These regions are today identified as uniquely favoured and have the potential to be prosperous due to the inflows of foreign capital.

Historically, all these regions had been lands of control and protectionism, cursed by overpopulation and plagued by natural disasters in which millions were trapped to live in extreme poverty with no hope to escape. Among other factors, the opening up of these economies and the subsequent increased inflow of foreign capital has contributed to the increase in their national income and the general well-being of the population. Across the three economies under study, this process began at different points in time and had different types of results.

The inflow of foreign capital depends on various economic factors but as described in the text, non-economic factors such as neighbourhoods, cultures and ethnic proximities also affect these flows. This may have strong bearing on the emerging service sector with its tradability options. Indeed, this sector is an important new area for FDI and there is indication that it may further enhance growth in both large and small economies.

The present work points to an alternative pathway that determines FDI flows between specific countries and this approach – presented in the form of neighbourhood and extended neighbourhood – may help in deepening and widening our understanding of FDI inflows. The neighbourhood model enlarges the scope of pure economic variables and introduces non-economic variables that may reduce the perceived risks (similar and familiar product/factor markets) as well as increase the expected returns (no major changes in product design) from the perspective of a foreign investing firm in its search for host destinations.

However, on closer scrutiny, one would appreciate that the neighbourhood concept is quite different from the concept of 'psychic distance' introduced in economic literature earlier. 'Psychic distance' presents a static concept, wherein investments and their sequence is attempted to be explained through the 'psychic distance' between the home country and the host country. In the neighbourhood model, the role and importance of 'psychic' or 'cultural' distance itself changes dynamically as investments move from the original to the intermediate and the extended neighbourhoods. Although developed in the context of the USA, the concept of original, intermediate and extended neighbourhoods may be equally applicable in explaining the FDI flows of other FDI sources.

The key question is why do the above arguments hold true across all countries in the world? The eclectic paradigm of Dunning (2001) seems to provide some explanation. The point he makes is that firms make their international production decisions based on perceived Ownership (O advantages), Location (L advantages) and Internalization (I advantages) related factors. When stretched from the micro to the macro, this leads to the concept of the investment development path (IDP). As a country develops, the attractiveness of its OLI advantages changes to potential investors (both inward and outward) and the country is likely to go through five relatively well-defined stages. The IDP is a useful heuristic model and attempting to find the position of a country on its IDP can lead to meaningful policy debates. In a way, the O advantages are related to the *push* factors of the home country, the L advantages to the *pull* factors of the host and the I advantages to the *how* of the involvement in so far as an international production decision is concerned. Although the basic structure of the model is very attractive, its details have been evolving over time (Dunning and Narula, 1996) and may contain too many explanatory variables – many with limited predictive value. On one side, this may be too general a theory and on the other it ignores the possibility of any special advantage for a pair of countries. Countries in the *neighbourhood* have a role in reduction of perceived risk. Indeed Dunning (1988) argues that firms from developing countries are likely to perform activities in neighbouring countries, which are politically and economically stable. Accordingly, while a substantial portion of FDI inflows may be explained by select economic variables, the country-specific factors and the idiosyncratic component account for more of investment inflows across economies.

It is well established now that one of the innovative features of the current phase of globalization is the fragmentation of production into production networks based on component specialization and intra-product trade. It offers groups of small countries opportunities to form open regionalism in order to enhance their productivity and competitiveness as well as the welfare of their nationals. This concept is equally applicable to the Caribbean, although Arndt (2001) justifies it for the Association of South East Asian Nations (ASEAN). As production networks grow in the ASEAN region, this provides opportunity for both China and India to participate in these networks in their extended neighbourhood with their respective component specializations. This represents the most likely scenario. However, it is an open question whether sufficient resources such as infrastructure and institutional framework will be forthcoming to achieve it.

The analysis presented in this book challenges the popular maxim that the inflows of FDI in China are explained by resource-seeking arguments. Quite evidently, the behaviour of foreign investors is different according to their origin. For example, Hong Kong based investors may have been motivated by resource-seeking arguments. In contrast, for US based investors it may be explained by market-seeking arguments. Interestingly, Hong Kong plays a dominant role as a source of FDI inflow to China. It is indeed to be mentioned here that many companies are investing in China from their 'regional' headquarters in Hong Kong.

Interestingly, the coastal regions are the most preferred destinations of FDI. Moreover, five of the provinces together (Guangdong, Jiangsu, Fujian, Shanghai and Shangdong) received more than 65 per cent of the total investment during 1996–2000. Shanghai alone for example, sucked in about US$6billion of FDI in 2000, more than a tenth of the total for the entire country. There are various forms of FDI existing in China such as: Chinese–foreign joint equity ventures, Chinese–foreign joint contractual venture, wholly foreign-owned enterprise, foreign invested joint stock limited company, foreign invested financial institution, compensation trade, international leasing, BOT, TOT, purchase of shares and transfer of enterprise property right.

The solely FIEs are rising in China compared to other forms of investment. It appears that the length of operation of an enterprise has been the single most important factor in the success of an FIE not only in terms of its profitability, but also in terms of its subjective performance.

In addition, FIEs are in industries consistent with China's comparative advantages. This study has examined the difference in access to technology between foreign and domestic firms in China with the help of certain parameters of technological advantage. The findings are revealing. The foreign firms in China seem to have advantages over the domestic firms in all parameters. It is thus likely that China has applied its abundant factor – labour – in achieving its comparative advantage.

In practice, R&D is only engaged in developing commercial applications for existing technologies, rather than creating new technologies. The spillover effect of FDI in China has been very slow. It remains to be seen as to how China will succeed with its massive rural unemployment in the long run.

Historically, at the time of independence India followed the path of self-reliance for her development. Nationalism played a contributory role in shaping its policies. In the Indian context, government economic policy was intended to shape the industrial structure by various interventions. Yet, despite significant policy interventions, empirical evidence on the actual economic performance negates the expected achievements. In fact, support by state to Indian industries distorted R&D, encouraged import of obsolete technology and discouraged innovation.

But in the new scenario after economic liberalization, the survival of a firm is determined purely by its ability to compete. In the Indian context, government support to industry was considered to be for ever in most cases. The post-liberalization time span is too short to examine the export performance of FDI. Interestingly, the rise of 'knowledge industries' is a new aspect of India's future development. This is the Indian edition of 'leapfrog' where human capital in the high technology sector has acted as a powerful engine of growth. The states (such as Gujarat, Maharashtra) which are relatively well-developed due to manufacturing have human capital in the low and medium technology sector, active economic facilitation by the state sector and are geographically closer to prosperous cities. As a result, these states are able to attract huge flows of foreign investment thanks to their excellent mix of low labour costs and decent productivity. The Southern states which are relatively well-developed due to high technology (computers, software), have enhanced the quality of their human capital from endogenous factors such as proactive policies and other interventions in the social infrastructure sector and have created economic clusters having favourable environment. Consequently, these states are now able to compete through services such as outsourcing and offshoring, their research, innovation and development. Now they need to upgrade their infrastructure to attract more quality investment. Northern states such as Punjab, Haryana, Delhi and Western Uttar Pradesh are reaping the benefit of agricultural development due to assured irrigation and government's support system. The states together are now able to grow faster than the Indian average.

With low labour costs and abundant high-tech and inventive human capital, West Bengal, historically, was able to compete at all India level quite efficiently. But now the state along with its other east-Indian counterparts failed to transform itself due to static policies. Uncertainty and fear of the future convinced many investors to put their money into other states. These states are also poor performers in the area of human development. Kerala, in contrast, has been able to perform much better in respect of human development although it has a political environment similar to that of West Bengal.

India is not free from a raging debate on spillovers from FDI, as these are issues of global concern and debate. It is natural to expect productivity spillovers through backward (OEM firms) and forward linkages (link between foreign suppliers of intermediate inputs and their domestic customers). The literature, though limited, addresses the key issues in the Indian context. For example, Kathuria's (2000) result shows that the productive efficiency and spillover benefits are associated not only with foreign firms but even domestic ones have also improved their position.

As regards spillovers in the rural sector, the time period is too short to measure the impact. Even then, the results show the positive effects in terms of poverty reduction. This aspect is more important if one may endeavour to study at the state level. In the past, the countless controls inhibited economic growth and thus failed to effectively implement poverty reduction strategies.

Foreign investors have been attracted to the Caribbean because of the strategic geographical position of these countries, and the prospect of marketing their products to a global market. The USA is the major export destination of Caribbean export. However, this trend is declining. In recent years tourism and infrastructure have attracted FDI in countries such as Guyana, the Organization of Eastern Caribbean States (OECS) and Jamaica. The Caribbean economies continue to follow open door FDI policies in the light of structural adjustment programmes aimed at economic liberalization. The dynamics of the labour market may be considered as a powerful ingredient in explaining the facets.

Our thinking reflects that higher education and the skill development strategy of the region lack vision. The institutional aspect of the Singapore model is relevant for the Caribbean. We have documented it and then tried to compare it with the Caribbean economies highlighting the differences. The system may play an important role in enhancing long-term growth. Moreover, by making effective use of electronic commerce, especially in the area of services, the Caribbean economies would be able to partly neutralize the advantage typically enjoyed by large economies. But the increasingly skilled and knowledge-intensive nature of the associated activities would require continuous upgrading of education and training. Unfortunately, the existing structure is too weak to transform the economy from low growth to prosperity. The Caribbean islands used to be the preferred destination of American, Canadian and European tourists looking for sun and cheap hotels, rum and calypso. Now they need to upgrade their infrastructure to cater to tourists with higher purchasing power as well as offer competitive prices because of availability of other competitive destinations.

In this book we argued that traditional models of innovation have not always been validated. It revealed that the balance between local and foreign sources of technology is closely entwined. Similarly, it argues that foreign channels are an essential feature of fast catch-up growth.

A number of key points emerge from the above view. For example, most latecomers are still distinct from followers and leaders. Although some have made the transition to follower and leader status in some areas, many are highly dependent on OEM and subcontracting for access to markets and technology. Through the 1990s and into the twenty-first century a variety of strategic options face the latecomer firms. As more of them approach the innovation frontier, they may require new strategies to acquire technology and to overcome remaining weaknesses. They may wish to take on characteristics of followers and leaders by increasing their R&D expenditure and improving their brand image abroad. Alternatively they may wish to expand their basic OEM activities into geographically neighbouring low-cost areas. They may even decide to pursue a mixture of both these strategies.

The evidence presented in this book suggests that there is no easy or automatic transition from latecomer to leader or follower. Indeed, production is developed and products are produced extremely rapidly and successfully on the basis of subcontracting, OEM and ODM. But some of these producers have retreated back to OEM/ODM after attempting to launch own brand products and suffering heavy losses. OEM/ODM could well remain the dominant feature of industrial growth in many industries in these developing countries for some time to come. A transition to leadership and follower on a broad front would require radical changes not only in the way latecomer firms operate but also in the environment in which they compete. For example, firms would have to develop strong marketing capabilities and invest heavily in creating brand images acceptable to worldwide consumers. Similarly, they would have to create a strong research culture within their companies and considerably increase their investment in basic and applied research to generate significant new innovations. Manufacturing firms would also need the support of a much stronger local capital goods sector and software industry than exists in most developing economies. The successful Caribbean cases presented in the book reveal the careful and strategic selection of firms that explain that the privileges granted were not wasted or abused. Their choices also at times reflected strategic rather than economic priorities.

Comparisons between India and China have often been made in the development literature. These comparisons can indeed be quite enlightening, given the similar challenges faced by the two countries in the late 1940s, and the different routes they have taken in addressing these challenges. In recent time FDI and economic growth has been a common focus of comparison between India and China. It is in this context to be mentioned here that the last two or three decades have witnessed marked changes in the global organization of industry with far-reaching effects for the evolving patterns of integration of developing countries into world economy. The Chinese government played a catalytic role for the industries by providing basic infrastructure such as roads, ports, and power and it has plans to develop these further ahead of the need for the investing companies. This is the ideal situation for China to remain competitive in industries such as consumer electronics, in which it's labour productivity is double that of India's (Farrel, 2004). The production processes of the manufacturing companies require efficient roads and transport networks. India is relatively poor in infrastructure but has an edge over China in terms of emerging industries be it in software, Business Process Outsourcing (BPO), biotechnology, or creative industries such as advertising. In the auto component sector, Indian firms with technological assistance from foreign firms have improved their technological capability. The auto industry of India as a whole has shown promise as they are manufacturing components based on MNCs' global design. This resulted in a need to transfer technology to local suppliers.

In the long-term scenario, the positive demographic backdrop weighs heavily for India. It has the only population in the BRIC countries (Brazil, Russia, India, China) that continues to grow until 2050. What is important here is that India's working age population (the share of population aged 15–60) exhibits a 'bulge' during the projection period.

Quite importantly, the future demographic pattern may be unfavourable for China. The one-child policy adopted by China in the last two or three decades will exact penalties after the next two or three decades when the ratio of working population to non-working population will be unfavourable for China. In fact the size of the population which will define the talent pool will be less for China at that stage.

The Caribbean will find it hard to compete with more open market regimes in areas like manufacturing and agriculture. The small economies, however, may be competitive in niche manufacturing. This book explores illustrative case studies in this context. The cases reveal that success is possible if the economies are moving to higher-end services such as call centres, tele-marketing and ICT enabled services. This requires high skill levels and underscores the emphasis on improving the quality and cost effectiveness of human resources.

In bringing this book to a close, there is a strong temptation to try to use what we have learnt to peek into the future of the three economies. These economies can grow faster given the potentialities they have. The alternative of reverting back to close and protected economic development seems improbable. This underlines the need for a theory of co-operation exploiting neighbourhoods resulting in a win-win situation for all. For example, 40 per cent of the population of Trinidad and Tobago is of Indian origin and the country is following the US time zone. It can exploit this competitive advantage and attract Indian investment in the BPO industry. The Caribbean islands, which are just three to five hours away from the US and Canada can pursue the groundwork to attract Indian investment.

The Caribbean region has potential for high-tech industries. The Free Trade Area of the Americas (FTAA) – tentatively scheduled for completion in 2007 – will encompass some 34 countries in the Americas, including the United States, creating a market with a population of approximately 800 million and a GDP of some $8.5trillion (Schott, 2001). The English speaking Caribbean economies, despite their small sizes may play an important role by providing fiscal incentives to foreign investors (with particular reference to Indian IT investors) in the areas of services and manufacturing. The decision is strategic since it will help the foreign investors to explore markets in developed economies like USA and Canada. In recent times Mexico is taking full advantage of its North American Free Trade Agreement (NAFTA) membership. Private investors are more interested in financing projects in the Caribbean due to low risks involved. None of this will help to reduce unemployment in the region if growth doesn't occur. In addition, small and medium-sized companies in Barbados and OECS economies seem to be getting worried because of possible implementation of FTAA. With globalization and high cost of labour, economies of scale are sometimes difficult to attain in the Caribbean. However, the region can follow the models laid down by countries such as Canada or Ireland that have built their industries on accommodation to the United States. In this context there may be bright prospects of establishing strong India-CARICOM trade and investment relationships in the form of extension of the extended neighbourhood model under the changing scenario.

With the objective of deepening its political and economic relations with the ASEAN countries, India launched its *Look East* policy in 1991. India graduated from being a sectoral dialogue partner in 1992 to a full dialogue partner in 1995 and went on to become a member of the ASEAN Regional Forum where regional security issues are discussed. India's evolving cooperation is reflected in India's participation in the annual ASEAN–India summit being held since 2002. In October 2003, India signed a framework agreement on comprehensive economic cooperation, leading to an ASEAN–India Free Trade Area in ten years. Earlier, during the ASEAN summit in November 2002, China signed a framework agreement on comprehensive economic cooperation, which included elements of the establishment of ASEAN–China Free Trade Area (ACFTA). The strengthening of the neighbourhoods may have some impact on future FDI flows of both India and China.

It is very difficult to attempt making any predictions regarding the future – but one thing is certain. The pace at which changes are taking place in the world economy, including changes in market structure, technology, customer preferences and new product development requires that companies and countries as well, respond to these changes. Strategies and choices that have yielded good results in the past may not be able to deliver in the future. In fact, the speed with which a country is able to respond to the dynamics of the world economy will be the hallmark of its success in future. The world as we know today will undergo major changes by the middle of this century. The countries that are unable or slow to respond will have to make room for others that can move quicker and innovation will be the key differentiating factor. In the long term, it may even be possible for some economies to survive only on the basis of their capital or technology, but labour alone may be unable to provide this sustenance. By bringing a large part of their population to the economic marketplace, India, China, the Caribbean as well as many other developing economies will set free their innovation potential which has so far not found any route to reach the market. When this happens, the world will surely be a different place.

Notes

Introduction

1. In general, foreign resource inflows can be viewed as an income transfer that can be either consumed or invested. In Obstfeld's (Obstfeld, 1994) model, for instance, a foreign resource inflow is no different from any other increase in income. Unless the rate of inter-temporal substitution is very high, the representative agent will respond to a permanent resource inflow with an increase in consumption. As the inflow affects income as well as consumption, saving may rise or fall. If the resource transfer is temporary or takes the form of a loan that must be repaid, the consumption effect is somewhat damped, but it is still likely to exceed the effect on investment. Thus, resource inflows may raise utility by allowing households to smooth consumption rather than by leading to a rise in investment and growth. However, it should be noted that this type of utility-based models miss some essential features of foreign capital inflows. In particular, the assumption of a single representative agent assumes a degree of capital market development – equalization of lending and borrowing rates – that does not exist in most developing countries, see Agenor (2001).

2 FDI: Global Trends and Assessments

1. Amiti and Wei (2004) made an interesting comment on job losses due to outsourcing in the context of the USA. To quote:

   > ... outsourcing does not lead to net job losses. ... For example, when disaggregating the US economy to 450 industries, there is a small negative effect on employment. But aggregating up to 100 sectors, there were no job losses associated with service outsourcing. This implies that a worker could lose her job due to outsourcing but then she, or an unemployed worker, may find a job in another form within the broader industry classification. Hence aggregate data would indicate that there are no net job losses when there is sufficient job creation in another sector, which indeed seems to be the case. (p. 39)

4 Foreign Investment: China

1. SEZ means 'special economic zone'. An authority of the country to practise a special administration system and implement special policies to achieves particular economic goals in its domestic and foreign activities establishes it. China's first economic zones, viz. Shenzhen, Zhuhai, Shantou, and Ximen were established in the early 1980s. Later in 1988 Hainan Island was also designated as the fifth special economic zone. The establishment of these zones aims at opening the four windows, namely, technology, knowledge,

management and foreign economic policy and also to the economic expansion in and outside China so as to promote the development of the export-oriented economy in the hinterland. The special economic zones are the signs of the opening of China's hinterland to the outside world. The special economic zones have been established as experimental zones for the economic reform in this country. Whenever a new policy is formulated, an experiment is first made in the SEZs before the new reform is carried out elsewhere.

2. However, China is obliged to open up its financial market for international competition since it has become a member of World Trade Organization (WTO). Hence the number of foreign banks and financial institutions in China is expected to increase and China may allow them to conduct Yuan business as well. Likewise, as China builds up its trade-related infrastructure, trade between China and other countries will be increasingly direct and will bypass Hong Kong. Hence, the demand for Hong Kong's entrepôt as well as transshipment services is expected to decline. Furthermore, some of the comparative advantages of Hong Kong's trade-related services are more artificial than real. For example, the intermediate role of Hong Kong in China-Taiwan as well as China–South Korea trade is mainly due to the restriction of direct trade between China and the two trading partners. With the improvement in diplomatic relation and direct shipping links between these trading partners, Hong Kong's comparative advantage in servicing indirect trade between them is again likely to be eroded (see Chai and Kwong, ibid.).

3. China's official figures of FDI may be an exaggeration. A large amount of China's FDI has been earned in mainland China but then booked to accounts in Hong Kong for tax purposes and subsequently comes back to the mainland as FDI, in a process of 'round-tripping'.

4. The coastal open cities are coastal port cities where special open policies are followed. In May 1984, the State Council decided 14 more coastal port cities, that is Dalian, Qinhuangdao, Tianjin, Yantal, Qingdao, Lianyyungang, Nantong, Shanghai, Ningbo, Wenzhou, Fuzhou, Guangzhou, Zhejiang and Beihai. The sole purpose of opening these coastal port cities was to achieve better industrial foundations, high level of technology, transport facilities, quick access to information, good network of economic cooperation at home and the channels for foreign trade so as to attract overseas investments. These open cities offer preferential policies to the investors. On technology-intensive and knowledge-intensive ventures or on energy and transport projects, the enterprise income tax will be collected at a rate of 15 per cent. On industrial and agricultural projects, the income tax will be collected at the rate of 24 per cent. No duties will be collected on equipment and machinery imported as overseas investments, the raw and processed materials imported for the production of export goods, means of transportation for their own use and office accommodation.

5. Recent research reveals that FIEs located in Guangdong performed better than those located in the SEZs, see Cheng and Wu (2000) and Fung *et al.* (2000).

6. Pudong is one of the Economic and Technological Development Zones (EDTZ). It has the characteristics of the other SEZs, but it goes farther in allowing foreign firms to import and export goods for use within the zone duty free (entrepôt free trade). A similar free trade zone has been established in Tianzin and Guangzhou. The choice of Pudong as an EDTZ applied the

special economic zone concept to a location up the coast, to a city renowned in generations past for its business and financial acumen. Unlike Shenzhen and the other SEZs which are literally fenced off from their surroundings, planners view the development as not only integral to the economic and social progress of Shanghai, but also as a way to boost the economics of the six provinces that comprise the greater Yangtze River area, home of 34 per cent of China's population (see Keijzer, 1995). In 2001, of the total 395 investment projects launched in Pudong, 26 registered an investment of over US$10 million each, with total investment coming to US$1.639 billion, up 249 per cent year-on-year. Furthermore, foreign investors, accounting for 85.8 per cent of the total, wholly own 339 out of the 395 projects. As on December 2001, there were 7,030 foreign funded enterprises (FFEs) in the area, and they were expected to invest a total of US$36.6 billion of foreign capital and that includes US$15.5 billion of contractual capital. In order to use foreign capital more efficiently, the Pudong SEZ is expanding its area with the area of software park to increase from the current 30,000 sq. km to 90,000 sq. km; the customs area of the Waigaoqiao Bonded Zone will expand from 6.4 sq. km to 7.52 sq. km; the microelectronic industrial belt will expand to neighbouring townships; and the urban area of Pudong will expand from 100 sq. km to 130 sq. km. One of the ensuing effects of the expanding is that foreign companies have seized the opportunity to increase investment. Official figures show that Hong Kong leads the way by launching 2,677 projects with US$3.4 billion of contractual foreign capital. It is followed by the United States, which has launched 987 projects with US$2.97 billion of contractual foreign capital; and Japan the third by launching 883 projects with US$1.62 billion of contractual foreign capital. Of the world's top 500 enterprises, 112 have shown presence in Pudong, launching 198 projects. In addition, there are other projects in this area such as a microelectronic project (US$300 million), a semiconductor project (US$400 million) and an Intel expansion project (US$300 million).

7. See *The Economist*, 15 Jan. 2004, p. 3.
8. See *China Economic News* (No. 21), 4 June 2001, pp. 11–13.
9. The future demographic pattern may be unfavourable for China. The one-child policy adopted by China in the last two or three decades will exact penalties after the next two or three decades when the ratio of working poulation to non-working population will be unfavourable for China. In fact the size of the population which will define the talent pool will be less for China at that stage.
10. On close examination, it reveals that China's 'high-tech' exports turn out to be not truly 'high-tech' according to international standard. The Chinese version of high-tech exports is defined by finished information technology products, DVD players and laser printers (Table 4.16). Interestingly, the high value-added brains of these products – integrated circuits – dominate the top high-tech imports into China.
11. According to the 'crowding-out' hypothesis, inward FDI might have a negative effect on domestic R&D activity, because purchasing technologies from abroad (by setting up joint ventures with foreign investors, for example) is a substitute for innovating on one's own. This substitute is more attractive

when conducting one's R&D is risky, or when the technology concerned is of high standard (such as invention).

5   Foreign Investment: India

1. See Lall and Streeten (1977).
2. For a recent comprehensive survey of the issues, see Kathuria (1995).
3. For detailed discussion see Sengupta *et al.* (1996).
4. UNCTC, 1994.
5. For a discussion of FERA and its implications see Martinussen (1988).
6. See Bhagwati and Srinivasan (1993).
7. See Kumar (1994).
8. Previous research rationalizes the low actual to approval ratio as due to:

(a) concentration of investment in a few large size projects,
(b) sizeable investment flows in infrastructure industries where gestation period high,
(c) large projects in organic chemicals, fertilizers and steel are being dropped or reviewed.

9. See US Embassy (2001).
10. The availability of information on them depends on their legal status. Limited information is available about their legal status. For example, very little information about the companies those registered outside the country, and in tax shelters, like Mauritius. Another case is the Enron's Dabhol Power Company – the largest foreign project yet – is incorporated in India as an unlimited liability company. But it is shell company that Enron controls through at least six holding companies registered in various offshore locations (see Mehta, 1999, Nagraj, 2003).
11. In his case data has been extracted from the Prowess package of the Centre for Monitoring Indian Economy (CMIE). Prowess covers all the firms listed in the Bombay Stock Exchange (BSE) with data from their annual reports. While extracting the data, two truncation rules were followed: (a) continuous data for a firm for all the years of the study period (that is the panel should be balanced); (b) the firm should not belong to any sector, which is reserved exclusively for small firms, such as match-sticks, leather products, and so on. After accounting for these two criteria, the initial data set consisted of 519 firms with data for eight years from 1989/90 to 1996/97 for 24 three-digit industries. Of these 519 firms, 32 firms had to be dropped, as they either had negative value added for more than three years of study period or were government owned or the Prowess reported zero fixed assets for the firms. Thus, the final analysis involved use of data for 487 firms belonging to 24 three-digit manufacturing industries. The selection of these industries is based on the matching of the Prowess industrial classification to that of SIA. The matching is necessary to facilitate an estimation of the impact of entry of foreign firms and FDI after liberalization. This is because SIA is the only source that gives industry-wise data on the collaborations and FDI after the liberalization and its classification is

different from that of the Annual Survey of Industries (ASI) or Prowess classification.

Of the 487 firms, 116 firms (that is nearly 24%) have a foreign equity participation of 25% or more (designated as FDI firm) during the study period. The distribution shows that the foreign firms' presence varies from zero to nearly 50% in different sectors with three sectors pulp and paper, vegetable oils, and industrial and scientific instruments having no foreign firm. The share of foreign firms varied from a little over 2% in sugar to over 63% in LCVs and the passenger cars sector for the year 1990 (Kathuria, 2002).

12. The HMI makes 120,000 cars annually in India and it is Hyundai Motor's largest production base outside Korea. India is the second largest overseas market for the company after the USA where it sells 500,000 cars a year. Unlike most multinational car companies in India, HMI invested in an aluminium foundry and also a transmission line so that it could increase indigenisation levels and cut costs. As a result, HMI has achieved indigenization levels over 85 per cent (see Park, 2004).

13. HMI was the first self-sufficient manufacturing unit and greenfield investment of an overseas automobile company in the Indian car industry. A greenfield investment is a start-up investment in new facilities. Such an investment can be wholly owned or a joint venture. It had invested Rs2,900 crore by 2001. HMI formed the industrial cluster with a strong subcontracting linkage between vendors. In 1997, the core companies (vendors) came from Korea with HMI. Most of the companies' headquarters are located in the Ulsan automobile cluster near Hyundai Motors, Korea (parent firm HMI). Under the umbrella of HMI, they had invested in joint ventures with Indian companies or in greenfield investment in the automobile industry.

14. The 'flying geese' pattern was originally conceptualised as a general theory of economic development. It explained the development of an industry from its introduction of its products to an economy through imports through the establishment of local production facilities to the emergence of growth in exports.

15. India is targeting one per cent share of world exports by 2007, see 'No Comparison', *Times of India* (2002).

7 Technology Transfer: Case Studies

1. This case is based on an article published in *Asian Business and Management*. For details see Chen and Ku (2002).
2. For details see Banik and Subbaymma (2000).
3. This case is based on company Annual Reports and write-ups in *Dataquest* (30 Sept. 2002), *Business India* (14–27 Oct. 2002b), *Business Standard* (26 Aug. 2003), *Economic Times* (14 Jan. and 28 Apr. 2004).
4. This case is based on company web sites and Annual Reports and write-ups in: *Deccan Herald* (7 Sept. 2004), *Financial Express* (18 Aug. 1998) and *Economic Times* (29 Oct. and 23 Nov. 2004).
5. This case is based on an author's visit to the Lenstec plant and discussions with its MD, Ian Hickling.
6. In a personal communication to one of the authors.

Bibliography

Agenor, Pierre-Richard (2001), 'Benefits and Costs of International Financial Integration: Theory and Facts', Working Paper No. 2699 – International Economics, Trade, Capital Flows, World Bank, Washington, DC.

Ahluwalia, I. J. (1991), *Productivity and Growth in Indian Manufacturing*, Oxford University Press, New Delhi.

Aitken, Brian J., Ann E. Harrison and Robert E. Lipsey (1996), 'Wages and Foreign Ownership: A Comparative Study of Mexico, Venezuela and the United States', *Journal of International Economics*, Vol. 40, No. 304, pp. 345–71.

Amiti, Mary and Shang-Jin Wei (2004), 'Demystifying Outsourcing – The Numbers Do Not Support the Hype Over Job Losses, *Finance and Development*, Vol. 41, No. 4 (Dec.), pp. 36–9.

Apoteker, Thierry (2002), 'FDI and Macroeconomic Performances in China: Issues Ahead', presentations for the EU Managers Programme, Beijing, Apr.

Arndt, S. W. (2001), 'Production Networks in an Economically Integrated Region', *ASEAN Economic Bulletin*, 18(1), 24–34.

Bacchetta, P. and Wincoop E. (1998), 'Capital Flows to Emerging Markets: Liberalization, Overshooting, and Volatility', NBER Working Paper No. W6530, Apr.

Bain, Joe S. (1956), *Barriers to New Competition: Their Character and Consequences in Manufacturing Industries*, Harvard University Press, Cambridge, Massachusetts.

Balasubramanyam, V. N., Salisu, M. and D. Sapsford (1999), 'Foreign Direct Investment as an Engine of Growth', *Journal of International Trade and Economic Development*, Vol. 8, 27–40.

Banik, A. (2003a), 'Foreign Direct Investment Inflows to China and India: Trends, Assessments and Determinants', *Savings and Development*, No. 1, Vol. XXVII, 5–22.

Banik, Arindam (2003b), 'An Assessment of the Caribbean Skills Development System: Does It Constitute a Viable Model for New Economy?', *Global Development Studies*, Vol. 3, Nos 1–2, Winter 2002–Spring 2003, pp. 283–98.

Banik, A. and Subbaymma G. (2000), 'Technology Transfer in Asia – Case of Latecomer Industries', paper presented in a conference on Globalisation and the Uniqueness of Asia, Euro-Asia Management Studies Association, INSEAD's Campus in Asia, Singapore, 23–25 Nov.

Banik, Arindam and Sunday O Iyare (2003), 'Globalization, Model of Competitiveness and Human Skill Development in the Caribbean', Conference Volume, Global Awareness Society International.

Banik, Arindam, Pradip K. Bhaumik, Sunday O. Iyare (2004a), 'Explaining FDI Inflows to China, India and the Caribbean – An Extended Neighbourhood Approach', *Economic and Political Weekly*, Vol. 39, No. 30, 24 July, pp. 3398–407.

Banik, Arindam, Sunday O. Iyare and Pradip K. Bhaumik (2004b), 'Neighbourhood Approach of Foreign Direct Investment Flows to the Caribbean Economies: Does the Present Structure of Caribbean Skill Development System Constitute an Impediment?', paper presented in a 3-day conference on Size, Power and

Development in the Emerging Power held on 3–5 Mar. at The Institute of International Relations, University of the West Indies, St. Augustine Campus, Trinidad and Tobago, conference proceedings.

Barclay, Lou Anne A. (2000), *Foreign Direct Investment in Emerging Economies – Corporate Strategy and Investment Behavior in the Caribbean*, Routledge, London and New York.

Barro, Robert J., and Xavier Sala-i-Martin (1999), *Economic Growth*, MIT Press, Cambridge and London.

Bekaert, G., Harvey C. R. and Lumsdaine R. I. (1999), 'The Dynamics of Emerging Market Equity Flows', NBER Working Paper No. W7219, July.

Belgrave A. and W. Ward (1997), 'Foreign Direct Investment and the Barbadian Economy', Working Papers, Central Bank of Barbados, pp. 56–75.

Berthelemy, Jean-Claude, and Sylvie Demurger (2000), 'Foreign Direct Investment and Economic Growth: Theory and Application to China', *Review of Development Economics*, No. 4, pp. 140–55.

Bhagwati, J. and T. N. Srinivasan (1993), 'India's Economic Reforms, Indian Council for Research on International Economic Relations (ICRIER)', New Delhi, mimeo.

Bhaumik, S. K., Beena, S. K., Bhandari, L. and Gokaru, S. (2003), 'Survey of FDI in India: Foreign Direct Investment in Emerging Markets', Centre for New and Emerging Markets, London Business School, DRC Working Paper No. 6.

Blomstrom, Magnus and Ari Kokko (1998), 'Multinational Corporations and Spillovers', *Journal of Economic Surveys*, Vol. 12, No. 2, pp. 1–31.

Blumenthal, Tuvia (1979), 'A Note on the Relationship Between Domestic Research and Development and Imports of Technology', *Economic Development and Cultural Change*, 27: 303–6.

Bordo, M. D., Eichengreen B. and Irwin D. A. (1999), 'Is Globalization Today Really Different than Globalization a Hundred Years Ago?', NBER Working Paper No. W7195, June.

Borensztein, Eduardo, Jose De Gregorio and Jong Wha Lee (1998), 'How Foreign Direct Investment Affect Economic Growth?', *Journal of International Economics*, No. 45, pp. 115–35.

Brainard, S. Lael (1997), 'An Empirical Assessment of the Proximity–Concentration Tradeoff Between Multinational Sales and Trade', *American Economic Review*, Vol. 84, No. 4, pp. 520–44.

Brezis, Elise, Paul Krugman, and Daniel Tsiddon (1999), 'Leapfrogging in International Competition: A Theory of Cycles in National Technological Leadership', *American Economic Review*, Vol. 83, No. 5, 1211–19.

Business India (2002a), 'Electrifying Growth', 14–27 Oct.

Business India (2002b), 'The Great Divorce', 1–14 Apr.

Business Standard (2003), 'Lunch with BS: Ratul Puri', 26 Aug.

Campbell, Trevor (2003), 'Foreign Direct Investment Inflows and Their Impact on Barbados' Current Account: Implications for Policy', in Harold Codrington, Ronald Craigwell and Darrin Downes (eds), *Facing Globalisation-Impact and Challenges for Barbados and the Caribbean*, Central Bank of Barbados, Bridgetown.

CARICOM (2000), *Caribbean Trade and Investment Report 2000*, Ian Randle Publishers, Kingston.

Carr, D. L., Markusen, J. R. and Maskus, K. E. (2001), 'Estimating the Knowledge-capital Model of the Multinational Enterprise', *American Economic Review*, Vol. 91, No. 3, pp. 693–708.

Caves, Richard E. (1982), *Multinational Enterprise and Economic Analysis*, Cambridge University Press, Cambridge, Massachusetts.

CDB (1998), Appraisal Report on Further Education, Report prepared for the CDB's 175th meeting of the Board of Directors held on 16 October 1997.

Chai C. H. Joseph and Charles C. L. Kwong (1996), 'Trade and Investment Relations with China', in H. C. Y. Ho and L. C. Chau (eds), *The Hong Kong Economy in Transition*, Asian Research Service, Hong Kong, pp. 109–18.

Chand, S. and K. Sen (2002), 'Trade Liberalization and Productivity Growth: Evidence from Indian Manufacturing', *Review of Development Economics*, Vol. 6, No. 1, Feb.

Chen, Tain-Jy and Ying-Hua Ku (2002), 'Creating Competitive Advantages Out of Market Imperfections: Taiwanese Firms in China', *Asian Business & Management*, Vol. 1, No. 1, pp. 79–99.

Cheng L. K. and Changqi Wu (2000), 'Determinants of the Performance of Foreign Invested Enterprises in China', Department of Economics, Hong Kong University of Science and Technology, Clear Water Bay, Kowloon, Hong Kong, May, mimeo.

Cheng, L. K. and H. Zhao (1995), *Geographical Pattern of Foreign Direct Investment in China: Location, Factor Endowments, and policy Incentives*, Department of Economics, Hong Kong University of Science and Technology, Feb.

Cheng, L. K. and Y. K. Kwan (1999), 'What are the Determinants of the Location of Foreign Investment? The Chinese Experience', *Journal of International Economics*, Vol. VIII, No. 45, pp. 235–65.

Cheung Kui-yin and P. Lin (2003), 'Spill-over Effects of FDI on Innovation in China: Evidence from Provincial Data', Department of Economics, Lingman University, Tuen Mun Hong Kong, mimeo.

Child, J., Sek Hong Ng and Christine Wong (2000), 'Psychic Distance and Internationalization: A Critical Examination', paper presented at the 2000 Annual Meeting of the Academy of International Business, Phoenix, Arizona (Nov.).

China Economic News, various issues, China Economic Information Agency, Beijing.

China Economic Quarterly (2003).

CIA World Factbook (2001).

CMIE (2004), Centre for Monitoring Indian Economy, Prowess, Corporate Information database available on line at: http://www.cmie.com/products/prowess/

Coase, Ronald (1937), 'The Nature of the Firm', *Economica*, Vol. 4, No. 3, pp. 326–45.

Codrington, H. (1987), 'Foreign Investment in the Private Sector of Barbados 1956–1985', *Central Bank of Barbados Economic Review*, Vol. XIV, No. 1, 14–29 June.

Das, Deb Kusum (2001), 'Some Aspects of Productivity Growth and Trade in Indian Industry', unpublished PhD Dissertation, Delhi School of Economics, University of Delhi, Nov.

Das, Deb Kusum (2002), 'Trade Liberalization and Industrial Productivity: An Assessment of Developing Country Experiences', Working Paper No. 77 (Apr.), Indian Council For Research on International Economic Relations (ICRIER), New Delhi.

Dataquest (2002), '*Mission Possible*', 30 Sept.

Davidson, W. (1980), 'The Location of Foreign Direct Investment Activity: Country Characteristics and Experience Effects', *Journal of International Business Studies*, Vol. 12, 9–22.

Deccan Herald (2004), *'Sona Koyo Plans EOU in Chennai'*, 7 Sept.

Desai, Asok V. (1980), 'The Origin and Direction of Industrial R&D in India', *Research Policy*, 9, 74–96.

Dunning, J. H. (1979), 'Explaining Changing Patterns of International Production: In Defence of the Eclectic Theory', *Oxford Bulletin of Economics and Statistics*, Vol. 41, pp. 269–96.

Dunning, J. H. (1984), 'Non-Equity Forms of Foreign Economic Involvement and the Theory of International Production', in Richard W. Moxon *et al.* (eds.), *International Business Strategies in the Asia-Pacific Region: Environmental Changes and Corporate Responses*, Jai Press, Greenwich.

Dunning, J. H. (1988), 'The Investment Development Cycle and Third World Multinationals', *Transnational Corporations and Economic Development*, Vol. 3, pp. 135–66.

Dunning, J. H. (1988), *Explaining International Production*, Unwin Hyman, London.

Dunning, J. H. (1993), *The Globalization of Business*, Routledge, London.

Dunning, J. H. (2001), 'The Eclectic (OLI) Paradigm of International Production: Past, Present and Future', *International Journal of the Economics of Business*, 8(2), 173–90.

Dunning J. H. and Narula R. (1996), 'The Investment Development Path Revisited: Some Emerging Issues', in J. H. Dunning and R. Narula (eds), *Foreign Direct Investment and Governments: Catalysts for Economic Restructuring*, Routledge, London.

ECLAC (2000), 'Implications of Hemisphere-wide Regionalism', *ECLAC Issue Brief*, No. 3, Sept.

Economic and Political Weekly (2004), 'Current Statistics', Vol. 39, No. 27, 3 July, p. 2939.

Economic Times (2004a), 'Electra Sells 3% Stake in Moser Baer to Warburg', 14 Jan.

Economic Times (2004b), 'It's a Long Road Ahead for Auto Part R&D', 23 Nov.

Economic Times (2004c), 'Moser Baer India to Setup Unit in Germany'.

Economic Times (2004d), 'Sona Koyo Opens EOU Plant', 29 Oct.

Eichengreen, B. (1999), 'Capital Flows: A Century's Perspective', A Draft Background Report, University of California, Berkley.

Esperanca, J. P. (1992), 'International Strategies in the European Service Sector: A Comparative Study', in M. Casson (ed.) *International Business and Global Integration: Empirical Studies*, Macmillan, London.

Farrel, Diana (2004), 'Sector by Sector', *McKinsey Quarterly*, pp. 117–19.

Fikkert, Brian (1993), 'An Open or Closed Technology Policy?: The Effects of Technology Licensing, Foreign Direct Investment, and Technology Spillovers on R&D in Indian Industrial Sector Firms', unpublished PhD dissertation, Yale University, New Haven, CT.

Financial Express (1998), 'Sona Steering Seeks Centre Go-ahead for Change of Name', Aug.

Fuchs, Deike Fuchs and Thomas Straubhaar (2001), *Economic Integration in the Caribbean: The Development Towards a Common Labour Market*, Social Protection Section, International Migration Programme, International Labour Organization, Geneva, 2001.

Fung, K. C., Hitomi Lizaka, Joseph Lee and Stephen Parker (2000), 'Determinants of U.S. and Japanese Foreign Direct Investment in China, University of California', Mar., mimeo.

Gao, T. (2005), 'Foreign Direct Investment from Developing Asia: Some Distinctive Features', *Economic Letters*, Vol. 86, No. 1, pp. 29–35.

Girvan, Norman (1971), *Foreign Capital and Economic Underdevelopment in Jamaica*, Institute of Social and Economic Research, UWI, Kingston, Jamaica, 1971.

Goldar, B. N. (1986), 'Import Substitution, Industrial Concentration and Productivity Growth in Indian Manufacturing', *Oxford Bulletin of Economics and Statistics*, Vol. 48, No. 2, pp. 143–64.

Goldar, B. N. and A. Kumari (2002), 'Import Liberalization and Productivity Growth in Indian Manufacturing Industries in the 1990s', Working Paper No. E/219/2002, Institute of Economic Growth, Delhi.

Grossman, Gene and Elhanan Helpman (1991), *Innovation and Growth in the Global Economy*, Cambridge, Mass., MIT Press.

Hachigian, Nina and Lily Wu (2003), *The Information Revolution in Asia*, Rand, p. 24.

Hagedoorn, J. and Narula R. (1995), *Evolutionary Understanding of Corporate Foreign Investment Behaviour: US Foreign Direct Investment in Europe*, MERIT, University of Limburg, Netherlands.

Helpman, E. (1984), 'A Simple Theory of International Trade with Multinational Corporations, *Journal of Political Economy*, Vol. 92, No. 3, pp. 451–71.

Hobday, Mike (1994), 'Technological Learning in Singapore: A Test Case of Leapfrogging', *The Journal of Development Studies*, Vol. 30, No. 3, pp. 831–53.

Hobday, Mike (1995), 'East Asian Latecomer Firms: Learning the Technology of Electronics', *World Development*, Vol. 23, No. 7, pp. 1171–93.

Hortsmann, I. J., Markusen J. R. (1992), 'Endogenous Market Structures in International Trade (natura facit saltum)', *Journal of International Economics*, Vol. 31, Nos 1–2, pp. 109–29.

Howard, M. and Banik A. (2001a), 'Private Capital Inflows to the Caribbean: Trends, Assessments and Determinants', *Economic and Political Weekly*, Vol. 36, No. 29, 2773–8.

Howard, M. and Banik A. (2001b), 'Patterns of Foreign Direct Investment in India, China and the Caribbean', paper presented in a seminar, Sir Arthur Lewis Institute of Social and Economic Studies, University of West Indies, Cave Hill Campus, Bridgetown (Barbados), 4 Apr.

Huang Yasheng (2000), 'Why is Foreign Direct Investment Too Much of a Good Thing for China', a lecture delivered at Harvard University Asia Center, Modern Asia Series, Spring 2000, 11 Feb.

ICICI (1997), 'Export Performance of Companies in the Corporate Sector – 1991 to 1995–96', Economics Research Division, Mumbai, mimeo.

India Investment Centre, *India Investment Climate*, various issues.

Inkpen, Andrew (1995), *The Management of International Joint Ventures: An Organizational Learning Perspective*, London: Routledge, chs 5–7, 10.

Inter-American Development Bank (IADB) (2001), *The Business of Growth: Striving for Competitiveness in Latin America*, Progreso Economico y Social de America Latina, informe annul.

International Monetary Fund (IMF) (1993), *Balance of Payments Manual*, Fifth edition, International Monetary Fund, Washington, DC.

International Monetary Fund (2004), *International Financial Statistics*, Washington, DC.

James, D., Sung, J., Green, F. and Ashton, D. (1999), 'The Role of the State in Skill Formation: Evidence from the Republic of Korea, Singapore, and Taiwan', *Oxford Review of Economic Policy*, 15(1), pp. 82–96.

Javorcik, Beata Smarzynska (2004), 'Does Foreign Direct Investment Increase the Productivity of Domestic Firms – In Search of Spillovers Through Backward Linkages', *American Economic Review*, Vol. 94, No. 3, pp. 605–27.

Johanson, J. and Vahlne, J.E. (1977), 'The Internationalization Process of the Firm – A Model of Knowledge Development and Increasing Foreign Market Commitments', *Journal of International Business Studies*, Vol. 8, No. 1, 22–32.

Johanson, J. and Wiedersheim-Paul, F. (1975), 'The Internationalization of the Firm – Four Swedish Cases', *Journal of Management Studies*, Vol. 12, 305–22.

Kamath, S. J. (1990), 'Foreign Direct Investment in a Centrally Planned Developing Economy: The Chinese Case', *Economic Development and Cultural Change*, 107–30.

Kamath, S. J. (1994), 'Property Rights and the Evolution of Foreign Direct Investment in a Centrally Planned Economy: Reply to Pomfret', *Economic Development and Cultural Change*, 419–25.

Kathuria, S. (1995), 'Competitiveness in Indian Industry', in Dilip Mukherji (ed.), *Indian Industry, Policies and Performance*, Oxford University Press, New Delhi.

Kathuria, Vinish (2000), 'Productivity Spillovers from Technology Transfer to Indian Manufacturing Firms', *Journal of International Development*, Vol. 12, pp. 343–69.

Kathuria, Vinish (2001), 'Foreign Firms, Technology Transfer and Knowledge Spillovers to Indian Manufacturing Firms: A Stochastic Frontier Analysis', *Applied Economics*, Vol. 33, pp. 625–42.

Kathuria, Vinish (2002), 'Liberalisation, FDI, and Productivity Spillovers – An Analysis of Indian Manufacturing', *Oxford Economic Papers*, Vol. 54, No. 4, pp. 688–718.

Katrak, Homi (1985), 'Imported Technology, Enterprise Size and R&D in a Newly Industrialising Country: The Indian Experience', *Oxford Bulletin of Economics and Statistics*, 47, 213–30.

Katrak, Homi (1989), 'Imported Technology and R&D in a Newly Industrializing Country: The Experience of Indian Enterprises', *Journal of Development Economics*, 31, 123–39.

Keijzer, Arne J De (1995), *China Business Strategies for the '90s*, Pacific View Press, Berkeley, California.

Kenevan and Xi Pei (2003), 'China Partners', *The Mckinsey Quarterly*, No. 3, pp. 12–15.

Kindleberger, C. P. (1969), *American Business Abroad: Six Lectures on Direct Investment*, Yale University Press, New Haven, Connecticut.

Kogut, B. (1983), 'Foreign Direct Investment as a Sequential Process', in C. P. Kindleberger and D. Audretsch (eds), *The Multinational Corporation in the 1980's*, MIT Press, Cambridge, Mass.

Kogut, Bruce and Zander, Udo (1993), 'Knowledge of the Firm and the Evolutionary Theory of the Multinational Corporation', *Journal of International Business Studies*, 24(5), 625–45.

Krugman, P. (1994), 'The Myth of Asia's Miracle', *Foreign Affairs*, 73(6), pp. 62–78.

Kumar, N. (1989), 'Determinants of Traditional and New Forms of Foreign Investments – The Case of Indian Manufacturing', RIS Occasional Paper No. 24,

Research and Information System for the Non-Aligned and Other Developing Countries (RIS), New Delhi.

Kumar, N. (1994), *Multinational Enterprise and Industrial Organizations – The Case of India*, Sage Publications, New Delhi.

Kumar, N. (2003), 'Liberalization, Foreign Direct Investment Flows and Economic Development: The Indian Experience in the 1990s', RIS Discussion Paper (RIS-DP) #65/2003, Research and Information System for the Non-Aligned and Other Developing Countries, New Delhi.

Kumar, Nagesh (1987), 'Technology Imports and Local Research and Development in Indian Manufacturing', *The Developing Economies*, 25, 220–33.

Kumar, Nagesh (1994), *Multinational Enterprises and Industrial Organization: The Case of India*, Sage Publications, New Delhi.

Kuruvilla, Sarosh, Christopher L. Erickson and Alvin Hwang, (2002), 'An Assessment of the Singapore Skills Development System: Does it Constitute a Viable Model for Other Developing Countries', *World Development*, Vol. 30, No. 8, pp. 1461–76.

Lall, S. (1983), 'Determinants of R&D in a LDC: The Indian Engineering Industry', *Economic Letters*, 13: 379–83.

Lall, S. (2001a), 'National Strategies for Technology Adoption in the Industrial Sector: Lessons of Recent Experience in the Developing Regions', Background paper for the United Nations Technology for Human Development, New York.

Lall, S. (2001b), 'New Technologies, Competitiveness, and Poverty Reduction', a paper delivered at the Asia and Pacific Forum on Poverty: Reforming Policies and Institutions for Poverty Reduction, Asian Development Bank, Manila, 5–9 Feb.

Lall, S. and Paul Streeten (1977), *Foreign Investment, Transnational Corporations and Developing Countries*, Macmillan, London, pp. 53–7.

Levinthal, A. D. and March J. G. (1993), 'The Myopia of Learning', *Strategic Management Journal*, Vol. 14, pp. 95–112.

Lochan, Samuel (2002), *Education for Productivity: Case Studies of Trinidad and Tabago, Jamaica and Barbados*, International Labour Organization, monograph, Mar.

Luo, Yadong (1998), 'Timing of Investment and International Expansion Performance in China', *Journal of International Business Studies*, Vol. 29, No. 2, pp. 391–407.

MacDougall, G. D. (1960), 'The Benefits and Costs of Private Investment from Abroad: A Theoretical Analysis', *Economic Record*, pp. 13–35.

Maitra, Ramtanu (2003), 'Why India's Economy Lags Behind China's', *Asia Times*.

Markusen, James R., and Anthony J. Venables (1999), 'Foreign Direct Investment as a Catalyst for Industrial Development', *European Economic Review*, No. 43, pp. 335–56.

Marston, R. C. (1997), *International Financial Integration: A Study of Interest Differentials Between the Major Industrial Countries*, Cambridge University Press, Cambridge.

Martinussen John (1988), *Transnational Corporations in a Developing Economy – The Indian Experience*, Sage Publications, London.

Majumdar, Dipak and Sandip Sarkar (2004), 'Reforms and Employment Elasticity in Organised Manufacturing', *Economic and Political Weekly*, 3 July.

McIntyre A. and B. Watson (1970), *Studies in Foreign Investment in the Commonwealth Caribbean*, No. 1, Jamaica Institute of Social and Economic Research. UWI, Kingston, Jamaica.

Mehta, Abhy (1999), *Power Play: A Study of the Enron Project*, Orient Longman, Hyderabad.

Nagraj, R. (2003), 'Foreign Direct Investment in India in the 1990s: Trends and Issues', *Economic and Political Weekly*, 26 Apr., pp. 1701–12.

Nollen Stanley D. and Thomas L. Brewer (2000), 'International Knowledge Transfer: Firms' Responses to Government Policy Liberalizations', Georgetown University, mimeo.

Nollen, Stanley D. and Thomas L. Brewer (2000), 'International Knowledge Transfer: Firms Responses to Government Policy Liberalizations', McDonough School of Business, Georgetown University, Washington, June, mimeo.

Obstfeld, M. (1994), 'Risk-Taking, Global Diversification, and Growth', *American Economic Review*, Vol. 84, Dec., pp. 1310–29.

Pantin, D. (1996), *Youth Employment Training Programmes in the Caribbean*, International Labour Organization, Caribbean Office, Port of Spain.

Park, Jongsoo, (2004), 'Korean Perspective on FDI in India – Hyundai Motors' Industrial Cluster', *Economic and Political Weekly*, 31 July, pp. 3551–5.

Pursell, G. G. (1981), 'Cost–Benefits: Evaluation of LDC Industrial Sectors Which Have Foreign Ownership', World Bank Staff Working Paper No. 465, July.

Ray, D. (1998) *Development Economics*, Princeton University Press, Princeton.

Redding G. S. (1993), *The Spirit of Chinese Capitalism*, Walter de Gruyter, Berlin and New York.

Reserve Bank of India, *Reserve Bank of India Bulletin*, various issues.

Roberts, Joanne (2001), 'Challenges Facing Service Enterprises in a Global Knowledge-Based Economy: Lessons from the Business Services Sector', PREST Discussion Paper 01–03, University of Manchester, UK.

Rosen, Daniel H. (2004), 'Low-tech bed, high tech-tech dreams', China Economic *Quarterly*, Vol. 8, No. 1, pp. 20–41.

Rugman, Alan M. (1982), *New Theories of the Multinational Enterprise*, Croom Helm, London.

Schott, Jefferey (2001), *Prospects for Free Trade in the Americas*, Institute of International Economics, Washington, DC, Aug.

Sengupta, Nitish, Arindam Banik and Rajat Kathuria (1996), 'FDI Inflows to India in the Post-Reform Period: An Analysis of Structural and Policy Impediments', Occasional Paper No. 3, IMI Research Paper Series, International Management Institute, New Delhi, Oct. mimeo.

Sharma, Kishor (2000), *Export Growth in India: Has FDI Played a Role?*, Economic Growth Centre, Yale University, July.

SIA Newsletter (2004), *Secretariat for Industrial Assistance, Department of Industrial Policy and Promotion*, Ministry of Commerce and Industry, Government of India, Apr.

Siddharthan, N. S. (1988), 'In-house R&D, Imported Technology and Firm Size: Lessons from Indian experience', *Developing Economies*, 26, 212–21.

Siddharthan N. S. and Stanley Nollen (2000), 'The Contributions of Foreign Collaboration and Technology to Exports from Firms in India', McDonough School of Business, Georgetown University, Washington, May, mimeo.

Siddharthan, N. S. (1992), 'Transaction costs, Technology transfer, and In-house R&D: A Study of Indian Private Corporate sector', *Journal of Economic Behaviour and Organisation*, 18, 265–71.

Sourafel Girma, David Greenway and Katherine Wakelin (2001), 'Who Benefits from Foreign Direct Investment in the UK?', *Scottish Journal of Political economy*, Vol. 48, No. 2, pp. 119–33.

Srivastava S. (2003), 'What is the True Level of FDI Flows to India?', *Economic and Political Weekly*, Vol. 38, No. 7, 15 Feb., 608–10.

Studwell J. (2003), 'Zhejiang: At Long Last, Capitalism, *China Economic Quarterly*, Quarter 3, pp.38–41.

Teece, D. J., Rumelt R. P., Dosi G. and S. Winter (1994), 'Understanding Corporate Coherence – Theory and Evidence', *Journal of Economic Behavior and Organization*, Vol. 23, pp.1–33.

Teece, David (1981), 'The Market for Know-how and Efficient International Transfer of Technology', *Annals of American Academy of Political and Social Science*, 458, 81–6.

Teece, David (1983), 'Technological and Organisational Factors in the Theory of the Multinational Enterprise', in Mark C. Casson (ed.), *The Growth of International Business*, Macmillan, London, pp. 51–62.

Economist, The (2001), 'The Rich Get Richer', 31 May.

Economist, The (2001), 'Islands of Quality' in *A Survey of India's Economy*, pp. 3–33.

Economist, The (2004), 'Shanghai' 04, 15 Jan.

Thurow, L. C. (1992), *Head to Head: The Coming Economic Battle Among Japan, Europe and America*, William Marrow, New York.

Times of India (2002), 'No Comparison', Editorial, 10 Nov.

Twomey, M. J. (2001), 'A Century of Foreign Investment in Mexico', UM-Deardon Economics Working Paper# 98, University of Michigan, Deardon.

US Embassy (2001), 'US Foreign Investment in India', New Delhi, mimeo.

UNCTAD, *World Investment Report*, New York, various issues.

UNCTC (1994), *Transnational Corporations in World Development*, United Nations, New York.

UNECLAC (1995), *Foreign Direct Investment in the Caribbean*, United Nations.

United Nations (2001), *Economic Survey of Latin America and the Caribbean*, Economic Social Council, New York.

United Nations (2002a), *Summary of the Economic Survey of Latin America and the Caribbean 2001*, Economic and Social Council, 17 Apr.

United Nations (2002b), *OECS Human Development Report 2002*, The OECS Secretariat, St Lucia.

Vahlne, J. E. and Wiedersheim-Paul, F. (1977), 'Psychic Distance – an Inhibiting Factor in International Trade, Working Paper, Center for International Business Studies, Department of Business Administration, University of Uppsala, Sweden, 1–19.

Vernon, Raymond (1966), 'International Investment, and International Trade in the Product Cycle', *Quarterly Journal of Economics*, 80, 190–207.

Virmani, Arvind (2004), *Accelerating Growth and Poverty Reduction*, Academic Foundation, New Delhi.

Williams, O. and S. Williams (1998), 'Foreign Direct Investment Flows to the Eastern Caribbean Central Bank Region', Working Papers, Central Bank of Barbados, pp. 179–94.

Wilson, Dominic and Roopa Purushothaman (2003), 'Dreaming with BRIC: The Path to 2050', *Global Economics Paper No. 99*, Goldman Sachs, New York.

Winter, Sidney G. (1987), 'Knowledge and Competence as Strategic Assets', ch. 8 in Teece, David (ed.), *The Competitive Challenge: Strategies for Industrial Innovation and Renewal*, Ballinger Publishing Co., Cambridge, MA.

World Bank (1994), *Global Economic Prospects 1995*, Washington, DC.

World Bank (1996), *Poverty Reduction and Human Resource Development in the Caribbean*, Latin America and the Caribbean Region, Washington ,DC.

World Bank (2002), *Global Economic Prospects 2003*, Washington, DC.

World Bank (2004), *Global Development Finance*, Washington, DC.

World Economic Forum (WEF) (2002), *The Latin American Competitiveness Report 2001–2002*, Geneva.

Wu, Yuan li and Wu, Chun-his (1980), *Economic Development in Southeast Asia: The Chinese Dimension*, Hoover Institution Press, Stanford.

Yeh, Andrew (2003), 'Chips ahoy', *China Economic Quarterly*, Vol. 8, No.1, p. 28.

Yoshihara, K. (1988), *The Rise of Ersatz Capitalism in Southeast Asia*, Oxford University Press, Singapore.

Zhihai, Zheng and Zhao Yumin (2002), 'China's Terms of Trade in Manufactures', Discussion Paper No. 161, United Nations Conference On Trade and Development, Geneva, June.

Name Index

Agenor, P., 3, 23, 50, 188
Ahluwalia, I. J., 104
Aitken, B. *et al.*, 114
Amiti, M and Wei, S. J., 15, 188
Apoteker, T., 51
Arndt, S. W., 48, 181
Asian Business and Management, 192

Bacchetta, P. and Wincoop, E., 27
Bain, J. S., 2
Balasubramanyam, V. N. *et al.*, 50
Banik, A. 29, 31, 123
Banik, A. and Iyare S., 123
Banik, A. and Subbayamma, G., 35
Banik, A. *et al.*, 123
Barclay, L. A., 13
Barro, R. J. and Sala-i-Martin, X., 149
Bekaert,G. *et al.*, 27
Belgrave, A. and Ward, W., 117
Berthelemy and Demurger, S., 3
Bhagwati, J. and Srinivasan, T. N., 191
Bhaumik, S. K. *et al.*, 40
Blomstrom, M. and Ari Kokko, 114
Blumenthal, T., 150
Bordo, M. D., *et al.*, 27
Borensztein, E. *et al.*, 3, 131
Brainard, S. L., 14
Brezis, F. *et al.*, 148
Business India, 192
Business Standard, 192

Campbell, T., 117
CARICOM, 13, 41, 117, 123, 137, 144, 208, 211
Carr, D. *et al.*, 15
Caves, R. E., 2
CDB, 142
Chai, C. H. J. and Kwong, C. L., 54
Chand, S. and Sen, K., 104, 106
Chen, T. J. and Ku, Y. H., 152
Cheng, L. K. and Kwan, Y. K., 49
Cheng, L. K. and Wu, C., 58, 59
Cheng, L. K. and Zhao, H., 29, 49

Cheung, K. Y. and Lin, P., 78
Child, J. *et al.*, 47
China Economic News, 11–13, 190
China Economic Quarterly, 77
CMIE, 160
Coase, R., 2
Codrington, H., 117

Das, D. K., 104
Dataquest, 192
Davidson, W., 24
Deccan Herald, 192
Desai, A. V., 150
Dunning, J. H., 3, 25, 47, 48, 58, 180
Dunning, J. H. and Narula, R., 48, 180

ECLAC, 137
Economic and Political Weekly, 90–92, 96
Economic Times, 192
Economist, The, 54, 79, 97, 111, 190
Eichengreen, B., 27
ESCAP, 27
Esperanca, J. P., 21

Farrel, D., 185
Fikkert, B., 150, 151
Financial Express, 192
Fuchs, D. F. and Straubhaar, T., 120
Fung, K. C. *et al.*, 189

Gao, T., 15
Girvan, N., 116
Goldar, B. N. and Kumari, A., 104, 106
Goldar, B. N , 104
Grossman, G. and Helpman, E., 3

Hachigian, N. and Wu, L., 72
Hagedoorn, J. and Narula, R., 25, 26
Helpman, E., 14
Hobday, M., 150
Hortsman, I. J. and Markusen, J. R., 14

Subject Index